MANNERIST FICTION

Mannerist Fiction

Pathologies of Space
from Rabelais to Pynchon

WILLIAM DONOGHUE

UNIVERSITY OF TORONTO PRESS
Toronto Buffalo London

© University of Toronto Press 2014
Toronto Buffalo London
www.utppublishing.com
Printed in Canada

ISBN 978-1-4426-4801-2 (cloth)

Printed on acid-free, 100% post-consumer recycled paper with vegetable-based inks.

Library and Archives Canada Cataloguing in Publication

Donoghue, William, author
Mannerist fiction : pathologies of space from Rabelais to Pynchon/William Donoghue.

Includes bibliographical references and index.
ISBN 978-1-4426-4801-2 (bound)

1. English fiction – 18th century – History and criticism.   2. French fiction – 18th century –
History and criticism.   3. Mannerism (Literature).   4. Mannerism (Art).   5. Formalism
(Literature).   6. Space and time in literature.   I. Title.

PR851.D65 2014   823'.509   C2013-908069-4

This book has been published with the help of a grant from the Canadian Federation
for the Humanities and Social Sciences, through the Awards to Scholarly Publications
Program, using funds provided by the Social Sciences and Humanities Research
Council of Canada.

University of Toronto Press acknowledges the financial assistance to its publishing
program of the Canada Council for the Arts and the Ontario Arts Council.

Canada Council
for the Arts
Conseil des Arts
du Canada

ONTARIO ARTS COUNCIL
CONSEIL DES ARTS DE L'ONTARIO
50 YEARS OF ONTARIO GOVERNMENT SUPPORT OF THE ARTS
50 ANS DE SOUTIEN DU GOUVERNEMENT DE L'ONTARIO AUX ARTS

University of Toronto Press acknowledges the financial support of the Government of
Canada through the Canada Book Fund for its publishing activities.

For my family

Contents

MANNERIST FICTION

Introduction

I feel that the future of writing is in space, not time.

William S. Burroughs[1]

The following study examines the idea of "deformation," and in particular deformations of the body, mind, and text in certain Western authors between the times of Copernicus and Einstein. I use the phrase "Mannerist fiction" in my title because the primary objects of study here will be literary fictions, and because I want to connect these deformations to the re-visioning of space in Mannerist painting in the early cinquecento. In bringing into juxtaposition "formalism" and the school of painting I would ask whether the former is not better understood as a type of artistic practice like the latter, rather than some critical or interpretive stance. The definition of "form" itself is borrowed from Kant, who famously referred to space and time as the "forms of perception" that organize our cognition of phenomena and, by extension, knowledge. So the term "deformations" in this sense carries much import. Heidegger, we should recall, went so far as to make time the very premise of Being. Space and time structure everything we say or do or think, without having any "being" in themselves, as Heidegger might say. The best comment on the matter by a writer of fiction that I can think of is in Henry James's story "The Figure in the Carpet," where the famous author, Vereker, responds to the young man seeking to discover what the secret "figure" is in his work by calling it "the very string [] that my pearls are strung on!"[2] Space and time structure the necklace, make it hold together, render its pearls visible as aesthetic objects, while remaining as invisible as Vereker's secret.

In the eighteenth century G.E. Lessing argued that space belonged to the painter, while time belonged to the novelists. While this is superficially true, it is always interesting to look at a painting's temporal quality, the moment in time it depicts, if it is representational, just as it is interesting to consider how a novel handles its spaces. The fundamental common parent remains "form." In discussions of art and literature we sometimes talk about a novelist's or painter's "material." What is it? We might understand it to be subject matter, and think of things like history, the Holocaust, nature, and so on. At an even more material level, we might say it is pen and ink, paint and canvas, or with today's multimedia artists, digital imagery, plastic, light, and sound. But there is something even more basic that novelists and painters all work with, and that is form: the string their pearls are strung on. One might say that over and above, as well as below, all other thematic or philosophical concerns, form itself is their material. The subject of a novel or painting is one thing, but it is really the way it is articulated in space and time that matters most. Form is the fundamental "material" that both Goya and Flaubert had to master. And while formal concerns are always historically and culturally conditioned, discussing those contingencies is more the work of the critic than the artist. The latter has something more immediate to deal with, and that is the problem of how to spatially and/or temporally render her subject in a way that makes it perceptible and vivid. The work may tell us something profound that can be paraphrased and called a "statement," but that will not elevate it to the level of art. Proficiency, ingenuity, and originality in form making and form breaking is what will accomplish that.

Paper and paint have their own material limitations, and their corresponding formal limitations when it comes to the treatment of space and time. Words like "figure" and "figural" come into play in both kinds of making, a figure meaning one thing in a painting (or carpet) and something else in a literary work. For Goya it is a matter of articulating his "figures" in the space of a setting. And the same might be said for Shakespeare as he envisioned his characters in the real space of a stage setting. As a writer, Shakespeare had the additional problem of having to deal with time. The dramatist thus sits halfway between the painter and the novelist in having to manage formal demands in both modalities. The poet, for her part, exists somewhere between the dramatist and the novelist in the restrictions she feels put upon her by the formal demands of spatio-temporality. Imagistic poetry looks to create a kind of *Gestalt* or picture in the reader's mind that may be literally timeless, while a narrative poem experiences some of the same temporal constraints that a novelist works under, and may be spatially conservative, or even conventional.

Regardless of the genre, if a work feels and looks spatially and temporally conventional, we call it "representational"; if it does not, we tend to look for another word. Perhaps we will call it "non-representational," "expressionistic," or "abstract." There are periods of stability and formal conservatism in art where the former dominates, and there are periods of instability and radical experimentation. In all cases, it is a matter of how the material of space and time are "articulated." Like the body's musculature, the art lies in making the moving parts work together. That is what puts the life in Pygmalion, and the "creative" in creative writing. When the parts fit together smoothly we might be looking at a Raphael painting, or reading a Tolstoy novel. When they don't, we might be looking at a painting by Bosch, or reading *Tristram Shandy*, both examples of Mannerist art.

"Formalism" is the term we use for a concern with form. It and "Mannerism" are big concepts, so it may be well to begin with some definitions and distinctions that go beyond Kant. The word "formalism" is employed by both art historians and literary scholars, while "Mannerism" is usually reserved for the school of painting that first appeared in Italy circa 1520 and includes painters like Pontormo, Bronzino, and Parmigianino, along with their followers in Germany and the Netherlands. In bringing the two terms together, I would like to suggest, first, that what are often judged mere exercises in "formalism" in literary art have a lineage and purpose that derives from the art world; and second, that both terms, "formalism" and "Mannerism," are about making art, not judging it. Formalism, in particular, is more than a school of criticism; it is a practice, an aesthetic, like Mannerist painting. This distinction has sometimes slipped from sight in literary studies as fashion has swerved away from New Criticism and subsequent formalist critical approaches such as Deconstruction, to the more socio-political orientations of New Historicism. It is good to remember that the first so-called formalists, the Russian Formalists of 1917, were practitioners, not critics; and that their point was that the treatment of form (space and time) had its own history.

Literary studies today nonetheless often work from a definition of "formalism" that underwrites the above shift in fashion to New Historicism. Rather than looking to what practitioners of the two arts do or say, we often locate our understanding of formalism next to a kind of art-for-art's-sake doctrine. This is the idea, familiar to literary scholars, that literary language is self-focused or (as the New Critics put it) "autotelic." Its function is not to tell us things by referring to the exterior world, but to offer a unique experience by drawing our attention to a work's own formal qualities. The focus is on the internal play of language itself.[3] This indeed makes it seem oblivious to historical or cultural influences (the lack of exterior world). The search for a text's literariness often defines the word, although this is the task of the critic, not the writer. The Marxist is also content with a definition that situates itself with the receiver of the text or artwork rather than the maker. Formalism here is the belief that the question of literature's specificity can only be answered by looking at the formal properties of literary texts.[4] Again, criticism rather than praxis is the focus.

For the best understanding of what follows I would suggest a slightly modified understanding of the word "formalism" that draws it closer to the world of "making" in art and painting, and in particular to de-forming rather than forming, de-formation and even dis-figuring or dis-figurement in the two arts. This perspective draws on the modernist moment in writing and painting for its best understanding, and it has usually been where art historians (always more interested in space than writers are) begin. I will come to art history in a moment, in that vein, but a good entry point lies in what T.W. Adorno said about abstract art. In his *Aesthetic Theory* he equates formalism to modernism as such. It is "abstractness, that irritating indeterminateness of what it is and to what purpose it is." Its object is "aesthetic distancing." And this "perspective" should ideally be that of both the critic and the "maker." "Formalism" for Adorno signifies that the maker is no longer working from the conventional epistemological given that knowledge is a matter of matching what one sees in the world to what it is, its truth – the notion that "appearance is meaningful." Something has occurred to make that (perhaps permanently, perhaps only temporarily) impossible. When that occurs, space itself is questioned. When we suffer "the catastrophe of meaning, appearance becomes abstract."[5]

Heidegger reminds us that the concern with form is more than just playing with language or line. We "frame" questions; we "frame" knowledge; and we depend on this *Gestell* or 'enframing' to live. But Heidegger points out in his later writings that whenever something is framed, re-presented or "pictured" – the "World" itself, for example, as *Weltbild* – Being is no longer present. The frame provides a misleading, false objectivity that comes to us from technology, but does not work when it comes to thinking about Being or art. Technology frames; but the spatial position it establishes between subject and object does not work in the world of thinking or of the viewer and the artwork. To represent thought in terms of figure and ground (*Gestaltung*) is to import a static, spatial stability into the world of spirit that it does not possess. What modernist art does is take the frame and break or deform it. The modernists tried to break open these boundaries, allowing the true Being of the represented object to shine forth, as much in language (the "house of Being") as in painting. Heidegger thus provides the basis for a kind of ethics of deformation in modernist art that has little to do with the Marxist accusation that so-called formalists are blind to history.[6] Picasso was a formalist, a painter concerned with form, just as Joyce, Sterne, and Rabelais were writers concerned with form and form breaking in prose fiction. The notion that they were somehow blind to history confuses *poesis* with *techne*.

My definition of "Mannerism" also focuses on the kind of "abstractness" Adorno notes in modernism. In Mannerist art spatial concerns trump animation of surface. Space in paintings often appears extended into infinity. Boundaries are removed.[7] In identifying the beginning of formalism per se in Western art with the Mannerist turn in painting in the age of Copernicus, I want to point out how both formalism and Mannerism are intimately connected to their historical moment in the early sixteenth century. Mannerist painting arrives on the scene right at the time when Renaissance space, stable for almost a hundred years as it developed from Giotto to Raphael, is at its best. And then the "just proportions" that define Renaissance space suddenly fall apart and give place to the disproportions and incommensurabilities of Mannerist art – a style that has been called by art historians expressionism before its time. It is the first moment in Western art when incommensurability becomes an explicit artistic intention.

Incommensurability is literally the lack of a common measure, but I use the term as another word for deformation, one that emphasizes scalar and spatial incongruities of the sort I will be looking at in Rabelais and Swift. It is the most accessible and familiar kind of deformation, and yet we often overlook its role. In Kafka's story, for example, the fact that Gregor Samsa wakes up to find he is an insect is one thing, but the true horror is in his size: the fact that he is big, human size and not small. If he were the size of an actual insect he could at least flip over and get out of bed. But he can't move. He is immobilized by his size and weight. And this horrible immobility is the first thing Gregor focuses on. An insect's body, one might say, is incommensurable with the gravitational demands placed on human ones. In "The Fly" the fly's head and arm on André Delambre are similarly human-size, out of all proportion to their original. It is this disproportion that makes them horrible. The effect, if Langelaan (who wrote the story) had made them fly-size, would have been merely grotesque, an artistic mistake. Similarly, Delambre's own head on the body of the fly must be in proportion to the size of the fly's body, disproportionate to his own. In other words, much of the horror in the story, if not all of it, derives from the incommensurability of forms and sizes.

This is the sort of spatial "abstractness" we see in Mannerism at the beginning of the sixteenth century. It was a time when "the catastrophe of meaning," as Adorno puts it, really meant something. Europe was wracked with the upheavals of the Reformation. But it was also the age that saw the invention of printing, and something that woodblock printing, and then moveable-type printing, made possible: the production and distribution of maps. Maps are about space, the space one lives in, and we like that to be stable. The voyages of discovery, however, were making that difficult, and had been doing so since the last years of the fifteenth century. In other words, on top of the horrors of the Reformation, this was a period when the public's notions of terrestrial space, of the very ground they walked on, was being shaken by the news being brought home by the explorers.

Indeed, one might argue that maps were the principal condition that made the spatial re-visioning of the world possible. Maps of the Old World, as we know, changed radically in the period. If one compares a Ptolemaic map from the late fifteenth century to one only forty years later the differences in scale are dramatic. In the latter, the point of view has shot up to a hundred miles or so higher in the atmosphere from where it is with Ptolemy, whose map covers a mere hundred and five degrees of longitude, or less than a third of the globe. The Ptolemaic maps suggest that a short sail off the western edge at Gibraltar will promptly bring one back at the other edge in the Ganges Delta, having sailed around a very small world. But by 1550 global space had ballooned out of all proportion. The world in the later maps has doubled in volume, with the appearance of the Indian Ocean, courtesy of the voyages of Bartolomeu Dias and Vasco da Gama, who rounded the Cape of Good Hope, respectively, in 1487 and 1497–8; and in the west as a result of the Magellan expedition, which rounded the tip of South America and made it all the way across the Pacific Ocean to the Philippines before returning to Spain in 1522.

This large-scale revision of global space was all about maps and mapmaking, and map revising, and would hardly have been possible without the printing needed to make the maps available. The new information coming in from the voyages was not just a matter of people having their age-old image of global space (as per Ptolemy) revised in the short span of a few years. Before 1475 (when the first Ptolemaic atlas with printed maps came out) the "average citizen" simply *had* no image – age-old or otherwise – of global space. Printing itself had only been around since 1460; up until then there were no maps as we know them in circulation, period. So the first thing that happened was the "map" itself, which made its appearance in 1475 as a new kind of public document. Not everyone had access. Nevertheless, a lot more people saw these printed editions than any earlier manuscripts of Ptolemaic maps.[8] The Bologna Ptolemy of 1475 came out in a run of only five hundred, which sold slowly. But revisions to the maps followed rapidly as reports from the explorers began coming in through the 1480s and 1490s. They continued for twenty years, with new maps appearing regularly in an attempt to keep pace with the steady flow of new geography. There was a craving for maps, which became almost talismanic objects in the century as global space became visible and familiar for the first time. A new spatial paradigm began to take hold.[9]

In other words, space itself underwent a change in the period, not in response to any scientific (or geographical) discovery, in the way Thomas Kuhn might argue, but in a way that made such discoveries possible to begin with. And people, one might say, saw space for the first time, represented on paper. Without maps the concept of a voyage of discovery has no real meaning.[10] Military campaigns changed as commanders suddenly had access to topographical maps. An attack or advance could be "mapped" over weeks or even days to show its progress, and these could be published in news reports for the public to see. Globes were the best representation of the earth, but difficult to produce. With the advent of printing all this changed as oval strips (gores) could now be pasted onto the round core.[11]

How did people respond to this respatialization of their world? They appear to have responded much the way readers respond to the publication of a great new novel, or art lovers to the discovery of a new painting by an old master. The aesthetic parallel is not an idle thought. Maps, it should be remembered, were more than charts: they were aesthetic objects where the illustrations and borders (the cartouche) were painstakingly drawn and coloured. So at the same time as people looked at them as realistic representations of the earth they lived on, they also looked at them as aesthetic objects. Space, in other words, first came into existence for many people as art – not as space, but as a kind of "painting" of space. The world was suddenly an aesthetic object, and space itself, a kind of fiction or representation, right at the moment when it felt most real to them.

But there was more. Although many were suddenly realizing that Ptolemy had been wrong about global space, it still felt safe to believe he had been right in his other mapmaking endeavour, to wit, his geocentric cosmography. In the turmoil of the day, that fact might have provided some comfort if people had been allowed to hold onto it. But they were not, because a few years later Copernicus appeared and took that illusion away from them as well, offering instead his heliocentric vision of the universe. One might say, indeed, that both Columbus and Copernicus were made possible by maps, and the new mapmaking that printing facilitated. Copernicus did not strike home in 1543 with the same force as the reports of the explorers. The conventional view is that he had to wait for Galileo and Kepler at the end of the century to make the radical nature of his contribution apparent. But it would be a mistake to think no one heard his news in the 1540s. And for those who did the sudden re-formation of both cosmological and global space must have been a true "revolution." It was a Big Bang that reverberated across the century and beyond.

Refiguring space was a central event in transitioning out of the Old World. Pico della Mirandola, in his "Speech on the Dignity of Man" (1486), writes: "I placed thee in the middle of the world, that thence thou mightest see more easily all that is in the world. We made thee neither a heavenly being nor an earthly being, neither mortal nor immortal, in order that thou, as the free and sovereign artificer of thyself, mightest mould and sculpture thyself in the form which thou shouldest prefer." The very name of Mirandola inspires the kind of wonder in looking around at the world that we associate with the Renaissance. In the company of a re-emergent Plato and Aristotle the educated "I" of Europe was once more in a position to survey and know, see and understand. But if Pico's formulation says something new, it also says something old, something old about the stability and continuity of medieval space that conditions his imagery. Because the spatial figure Pico employs is still the medieval centre-periphery model. The radical departure, one might say, is not at the level of the system but only at the level of personnel, with Man replacing God at the centre. Space itself has not changed.

The stability of Pico's spatial model is everywhere evident in Renaissance art, especially in the use of "perspectivism" by painters and architects to achieve realistic visual effects.[12] This stability reaches a kind of apotheosis in the High Renaissance. Antonio Manetti, writing after Brunelleschi, claimed, quite rightly, that perspective was a rational, mathematical concern with correct spatial relations based on a single point of observation. The goal, he wrote, was to create an illusion. And Leon Battista Alberti, writing in *Della pittura* (1435), claimed that "naturalism" of this kind was appealing because it domesticated an otherwise dangerous and mysterious world. Space, at best, is seen as a neutral tool, like paint. Da Vinci said he preferred painting to sculpture because the lines of perspective in a sculpture did not look authentic, while in a painting perspective could reach way out beyond the work itself. Plus, he pointed out that painting could provide aerial perspectives in a way impossible for sculpture.[13] He was the first to notice that space could be as amenable or conditional to what inhabits it as paint.[14]

"Things fall apart," Yeats wrote in 1920, "the centre cannot hold." This was even more true in 1520 as maps dissolved the medieval centre-periphery model. In 1520 the centre quite literally did not hold once explorers and their maps began circulating. This is not to say that these changes had a more direct effect on people's lives than the Protestant Reformation, whose effects were felt on every level of existence. Jacob Burckhardt writes that the sixteenth century, as a result, was a time of narrow fanaticism. And the Reformation had as profound effects on art as anything else.[15] It is hard to overstate the importance of the religious fight that followed Luther's declaration. Nonetheless, "narrow fanaticism" does not quite do justice to some of the work done at the time, either in painting or literature. And André Chastel's feeling (see n. 15) that many (apparently including painters) might have given up on putting ideas and concepts in visible form is also questionable. What happened was merely that "form" itself, as an idea, was changing.

The upheaval in the Church certainly added to the kind of instability Chastel refers to, but the specific spatial revisions I have been discussing can also be connected to other factors. Stephen Greenblatt refers to "the great 'unmooring' that men were experiencing" – an apposite metaphor. He points out that the impressive number of conduct manuals published during the period – coming from the pens of Machiavelli, Castiglione, Erasmus, and Tyndale – shows just how adrift everyone was, men and women alike. The "unmooring" had very real effects on the ground, as Greenblatt points out, in farming and the agrarian economy, sparking population shifts and urban growth.[16] These were material not intellectual factors, and felt as such by everyone. But they must have been aggravated for many by the rapidly changing visions of terrestrial space forced on them by the explorers. The 1520s and 1530s witnessed a rash of comets, and in 1533 there was a lunar eclipse, prompting astrologers to predict disaster. This was the unstable state of the spatial union when in 1543 Copernicus published his *On the Revolutions of the Celestial Spheres* – a book that promptly did to the universe what Magellan and the others had done to the planet. With Copernicus, the "unmooring" went cosmic, and the whole spatial grid of the Renaissance lost its hold. Greenblatt might be thinking of the fate of Ptolemy's globe as the centre of the universe as much as anything else when he refers to people's "sense that fixed positions had somehow become unstuck."[17]

Critical studies of formalism today usually align it with the modernist period. In juxtaposing Copernicus, Newton, and Einstein I want to suggest not so much a "history" as some family resemblances that run through the three, and that makes a slightly different "dating" possible. Much has been written about Sterne as an example of postmodernism before its time, just as art historians write of Mannerism as expressionism before its time. Newton saw his cosmological interests as furthering and supporting those of Copernicus, and Einstein saw himself as the third in that great line. Joyce looked back to Sterne, and both looked back to Rabelais. Revisions to contemporary ideas of "space" took place in all three periods. So there are some family ties among the three cosmologists, as well as among the writers and painters in the three periods. But the view that formalism is exclusively a modernist phenomenon has strong support from those who see its "abstractness" as a kind of necessary, even inevitable, reaction to what might be called the "long march" of, or towards, "realism" in Western art. A brief reminder of the scholarly record on the topic can show us why this view carries such weight.

Eric Auerbach, for example, argues brilliantly in *Mimesis: The Representation of Reality in Western Literature* that the progress away from and out of a Romance-based prose fiction is clear if we compare Homer to the Bible. His erudite exposition in "Odysseus' Scar" comparing the story in Homer to the Biblical tale of Abraham and Isaac is required reading on the topic. In real space, people age in real time; this does not happen in Homer, where Odysseus is pretty much the same fellow when he gets home that he was when he first left to go to war. Interestingly, for what I am thinking about here, Auerbach uses a spatial metaphor to describe the difference between Homer and the biblical text. The former is all foreground and no background. There is no depth (of field), but rather a kind of mural that one moves across in Homer, rather than into and out of, as one will do in the subsequent works of realism, the first example of which is the Abraham and Isaac story, where the reader must actually interpret (read for background) and not simply look and see and accept, as with Homer. And Auerbach offers the long digression in *The Odyssey* that cuts away from a scene of high tension and fills in the backstory on how Odysseus got the scar on his leg, as an example of this narrative "flatness." Thus begins, in Auerbach's view, the long march towards the everyday in Western literary art. And its main feature is real, everyday space, as we will eventually get it in Renaissance painting. Auerbach's book is a major critical accomplishment, although recent trends away from literary history have produced critics of the teleological nature of his overall argument.[18]

Rabelais is an important way station on the road to realism that Auerbach posits – a place the French author earns through his devotion to the details of various bodily fluids and functions, and despite the spatial unrealities of his stories. Bakhtin also subscribes to this view, and likewise overlooks Rabelais's distortions in order to enlist him on the same long march. His 1920 "Forms of Time and Chronotope in the Novel" tells the story of the gradual coming of age of realism in the novel, from Greek Romances where space and time ignore the rules of everyday life, to Rabelais, where the everyday, in all its noisy glory, triumphs. Bakhtin cites the great nineteenth-century realists – Stendhal, Balzac, Dostoyevsky – but Rabelais is decidedly the epigone. Rabelais in this master narrative is both a Renaissance man and a realist, but certainly not a Mannerist. Bakthin's critics, like Auerbach's, have noted the distressingly teleological nature of his argument – one that first presumes that realism is the goal, then looks back and places things on the road to that end.[19]

The most influential contemporary history of space remains Henri Lefebvre's *The Production of Space*. This and works that follow its lead take a materialist approach (historical materialism) where the word "space" is used almost figuratively in a focus on "social spaces" that is reminiscent of Foucault. Such works operate within a Marxist sociology of space where space is (paradoxically) less material than figural, less a mode of perception than a word for "site" or "cultural construction."[20] As such, it is a superstructural element subordinated and secondary to the base, an effect that is prompted by prior social movements, such as the shift in power from country to city. Marxist writers like Daniel Bell

(*The Condition of Postmodernity*) and Fredric Jameson see respatialization as an exclusively twentieth-century phenomenon. Jameson's position that spatial categories have come to dominate temporal ones in the late-capitalist period is well known. Interestingly, Jameson echoes William Burroughs on the topic (see epigraph).

Spengler in *The Decline of the West* noticed, nonetheless, that something drastic happened to our sense of space in the early sixteenth century. He sets the classical soul opposite the modern soul, with the former in a comfort zone of controlled and comprehended space, while the latter is Faustian and doomed to endless and hopeless striving. And this is because space, following Copernicus, is now limitless. Limitless space, Spengler argues, represents that lost Faustian soul. He claims that depth of field in painting denotes self-confidence and a trust in human knowledge. The purpose of perspective in Renaissance art, for example, is to bring the world to heel under the human gaze, to subject phenomena to the "I," which in ordering comprehends them.[21] The Mannerists do not enter the picture, so to speak, in Spengler's account.

His position is similar to that of the influential early twentieth-century art critic Wilhelm Worringer, who was the first to write about the distortions of modernist painting in his 1908 *Abstraktion und Einfühlung* (first translated as *Abstraction and Empathy* in 1953). In it he enlarges on Riegl's idea of a *Kunstwollen* or *Zeitstil* to argue that when people lose faith in the solidity or reality of their world, the third dimension in painting (depth) disappears and we are left with art that is flat and abstract.[22] Space loses its coherence:

> It is precisely space which, filled with atmospheric air, linking things together and destroying their individual closedness, gives things their temporal value and draws them into the cosmic interplay of phenomena; most important of all in this connection is the fact that space as such is not susceptible of individualization ... Space is therefore the major enemy of all striving after abstraction, and hence is the first thing to be suppressed in the representation. This postulate is inseparably interlocked with the further postulate of avoiding the third dimension, the dimension of depth, in the representation, because this is the authentic dimension of space.[23]

Depth of field for Worringer is the true dimension of space. The spatial incommensurabilities of Picasso are symptomatic of a breakdown in communication between the inner and outer life, and reflect alienation. As an art historian Worringer is principally concerned with space, but he notes that detaching an object from its natural spatiality is also to detach it from time, producing a loss of temporal value. The identification of spatiality with the third dimension, the dimension of depth, is compelling and feels generally right when one thinks of alienation and flatness in much modernist art. Klee's images, one might say, are as flat as Homer's narrative. Others, however, that are almost clinical examples of "alienated art," have depth of field. Most of Dali's paintings have it, and even Munch's *Scream* has a foreground and background.

More than depth of field, the larger issue in these paintings has to do with a particular spatial logic and its disarticulation that is first apparent in Mannerist painting and literature. Worringer follows the "long march" model and argues for an unbroken tradition of developing realism (he calls it "naturalism") all the way through the Renaissance, ending only with Cézanne at the end of the nineteenth century.[24] He does not mention Mannerism. And other art critics have echoed the view that modernism is the first occurrence in Western art of abstract "formalism."[25]

Despite these histories, with their *telos* in modernism, I would suggest that the first large-scale manifestation of disproportion and incommensurability in Western art came with the rejection of quattrocento space by painters in the early sixteenth century. Nor was this rupture an isolated formal event; it was tied into the larger shift in the tectonic plates of space and time that took place in the period, including the Copernican revolution and the revolution in mapmaking occasioned by the European voyages of discovery. Erik Erikson writes that "some periods in history become identity-vacua" where one cause is "fears aroused by discoveries and inventions ... which radically expand and change the whole world image." This is a good description of the age of Luther (which Erickson mentions), and of Copernicus and the Explorers.[26]

Space and time may be invisible but they are not universals, as we well know; they have a history and can change. And since they are our "modes of perception," as Kant said, the world we see and represent in art changes when they do. They can be changed by events, as Erickson suggests, or even a singular event. Art historians all agree that space has a history. Spaces are born and die and have their own history.[27] Erickson's notion of events provoking a shift in the space-time image is Kuhnian. A "paradigm shift," according to Kuhn, is a definitive change in what counts as knowledge at the time of major scientific discoveries. The discoveries provoke the "shift," as per Erikson. For people to understand them something about the rules for what qualifies as knowledge has to change. The "paradigm" in use that determines what counts as truth has to shift in order to accommodate and make visible the new facts.[28]

It might be argued, however, that this particular *Gestell* is a rather undialectical, linear, and even teleological model for something that happens in many different ways. For example, it seems equally reasonable to believe that instead of a cultural crisis in identity formation (Erikson) producing a shift in "the whole world image," the shift in the space-time image was the condition for the possibility of that crisis in the first place. These processes are impossible to peg out on a clothesline. Nonetheless, Kuhn and Erickson do notice something important, which is that space and time changed in the early sixteenth century.

Kuhn, for example, discusses his "Copernican revolution" as a shift in the space-time image that took place at the time. In painting, the shift is visible as early as the hallucinatory *Garden of Earthly Delights* (ca 1510) by Bosch, and in writing, as late as 1650 in Marvell's "To His Coy Mistress," where the poet writes: "Had we but world enough, and time, / This coyness lady were no crime," implying that space as well as time is in short supply. The final couplet of the poem reads: "Thus, though, we cannot make our sun / Stand still, yet we will make him run." The question of whether it was the earth or the sun that stood still was the one Copernicus raised in the 1540s. Marvell need not have had that in mind to write his lines, but they do depend for their effect on the reader's awareness of the heliocentric hypothesis and debate. Clearly, it was still news. Marvell wrote the poem not long after Copernicus's *De revolutionibus orbium coelestium* (*On the Revolutions of the Celestial Spheres*) had been put on the Index of banned works by Rome, which happened in 1616, so he probably knew about it.

Kuhn points in like manner to the work of Donne for evidence that something profound had taken place and needed to be acknowledged. In "Ignatius, his Conclave" Donne has Copernicus as the first inhabitant of Hell. Ignatius Loyola tells him he might be right in his new thinking. Even in your day, Loyola admits, yours was a "truth, which [] was creeping into every mans minde."[29] In "The First Anniversary" Donne writes:

[the] new Philosophy calls all in doubt,
The Element of fire is quite put out;
The Sun is lost, and th'earth, and no man's wit
Can well direct him where to look for it.
... [the universe]
Is crumbled out again to his Atomies.
'Tis all in peeces, all cohaerence gone;

All just supply, and all Relation:
Prince, Subject, Father, Sonne, are things forgot.   (ll. 205–15)[30]

Kuhn notes that in the 1600s atomism made a comeback because it was basically just Copernicanism, and that the "new Philosophy" Donne refers to was a merger of atomism and Copernicanism.[31] Atomism, originating with Democritus, took a mechanical view of the universe as a large machine-like operation made up of particles obeying purely scientific laws – that is to say, with no one in control, such as God. So it was not wrong of the Church to see the juxtaposition here of atheism (although paganism would better correspond to the time of Democritus) and the new cosmology. Giordano Bruno, who followed Copernicus in the late 1500s, noticed the similarity of Democritus's world to the Copernican one. Following Copernicus, he claimed that there were other solar systems scattered across infinite space; that nature was a system of atoms that had no order and no centre; and that God was therefore both everywhere and nowhere. This is the blend of atomism and Copernicanism Kuhn has in mind, and that Donne probably did as well when he referred to the "new Philosophy." Bruno was more direct about it than Copernicus, and was burned at the stake for his frankness. Naturally, not all Catholics in England were agonizing in 1600 over a book written by an unknown Polish astronomer sixty years before – especially one that had not been translated into English. Many in England had never heard of the book. And those who probably had, like Milton, could choose to ignore it. At least there is no evidence in *Paradise Lost*, written in 1667, that the Ptolemaic universe is in any danger.[32] Arthur Koestler, early in the twentieth century, famously called *On the Revolutions* "the book nobody read."

While there is clearly a history of science through-line from Copernicus to Newton to Einstein that this study rests upon, my arrangement of authors is not chronologically ordered and does not move ahead in the same way. This is because doing so would imply a narrative, a history of ideas, or literary history approach foreign to my goal here. Rather than a history of ideas, the book is really about one idea, the Mannerist idea of space, which first comes up around the time of Copernicus and reappears in the work of later writers and painters, with perhaps a little more emphasis in the other two periods, when cosmological revisions were also front and centre. Instead of a chronological ordering I have therefore chosen a different way of grouping these disparate authors that corresponds roughly to what I said at the outset here about deformations of the body, mind, and text. The study brings together physiology, psychology, and textual analysis in what might be called an applied spatial critique of the works examined.

I begin in part 1 with Rabelais and Swift, in what is at least partly a shameless attempt to underline the Copernican and Newtonian family ties. If this were an art history monograph I would include plates of the wonderful ceiling paintings done in Newton's day, where space itself is the subject. Ceiling art experienced its own renaissance in the period. However, the real reason for my juxtaposition is that our two narrators are doctors, men of science (Rabelais and Gulliver), who both give us big people and little people. Rabelais, however, is a Mannerist who delivers a hundred variations on the theme of spatial incommensurability, while Gulliver is surprisingly accurate, the perfect Royal Society man who delivers his big and little worlds in their proper proportions.

Part 2 of the study brings together Ben Jonson, Sade, and Pynchon. Here we have a combination of different kinds of deformation of mind, body, and text that I range under the headings of narcissism, sadism, and hysteria. The deformation is one of mind in Jonson, whose plays I will discuss in chapter 3 through the lens of a psychological spatial analysis (object relations theory); in Sade it is physiological, psychological, and textual. I will suggest in chapter 4 that it is Sade's deformed body that furnishes the key to understanding his spatial eccentricities. And in chapter 5, in Pynchon "de-formation" takes the shape of a textual battle between two kinds of space: real and fantastic. Hysteria in Pynchon is both the cause and the effect of his spatial juxtaposition of two absolutely antithetical textual spaces: the space of realism and the space of cartoon.

In the third and final section I focus on two moments that might be called the historical bookends for the concern with space and time in the Western tradition. In chapter 6 I look at some exemplary texts from the modernist moment. These were the years when Einstein's thoughts on the space-time continuum started to become known. In this chapter I look at how spatial and temporal incongruities, for example, appear in novels by Faulkner, Joyce, and Mann. For the reader who wants to know what this looks like, I recommend going immediately to chapter 6 for the analysis of two spatial and temporal deformations in Faulkner's *As I Lay Dying*. In chapter 7 I argue that while Heidegger and especially Bergson are key to our understanding of the temporal experiments of much modernist fiction, the notion of *durée* that Bergson introduced is essentially the prophetic time of the Old Testament. I look at some of the linguistic evidence for this, and also suggest that Einstein's notion of time as a continuum that cannot be dissociated from space can be found *in vitrio* in Aristotle's *Physics*.

In concluding the study with this turn to the past – from modernism to Moses, so to speak – what I want to suggest is not only that we need to think more about what "formalism" is, and its real history as a practice rather than theory, but to ask what it might mean for studies of modernity, and especially modernist art, to think that its central philosophy of time has so much in common with the prophetic time of the Old Testament. We are the children of the Greeks in so many ways, and Western art and science, from Copernicus to Einstein, derives much from the ontological obsessions of Greek philosophy. What then happens if we begin to entertain the possibility that the main artistic innovation of the last century might well have been a rejection of the entire conceptual underpinning of that heritage?

Part One

Big People and Little People:
Two Cases of Disproportion

1 Rabelais and Mannerism

There is too much eating. There is too much drinking. Lewd, leaping and cavorting women gather in the towns.

16th-century German pamphlet

In Western Europe circa 1500 space changed, and the availability of maps allowed people to see it changing. They were fascinated. *The Cosmographiae*, for example, were writings about the cosmos that had been appearing with some regularity well before Copernicus published *On the Revolutions* in 1543. They included information on geography, history, and natural science in addition to astronomy, and were liberally illustrated with maps. The earliest and best known was by Petrus Apianus, which appeared in 1524 at the peak of interest in accounts of the explorers, and it went through fifteen editions. Readers were interested both in the new terrestrial space and the new heavenly one.[1]

Copernicus would make the word "revolution" mean something special, but his own work was part of a bigger revolution in the world of space. In *The Structure of Scientific Revolutions* Thomas Kuhn claims that Copernicus and the calendar are evidence of how external conditions can help transform an anomaly into a crisis.[2] It may seem odd today to think of the heliocentric universe as springing forth from the status of an observed anomaly, but that would probably be Copernicus's description of events: one day a small problem with calendar calculations, an observation through a telescope, the next, a new world. But much weight rests on the external conditions that Kuhn notes as catalyst. The conditions must be right for a thought to occur, let alone a scientific discovery. It is the former that enables the latter, not the latter that provokes the former. A thought occurs that could not have occurred at another time, or if it did, the external conditions were not there for it to be heard and become part of public consciousness. We know that others had suggested before Copernicus that the sun was the centre of the universe. Aristarchus of Samos, Pythagoras, Pliny, Averroes, even Nicolas of Cusa had written in the preceding century of the possibility that the universe might be infinite.[3] But external conditions were not such that the thought could take hold.

This is a more indeterminate dynamic than the one usually ascribed to Kuhn, where the discovery of a new fact necessitates a paradigm shift in what counts as truth. That is a kind of cause-and-effect relationship that is difficult to prove. Copernicus was not the effect and some newly discovered fact the cause, any more than he was the cause of some paradigm shift in what counted as astronomical truth. Nor did external conditions, as such, "cause" his discovery. His new planetary scheme was merely made possible by those conditions.[4] I would agree there was a "paradigm shift" in space itself in the period, but if anything, it came first, making possible everything else that followed. And that had as much to do with printing and the appearance of maps as anything else. These were the external conditions, a bit like a change in the weather that allows new things to happen and grow, but difficult to tie to any single cause. In this case it was more as if a new ecosystem of space took hold that made old boundaries of all kinds impossible to maintain.[5]

Copernicus's book was modest in its claims. Written in response to a request by the Church for a more exact calendar, it was an attempt to correct Ptolemy on that heading, but also to predict eclipses more accurately. The wholesale revision of cosmological space that accompanied it was almost a footnote to that aim, but nonetheless entailed accepting the sun rather than the earth as the centre of the planetary revolutions. With this assertion, cosmological space suddenly expanded exponentially.[6] It used to be thought that few read Copernicus's book. Arthur Koestler, in his 1959 *The Sleepwalkers*, famously called it "the book nobody read." Frederick Copleston, in his *History of Philosophy*, downplays its influence, while C.S. Lewis insists that neither Copernicus nor the discovery of the New World had any demonstrable effect on writers in England or Europe.[7] Rome itself did not see the danger of *On the Revolutions* until 1616, seventy-three years after its publication, and did so only then thanks to Galileo and Kepler, whose work at the end of the 1500s began to make the true import of what Copernicus had written apparent. Kepler himself said that Copernicus merely re-presented

Ptolemy, not nature, although he was kind enough to add that in so doing Copernicus came closest to the truth. Copernicus cannily dedicated
his book to Pope Paul II, and this, combined with its heavily mathematical nature, and a preface written by a Lutheran clergyman who decided
to change Copernicus's claim to a mere suggestion or "what if," further
attenuated its shock value. But today we know that all the important
thinkers and astronomers read the book when it came out, and did not
miss its point. Around four hundred copies were printed in the first edition and took roughly twenty years to sell.[8] The book was widely known.

To get a sense of the "new" space that comes into the world in
Rabelais's day, it can help to remember a couple of literary treatments of
the older Renaissance space, which for all of its devotion to the realism
of depth of field and perspective still relies on medieval notions of centre and periphery. Consider More's *Utopia*, for example, written in 1517.
It deals in pre-Copernican space and presupposes a medieval *Gestalt*.
As a pillar of the Church of Rome and a man whose convictions led him
to oppose the king, More was not easily moved, or even particularly
impressed by minor shake-ups in the world like Luther. Copernicus did
not faze him. His island utopia displays none of the spatial tensions and
deformations that were beginning to eat away at the edges of Ptolemaic
space in the period. It still inhabits a pristine Renaissance space: "The
island of the Utopians is two hundred miles across in the middle part
where it is widest, and is nowhere much narrower than this except toward the two ends. These ends, drawn toward one another as if in a
five-hundred-mile circle, make the island crescent-shaped like a new
moon. Between the horns of the crescent, which are about eleven miles
apart, the sea enters and spreads into a broad bay."[9]

The *Oxford English Dictionary* defines "proportion" (from *pro portione* :
"for or in respect of [his or its] share") as "comparative relation"; "a portion or part in relation to the whole"; and "proper proportion" as the
"due relation of one part to another ... between things or parts of a thing
as renders the whole harmonious; balance, symmetry, agreement, harmony."[10] This also defines the Renaissance notion of *commensuratio* in
painting: a matter of just proportions. A circle cannot rightly be said to
display just or proper proportions because of its singularity; its display is
a sum of its parts, or better, the condition of particularity. Beginning from
a point, the line that will become its circumference is by necessity straight
before becoming curved, its curvature only becoming apparent by degrees, its angle of curvature constant, until it rejoins its beginning, making it henceforth impossible, as of that moment, to speak any longer

about beginnings and endings, the circle now being complete and identical to itself, its circumference identical at all points to all other points. Proportion and proportionality, however, become very much operative in the case where not one line, but two, depart from the above-mentioned point, one describing a smaller circle, one a larger circle, as if the point leading the outer line were moving faster to keep abreast of its slower inner counterpart, the two destined to be furthest apart (on More's island, two hundred miles) directly opposite their starting point, and meeting again where they started out, the diameter of the outer circle thus formed (in More's case) being five hundred miles. The crescent is perhaps the perfect example, not of perfection itself, but of proper proportion, the perfect agreement and harmony of two parts, beginning and ending as one.

More's literal "no-place" is spatially organized and stable in this sense. Its proportions are perfect, and perfectly conventional. The author describes the river that runs through its capital: "The Anyder rises from a small spring about eighty miles above Amaurot, but other streams flow into it, two of them being pretty big, so that, as it runs past Amaurot the river has grown to a width of half a mile. It continues to grow even larger until at last, sixty miles farther along it is lost in the ocean. In all, this stretch between the sea and the city, and also for some miles about the city, the river is tidal, ebbing and flowing every six hours with a swift current."[11]

The voice of the surveyor here is as reliable as an accountant's bookkeeping. More's objective is rational and precise, as is his sense of space. He wants his readers to suspend their disbelief and take this as a real account of a real city. The good geographer notes beginnings, middles, and endings, Amaraute being located roughly halfway between source and outlet to the sea, the river growing progressively wider as it goes. More uses detail the same way Defoe later would writing *Robinson Crusoe*: as a way of establishing the scientific tone, and thus making easy the suspension of disbelief. He wants his readers to be struck by the facticity, the historicity, the verisimilitude of the "place." So he takes great pains to present it as spatially familiar. He was not out of touch with what was happening on the Continent, in particular with news coming in of the voyages of discovery in the New World. His *Utopia* is nothing if not a response to that news, especially with a narrator who sailed with Amerigo Vespucci. But his attention is on the human meaning of the voyages, not their effect on global space. And he retains what might be called a philosophically flat space in which to set his speculative tale of an ideal community.

It is one he wants readers to find credible, even if they see the whole piece as a hoax. It is pointedly lacking anything we might call "irony," or any sense that it is meant as a jest. So we are encouraged to take it as fact, not fiction.[12] Its historicity, or factual feel, is to a great degree the result of More's attention to just proportions in its geography. The lunar metaphor in its crescent construction, like the mention of the tides that reach Amaraute, emphasizes rhythm and harmony. Some critics today have deconstructed the island's "harmony" by noting, for example, its creation as an act of violence that is then hidden; just as the inner harbour, womb-like, is both a positive birthplace of energy and a lack, an emptiness. The circle itself is broken, one might say, by the crescent. It is open on one side, and thus incomplete. There are also some minor irregularities in topography, and in the spatial and visual coordinates.[13] The average reader, however, probably does not notice such things.

Ariosto provides another example of pristine Renaissance proportions. *Orlando furioso* is stylistically interesting, but it displays the same medieval "enframing" as *Utopia*. Completed in 1509, it trades on the twelfth-century legends and chivalric tales of Arthur and Charlemagne and has no more interest in space than *Tristan*, the *Chanson de Roland*, or the works of the Byzantine painters. Characters and actions are located in a static, universal space and time. And when the author needs to be precise about the two forms, he is utterly conventional. In canto 16, for example, Rinaldo brings his English troops against Rodomont by crossing the river above the town:

> Three leagues above, he o'er the river's bed
> Had cast a bridge; from whence his English power
> To the left-hand by crooked ways he led;
> That, meaning to assail the barbarous foes,
> The stream no obstacle might interpose.   (16.29)

This has the necessary precision of a military campaign, written in a world whose temporal and spatial axes were firm and unquestioned. When necessary, Ariosto can number and itemize as well as More. He tells us that

> Rinaldo had, with Edward, sent a force,
> Six thousand strong, of archer-infantry,
> And sped, with Ariman, two thousand horse
> Of lightest sort; and foot and cavalry

Sought Paris by those roads, which have their course
Directly to, and from, the Picard sea;
That by St. Martin's and St. Denys' gate,
They might convey the aid the burghers wait.   (16.30)

The poem's space is rational and can be mapped. It has the precision of a military history.[14] Ariosto's calm disposition of forces through the literary spaces of his story shows no sign that contemporary shifts in the tectonic plates of space and time have sent any tremors his way. Like Milton, he might have been aware that changes had taken place in the world, but he chose to ignore them. For More and Ariosto, the sea is calm, and the stars are firmly placed in the firmament.

With Rabelais all these bets are off. And this is interesting since Rabelais-as-narrator was a man of science, a doctor, like Gulliver. Doctoring patients' needs in 1700 meant something quite different from what it meant in 1500, but the fact remains that the voice in each case is comfortable with numbers, mathematics, and geometry. Both narrators are men of science who parody their own Pythagorian proclivities but depend upon them nonetheless for their effects. It is interesting to compare how each crunches their respective numbers. In Rabelais we see the first seriously careful disfigurement of *Gestell* (enframing) in Western literature. *Pantagruel* (1532) appeared first and was popular enough to prompt Rabelais to write a prequel, *Gargantua*, probably in 1535. Both books feature giants, a perennial folk motif. But Rabelais was not a folklorist; he was a Mannerist who dealt in the same kind of spatial incommensurabilities as the painters of his day. He continued with a book 3 and book 4, which try to ring as much change as possible on the trope of spatial disproportion, and there is a book 5, published after Rabelais's death, that may or may not be his. When the first two were later published as a whole, books 1 and 2 were reversed to follow the chronological order of the story, with *Gargantua* as book 1 and *Pantagruel* as book 2, which is how they are now referred to.

Spatial incoherence is central to Rabelais's effect. He was hardly a conscious formalist, experimenting with self-reflexivity before its time. As Bakhtin and Auerbach point out, he is a "realist" insofar as the world does indeed come pouring in on his story at every turn. And yet, he was aware of the space-time *Gestalt* of his day. He often refers to the New World (*nouveau monde; terre neuve*), for example; and he picks up the word "utopia" from More and uses it as the name of the country his big heroes live in – somewhere off the northeast coast of Africa, we are told in book 2.[15] Its people are called Amaurotes, after the capital of More's *Utopia*. And there is the famous debate in chapter19 of *Pantagruel* between Panurge and a "learned Englishman" called Thaumaste who seems to be Rabelais's parody of More himself. In book 4, the whole Pantegrueline cast goes off on its own voyage of discovery into the New World, in search of the elusive northwest passage to China. Rabelais even has them giving little pen knives to the natives along the way, a touch he pulled from the accounts of Cartier, who had just returned from sailing up the St Lawrence River in Canada. So Rabelais was fully aware of the changes to the world image (*Bild*) going on around him.[16]

The question is, how does he present it, and what does he do to it? Certainly, there is no shortage of wonders in Rabelais's books. But the one that holds centre stage throughout is the fact of size. We are in the presence of giants, of big people and little people. As in Gulliver's stay with the Lilliputians and Brobdingnagians, it is this strange incommensurability more than any political or religious allegory, more than any satirical attack on the Church or higher learning, that carries the story in Rabelais and holds our attention. Histories of literary influence are quick to point out Sterne's debt to Rabelais. and Swift's debts as a satirist to Rabelais have also been noted. It is hard to imagine two more dissimilar writers than the misanthropic Swift and the carousing Rabelais, and yet both were fascinated by the measurements of human bodily functions and secretions. Swift took his lead from Rabelais here as well. Have any writers, besides these two, given us representations of giants relieving themselves in public? Gulliver does so on the queen's apartment to put out a fire; Gargantua lets loose on the Parisians for no good reason at all, from the bell tower of Notre Dame, "so fiercely that he drowned two hundred and sixty thousand, four hundred and eighteen persons, not counting women and children" (*G* 17). Swift's debt to Rabelais, in other words, runs deep.

In Swift, the argument between the Big Endians and Little Endians, and its political subtext, has not stood the test of time as well as the more striking spatial disorientation that follows from Gulliver being vastly out of proportion to his environment. The same can be said of Rabelais's work. He parodies and pillories an array of pedantries and policies, but nothing holds our interest like the phenomenal disproportion of his spatial constructions. The difference is that while Rabelais's hero makes water beyond all possibility, given his body size, Lemuel does not; given his own body size, relative to the Lilliputions, he pisses in proportion.

Rabelais appears to have felt the changing times in ways that look ahead to Copernicus and his astronomy. When he tells us how the race of giants came into being, for example, in the opening chapter of *Pantagruel*, the explanation includes a variation on the age-old theme of the heavens being out of joint. A star does not appear in the East, and no comet shoots across the sky, but the account nonetheless links the founding spatial deformity of the giants with a cosmic dislocation. First comes time:

> En ycelle les kalendes feurent trouvées par les breviares des Grecz, le moys de Mars faillit en karesme et fut la myoust en May. On moys de Octobre, ce me semble, ou bien de Septembre (affin que je ne erre, car de cela me veulx je curieusement guarder), fut la sepmaine des troys Jeudis ...

> [That year, too, the Greek kalends first figured in the almanacs. March coincided with Lent, it was mid-August in May. The week famed in the *Annals*, the week of the three Thursdays, fell in October – or September, to exclude all possibility of error, since I am bound to remain scrupulously accurate. Three Thursdays it had ....]

The distortion of time is then connected to a distortion of space:

> ... car il y en eut troys, à cause des irreguliers bissextes, que le Soleil bruncha quelque peu comme *debitoribus* à gauche, et la Lune varia de son cours plus de cinq toyzes, et feut manifestement veu le movement de trepidation on firmament dict *Aplane*: tellement que la Pleiade moyene laissant ses compaignons declina vers l'equinoctial et l'estoille nommé l'Espy laissa la vierge se retirant vers la balance: qui sont bien espoventables et matieres tant dures et difficiles, que les astrologues ne y peuvent mordre. (*P* 217–18)

> [... because of the irregular bissextile. The sun swerved a little towards the left, like a debtor ducking the bailiffs. The moon shifted about five fathoms off her course. The firmament called Aplanes (the heaven of fixed stars surrounding the seven heavens of planets) showed distinct signs of trepidation. As a result the middle Pleiad abandoned her fellows and declined toward the equinox. The star called Spica, in the constellation of the Virgin, moved over to the neighboring constellation of the Balance or Libra. Dreadful events these, matters too hard for astrologians to set their teeth in ...] (165)

Joyce must have enjoyed this passage, since he produced one quite like it in *Ulysses*, which I will look at later. Rabelais, in short, connects the birth of his principal piece of spatial disproportion – his giants – to cosmological turbulence.[17] He does so in a joking way, but the fact is that he cites a shift in the spatial and temporal coordinates as the source of his own spatial mutation. He also has More and *Utopia* on his mind, and certainly the explorers – Vespucci, Cartier, and others – but his imagination takes him from the terrestrial to the cosmological as the sun strays and the heavens are suddenly full of "alarming happenings."

The gigantism is caused by eating magic medlars – a kind of crabapple that is only edible when overripe and decaying. As an ex-Franciscan, Rabelais must have enjoyed rewriting this part of the story of the Fall, using his own fruit. Eating the magic medlars causes various parts of the anatomy to grow, and with the giants it happens to be the length of their bodies. The physical descriptions stress the disproportionate swellings; one part of the body is affected, but not others. The result is a hallucinatory disproportion. Exaggerations, monsters, mutants, giants, and the like had been around before Rabelais; he himself cites Lucian and Pliny. And there was *Baldus*, written before Rabelais, by Teofilo Folengo, which had already brought onto the page much that was Rabelaisian in this regard, including fantastic characters and scatological adventures.[18] But Rabelais takes things a step further.

Bakhtin calls Rabelais the ultimate realist because of the bodily fluids and functions (humanism, at a physiological level), but he has nothing to say about the presence of giants; or, given giants, that they should do things that they logically could not do because of their size. Giants in Rabelais's time would have been seen as frightening manifestations of otherness, symbols of what everyone feared and hated, certainly not their ideals of themselves.[19] All the more so if their spatial proportions seemed to obey some mysterious law. In *Beowulf*, by contrast, Grendel and his mother are monstrous and terrifying, but given their size, they do not violate any known laws of right proportions. The same holds for Polyphemus in *The Odyssey*. That is the difference that matters in Rabelais: his geometry is intentionally deformed. Huwawa in *Gilgamesh* and Error in *The Fairie Queene* are there to illustrate an allegorical point, like More's island realm, so it is important they obey the laws of spatial logic. Rabelais' giants are more of a threat – not to people, for they are not killers, but to the sixteenth-century *episteme* itself, because their defiance of spatial logic is a threat to the whole system.

It is important to note that in myth and folklore we never get the impression that space itself is an issue. Polyphemus, once the scale is established, behaves in keeping with its alignment. He may grab and eat some of the sailors, but he does not have a tongue six miles long, as in Rabelais. Once scale is established, it is adhered to. In Rabelais, by contrast, scale itself becomes the subject. For example, Pantagruel, when he is born, is so big he crushes his mother to death. This establishes one order of relative size. A newborn – instead of weighing, let's say, six pounds – would need to weigh several hundred to crush his mother. But then we learn that prior to the birth, out from Badabec's womb came "sixty-eight muleteers" leading mules "laden with salt," followed by "nine dromedaries loaded with hams ... seven camels ... and twenty-four cartloads of leeks, garlics and onions" (P 2.2). This calls for some recalibration. Badabec is large indeed – around the size of an apartment building. So that Pantagruel himself must be around the size of the Chrysler Building.

But this new adjusted scale soon mutates. The same is true of geographical space. Africa is named as the place of Pantagruel's birth, but space is fungible to the point where movement through it takes on a surreal quality. One moment we are in one location, the next, somewhere else. Often enough we are in the area around Touraine, Rabelais's birthplace. But when Pantagruel is old enough to go to school Gargantua, his father, sends him to Poitiers as if it were just up the road – as if the whole world were made up of giants just like him, with giant children going to giant schools.

Pantagruel varies in size and location almost arbitrarily. At one moment he seems twenty feet tall, then at another he is able as a boy to pick up a stone that is fifty foot square and ten feet thick, which would mean he would have to be more in the order of two hundred feet tall. When he is at school Rabelais has him travel about like any normal student or tourist, visiting Toulouse, Bordeaux, and other cities, without apparent incident, and even has him contemplate studying medicine, as if he were an ordinary mortal. A normal book for someone this size would be the size of a golf ball, too small to decipher. Rabelais even has Pantagruel playing tennis with his fellow students (P 2.5). At the same time he is able to pick up a huge church bell with his little finger – a bell so big that for hundreds of years it could not be moved. These disfigurements run throughout Book Two.

Panurge, the friend and future travelling companion that Pantagruel develops in Paris, is a normal-size man, like everyone else in the city.

When news arrives that Gargantua has died and the Dipsodes have invaded Utopia, the two set out immediately for Pantagruel's home. At this point we assume that for the Dipsodes to invade, they too must be a race of giants. But then we learn in chapter 24 that Panurge plans to infiltrate their ranks, "to banquet with them and lecher at their expense without being noticed by anyone" (P 2.24). So they are his size. But then, at the same time, they are so small that one in Pantagruel's mouth "would not have amounted to more than a grain of millet in an ass's throat" (P 2.25). And these mites have invaded Utopia. The explanation for this, as if there could be one, is that not everyone in either Utopia or Dipsodia is a giant, only the ruling class.

The Dipsode king, however, is not a giant. But he has three hundred giants in his army (P 2.26). Bakhtin may call this the logic of the folktale, but folktales are more spatially coherent. The battle between the Dipsodes and Utopians that concludes Book Two is described in some detail, with a surprising attention to spatial and geographical coherence, although this is the sequence where we learn that Pantagruel's tongue is six miles long and his mouth cavernous enough to hold an entire country. This is nonsense in a non-place of the sort Thomas More never dreamed of.

The tale of Pantagruel worked so well that Rabelais brought out the story of his father, Gargantua. He repeats the formula: story of birth; boy grows up and goes to Paris to be educated; war breaks out at home; boy returns home. This time round we are told that a cart brought Gargantua's rosary to the church and that each bead was "as big as a hatblock"; that his breviary weighs eleven hundred pounds; that he eats "dozens of hams" at a sitting; and so on. But then Gargantua enters the church like anyone else. Once Ponocrates takes over his education, Gargantua trades the scholastic approach for a humanist education that stresses the body as much as the mind. And again Rabelais has him interacting with his fellows without any indication that size is an issue. He even repeats the tennis match scenario that he used in the former story.

What makes this instalment special is the way spatial dislocations and disruptions dominate Rabelais's ostensible humanist agenda. Gargantua is put to school learning Renaissance skills, like music. The size of the trombone he needs might have given Rabelais a good excuse for a joke if he had thought of it (G 1.23). Gargantua learns to ride different kinds of horses as well without there being any hint that these cannot be normal-size horses. And he learns how to handle various weapons, like the pike, the rapier, and the dagger, again without Rabelais giving any indication that he sees that size must be of the essence here. Perhaps we are to assume that all of the above instruments and implements were made in large to accommodate the giant. But that would be difficult to accept when it comes to the beasts of the field, since Gargantua's new education also includes hunting. If Man Mountain, as Gulliver was called, is chasing a boar it would be roughly the size of a mouse to him. Gargantua is a giant but we are told it is a real accomplishment for him to scale a six-foot wall. He learns, Rabelais writes, to "run up the wall of a house like a rat"; "climb[s] trees like a cat"; jump "from one to another like a squirrel" (G 1.23); and so on. No sooner are we told this than we learn that he lifts weights that are 870 tons each; then, like a botanist, he goes out into the fields to examine plants. The humanist agenda here goes down under the more obvious concern with spatial proprieties.

When the military call comes for Gargantua to return home and help his father, we learn that Picrochle, the invader, is allied to Grandgousier (father of Gargantua) by blood (G 1.28), which would have to make him a giant too, one would think. But this logic is equally void and Picrochle turns out to be one of the Little People. Like Anarch, the king of the Dipsodes in Book Two, he is a mini-man out to attack giants. It is all good fun, as always, and at one point Gargantua even has to comb the cannonballs out of his hair, which have lodged there like grape seeds, he says, which again gives us a clue to the difference in scale. The battle itself is set in the countryside around Touraine again, but if the leader is so big that cannonballs are the size of grape seeds to him, the battle should not really be one.

The effect of these spatial shifts and incongruities is complex. The comic is given a strange twist that makes the story less comic than dreamlike, even slightly Daliesque and upsetting. Compare the story of Little Red Riding Hood, which is supposed to be much more terrifying. In that story spatial logic is observed and everything fits. The story is fanciful but spatially coherent. Red goes into the woods and comes out of them; her basket is not said to contain 870 sandwiches because no basket would hold that many; and the wolf is not too big to get into bed. In Rabelais such laws of just proportion are ignored. Instead, we are in the world of painters like Bosch.

Rabelais is our first literary formalist, and first Mannerist fictioneer, more than the apogee of Renaissance man. One art historian compares him to Rosso Fiorentino and Breughel, although a shared sense of humour rather than space is the point.[20] But it is not humour that Rabelais has in common with Mannerist painters; it is his spatial disjunctions and deformations. Rabelais stood alone under that mutant sky. More and Ariosto are part of an older world. We see none of his deformations in Marguerite de Navarre's *Heptameron* (ca 1550), which is as precise in its spatial sense as its model, Boccaccio's *Decameron* (1353); nor in Marot, du Bellay, Labé, or Desportes – other French writers of the period; nor in Spanish works of the time like *La Celestina* and *El Abencerraje*. Rabelais, like Sterne and Joyce after him, was on his own planet, and living in a space of his own.

2 Swift and *Commensuratio*

He who thro' vast Immensity can pierce,
See Worlds on Worlds compose one Universe,
Observe how System into System runs,
What other Planets circle other Suns?

Alexander Pope

If a poet looks through a microscope or a telescope, he always sees the same thing.

Gaston Bachelard

It took about sixty years for the echo of Copernicus to return. It came finally in the work of Galileo, who used the telescope to prove his precursor had been right. Galileo's first interest had not been astronomy per se, but the tides. In 1595 he realized that Copernicus's "theory" explained how they worked. Ten years later he was studying the phases of Venus and found that they too confirmed what Copernicus had said. In 1613 he published a work on sunspots in which he explicitly mentioned Copernicus's "theory" as not a theory but a fact. At this point the Church could no longer ignore things, and in 1616 the pope put Copernicus's *On the Revolutions* on the Index of banned books. Galileo was forced to promise he would henceforth cease and desist from mentioning in any way, shape, or form the Copernican heresy.

Reluctantly, Galileo complied. However, he went on working on his theory of the tides. In 1632 the work was ready to be published. It passed the Roman Catholic censors and came out as *Dialogue Concerning the Two Chief World Systems – Ptolemaic and Copernican*, for the modern edition of which Einstein wrote the foreword. In it, Galileo made clear what he had first discovered in 1595, to wit, that the Copernican system explained the tides where the old geocentric model of the universe could not. No one knows what happened to the censors, but Galileo was promptly called before the Inquisition and reminded of his promise to cease and desist with Copernicus. The book was ordered to be publicly burnt, and Galileo was put under permanent house arrest.

But the issue was now a public one. The Church felt the heresy was another arrow in its back as it battled Protestantism. The necessity to counter Luther had drawn Europe into nasty religious wars in the century, and things had taken an ugly turn in Spain with the Inquisition. Many artists in the baroque period responded with a fervent and fervid Catholicism in Counter-Reformation painting and sculpture that most decidedly did not display any spatial or Mannerist incongruities. Bernini was a favourite of the Papal See for his religiously swooning subjects, but whether Christian or pagan all of them had their feet planted firmly on the ground. Caravaggio's 1601 *Supper at Emmaus* is so "realistic" one can almost taste the chicken.

But Mannerist space did not disappear. In many of El Greco's works it might be argued that a Counter-Reformationist zeal and ecstasy is responsible for the formal disfigurements in his characters and settings. However, the same spatial treatment is afforded a pagan subject like his *Laocoön*, done around 1608. The dream-like quality of the spatial contours is a quality unto itself, a purely formal matter. His handling of space looks back to the Mannerists and ahead to painters like Chagall.[1] A similar violation of *commensuratio* appears in the ceiling painters – the *quadraturisti* of the day.

It also recurs in literature. In baroque poetry, spatial distortions and disproportions are the main features. The swooning and ecstasies in much of this Counter-Reformationist work is patent, but the excesses are both spiritual and spatial. In Agrippa d'Aubigné, for example, we are in a kind of Brobdingnag of giants where everything is of "colossal proportions." Striding across the landscape like Gargantua, the protagonist of *Le Printemps* complains that "thousands of night birds, a thousand mortal songs / Encircle me, passing in order across my brow," and so on. By contrast, in the poetry of Théophile de Viau, everything is Lilliputian. A world in a grain of sand or goldfish bowl. And there is much about the stars and collapsing heavens. It is part of the "dance of death" of the age, but it uses Mannerist space. In d'Aubigné's *Les Tragiques* "the stars die ... Everything hides in fright: fire runs into air, / Air into water; water into the earth." Saint-Amant writes: "The stars fall from the sky, / Flames devour the earth." Reality is utterly dislocated and disorganized. Viau writes in a similar vein: "Et ce grand desordre du monde / Puet-estre arrivera demain" "and this immense disorder of the world / Perhaps it will arrive tomorrow"). This is partly religious swoon, an excess of feeling, but the spatial correlative should be noted.[2] To quote the Donne passage again from "The First Anniversary," "[the] new Philosophy calls all in doubt / The Element of fire is quite put out; / The Sun is lost, and th'earth, and no man's wit / Can well direct him where to look for it."

The implication of infinite space (the sudden new possibility) was that there might be any number of other worlds out there. Thus began the theory of the plurality of worlds that runs on for a good century. There might be another world on the moon, and others further off in space. The possibility is presented as early as 1602 in Tommaso Campanella's utopian piece *La città del sole* (*The City of the Sun*). Galileo, author of *The Starry Messenger*, was the messenger, but the conditions necessary for that message to be understood involved a fundamental shift in the space-time image of the world.

Einstein claimed that Galileo made Newton possible. Galileo provided Newton with Jupiter's moons. He gave him science, which Newton took and improved, demonstrating mathematically and beyond any doubt that what Galileo argued about Copernicus was true. To say that Newton was important in the eighteenth century in England and France would be an understatement. "All Nature and her laws lay hid in Night," wrote Alexander Pope, "God said, Let Newton be: And all was Light."[3] His *Philosophiae Naturalis Principia Mathematica* or *The Mathematical Principles of Natural Philosophy* (1687) attempted to shine that light on the problem of what holds the astral clockwork together. With Newton it is not about "why" but always and only about "how." He is all mechanics, physics, and mathematics when it comes to studying the orbital dynamics of planetary motion. His three laws of motion used gravity to explain exactly how the things worked that Copernicus and Galileo had talked about. Galileo had discovered Jupiter's moons but Newton made better use of them. In book 3 of the *Principia*, on the "System of the World," he says that just as gravity explains the moon's revolution about the earth, and the orbiting moons of Jupiter, it explains the heliocentric universe.[4]

Gravity varies inversely as the square of the distance between two bodies and is proportional to the product of their masses; this answered another question people had about Copernicus's heliocentric model: if the planets are orbiting the sun, why do some appear to go around it faster than others? Why do we see the so-called retrograde motion of a planet like Mars relative to the earth, for example? The answer is that Mars is further from the sun than the earth. "As parts of the Earth mutually attract one another," Newton wrote, "so do those of all the Planets." If Copernicus provided a new world of space, it took Newton to write its constitution. "The forces," he writes, "which are as the matter in terrestrial bodies of all forms, and therefore are not mutable with the forms, must be found in all sorts of bodies whatsoever, celestial as well as terrestrial, and be in all proportional to their quantities of matter."[5]

Newton distinguished between absolute and relative space and time. He believed like Plato that the changing world of time and space was distinct from their absolute siblings in the heart of God, where they were as unknowable, immeasurable, and unchanging as He was. "The last of the magicians" is what John Maynard Keynes called him. The universe, or the Eternal, was God's "sensorium." In his *Opticks*, written in 1704, Newton asks whether it "does not appear from phenomena that there is a Being incorporeal, living, intelligent, omnipresent, who in infinite space, as it were in his sensory, sees things themselves intimately, and thoroughly perceives them, and comprehends them, wholly by their immediate presence to himself."[6]

In Voltaire's 1741 *Elements of the Philosophy of Newton*, chapter 2 is called "Space and Duration as attributes of God." In it Voltaire writes that "Newton sees space and duration as two beings whose existence flows necessarily from God's."[7] The comment on God in the *Opticks* comes at the very end of the work, while in the *Principia* God is not mentioned at all, at least in the first edition. In the second He is, but only as part of the "argument from design" at the end, in the General Scholium. "This most beautiful system of the sun, planets, and comets," Newton writes, "could only proceed from the counsel and dominion of an intelligent and powerful Being." And again later: "All that diversity of natural things which we find suited to different times and places could arise from nothing but the ideas and will of a Being necessarily existing."[8]

Newton was the Columbus of the Enlightenment, and almost as eccentric. He believed, for example, that Moses already knew about his theory of gravity. Moses (he believed) also knew that the sun was the centre of the universe. Newton tried to use his knowledge of orbital dynamics to give a scientific basis to the chronology of events in the Bible, and concluded "that the first celestial sphere was drawn in 939 B.C. by Chiron the centaur for the benefit of the Argonauts." He went so far as to say that if science or philosophy should ever throw into doubt any of Christ's "interpretations" we should always believe what the Old Testament tells us.[9]

According to Kuhn, "scientific revolutions" are caused by a growing feeling that an existing paradigm has ceased to function adequately in the exploration of an aspect of nature to which that paradigm itself had previously led the way.[10] Newton's accomplishment was not so much the revision of Copernican space as it was the drawing out of its laws, giving it an unimpeachable scientific basis. He was part of the second great wave, the second notable shift in the tectonic plates of space and time after Copernicus. Before him, Descartes had proposed a theory of vortices to account for orbital dynamics. Fontenelle, in Newton's day, picked up on the "vortex" idea and asked: "Is every star the center of a Vortex, as big as ours? Is that vast space which comprehends our Sun and Planets, but an inconsiderable point of the Universe?" Fontenelle talks about "the infinite diversity and variety which is to be observed in the works of nature," and insists that the idea of life existing on other planets or worlds "cannot be contradicted by any Philosopher," adding, somewhat surprisingly, that the plurality of worlds would not contradict "either Reason or Scripture."[11] Again, we have the plurality of worlds. And what might people look like on those other worlds? In the New World they had red skins and wore feathers in their hair, so many speculated that would be the answer. Swedenborg, the eighteenth-century mystic, thought so, and so did many others.[12] Newton, like Copernicus before him, did not invent this new line of thought; he was merely part of it.

Nonetheless, with Newton the word "revolution" in relation to science starts to be heard for the first time since Copernicus. That was a word that had not been used in relation to scientific events before, but the *Principia* changed that and was soon being called a revolution in physics. Fontenelle uses the word in 1727 in reference to the new infinitesimal calculus discovered by Newton.[13] Or perhaps it was discovered by Leibnitz, since the two argued about it. Newton's management skills aside, his theory of gravity built on Galileo's contributions to make Copernican theory a fact of life. The anxieties this produced were of a different order and magnitude from those of 1600, or 1500, attenuated as they were in the eighteenth century by an age devoted to science, and to a new concept called "progress." The rational tone, for example, is evident in 1778 in James Ferguson's statement: "Instead then of one Sun and one World only in the Universe, as the unskillful in Astronomy imagine, [the new Science] discovers to us such an inconceivable number of Suns, Systems, and Worlds, dispersed through boundless Space, that if our

Sun with all the Planets, Moons, and Comets, belonging to it, were an-
nihilated, they would be no more missed, by an eye that could take in
the whole Creation, than a grain of sand from the sea-shore."[14]

With Newton's imprimatur, however, the "new Science" threatened
traditional beliefs in the Church and God even more seriously than
"science" had in the time of Copernicus. Leslie Stephen notes the principal disproportion that Copernican theory brought with it, and what it
did to people. "The scenery," he writes, "had become too wide for the
drama," to the point (he suggests) where people "began to suspect that
the whole scenery was but a fabric woven by their imaginations."[15]
Stephen's choice of words is illuminating. Reality at these moments
("the whole scenery") and fiction (it is just "scenery") start to lose their
definition and meld into one another, reproducing the same unease
over the distinction between artefact and reality that must have been in
play when the new maps began appearing in the late fifteenth century.

In novels, where time is of the essence, the age produced a second
Rabelais in Laurence Sterne, author of the temporally avant-garde
Tristram Shandy (1769) – a work that not only revels in *incommensuratio*
at the temporal level, but makes it the central point of discussion by the
narrator. Tristram's anti-narrative follows metonymic and associational
chains of logic that defy temporal coordinates. The book is Rabelaisian
in its bawdy physicality and send-up of erudition and pedantry; but
not, interestingly, in its treatment of space. Space in *Tristram Shandy* is
not an issue; it is as domesticated as Uncle Toby's fortifications. In
Sterne, only time is out of joint.

The most spatially interesting book in the period is *Gulliver's Travels*
(1726), where effects of scale rival those in Rabelais. Lemuel Gulliver, a
fictional medical man as much as Rabelais was a real one, could not,
however, differ more from his precursor in the way he handles proportion. While Rabelais has a healthy dose of what can only be called ex-
pressionism-before-its-time in his work, Swift's volumes and measures
are for the most part laboratory precise. Gulliver's disproportionate
size in his first two voyages makes it easy to find him ridiculous, but
that would be a mistake. Gulliver seeks to inspire the same kind of con-
fidence that More did in *Utopia*. He remains within himself, never gets
excited, and earns our trust. In the Age of Newton, no less would be
expected from a ship's surgeon. His political views ultimately prove
naive, but his science and sense of space are generally sound.

This might seem hard to accept given the voyage to Laputa that follows his visits to Lilliput and Brobdingnag, where we get the Academy

of Lagado; or the fact that Gulliver ends up accepting that he is a Yahoo. Nonetheless, the figural representations and geometry of the first two parts of the book observe the principle of *commensuratio* with a surprising fidelity. The later send-up of science may contradict the spirit of this precision, but it does not succeed in discrediting it. In Brobdingnag, for example, Gulliver is so small that he is like a microscope, and what he sees may be horrific, but it is always true. The Lilliputians in the previous part have the same microscopic virtue when it comes to Gulliver himself, who looks as gross when writ large as anyone would.

If one looks closely at the spatial descriptions in the first two voyages it is clear that while Gulliver does crunch his numbers accurately, he is not always perfect. In Lilliput, for example, there is something spatially amiss with the scene where the envoy "from his Imperial Majesty" marches up Gulliver's stomach and presents his credentials, sticking them, Gulliver says, "close to my Eyes."[16] If just proportion rules, the ratio of the size, in height, of a written character to a six-foot-tall human would be about a half-inch (roughly the height of the written character) to seventy-two inches, or 1:144. So anything written on a piece of paper by someone six inches tall would be about .05 inches high, quite impossible for someone Gulliver's size to read, even with his glasses.

And then there is the awkward business of Gulliver pulling home across the channel the entire enemy fleet from Blefescu. He says that he "with great Ease drew fifty of the Enemy's largest Men of War after me" (34). We have already learned something about the Lilliputian king's navy – that "some" at least of his "largest Men of War" are "Nine Foot long" (10). If the enemy also has nine-foot ships, it would seem hard to imagine Gulliver, who is six feet tall, being able to tow them all home like that, even if they were made of balsa wood. Has Swift made a mistake, or is Gulliver just bragging?

Another instance that might seem spatially wrong is when twenty-four of the king's horse guard conduct military exercises on a "two Foot and a half square" handkerchief that Gulliver stretches between stakes and makes into a raised platform (23). The Lilliputians are six inches tall and Gulliver has by this time told us that their biggest horses are four and a half inches high. While it would indeed be hard for twenty-four of them to do much manoeuvring on a two-and-a-half-foot-square space, they would nonetheless have enough room at least to form a couple of lines and charge each other, and even engage in some of the mock battle scenes Gulliver describes.[17]

Distortions here would diminish the effect of the one great disproportion Swift wants to keep constantly in front of us: that of Gulliver himself. The chapter describing the Lilliputian metropolis is illuminating.
Where Rabelais takes a delight in never giving us anything in the way
of rational measurements or numbers, Swift behaves here like a real
surveyor, giving us exact numbers, all of which make proper spatial
sense. He tells us how high and thick the city wall is, and that he went
"sideling" through the streets "only in my short Waistcoat, for fear of
damaging the Roofs and Eves of the Houses with the Skirts of my Coat."
The city is laid out with a care that would make Thomas More proud.
Two streets, five feet wide, divide it into quarters; the lanes are twelve
to eighteen inches wide; the town can hold five hundred thousand resi-
dents; the houses are three to five stories; and the palace is right in the
centre of the city where the two streets meet. It is "inclosed by a Wall of
two Foot high and Twenty Foot distant from the Buildings" (28) and so
on. We get measurements of the court and an exact description of the
apartments. The Emperor wants Gulliver to see the inner court, but the
wall enclosing it is five feet high so Gulliver has to build himself something to get safely over it. He then lies down and looks in the windows.
The Empress appears and allows him to kiss her hand. The effect of a
just fit here is one of contrast between the rationality of the scale and
accounting, and the complete and utter irrationality of the one fundamental spatial distortion that is Gulliver himself, which is probably
what Swift wanted.

Scale is the main issue, as it is in Rabelais, and Swift knows this is the
first thing to establish when Man Mountain arrives in Lilliput. When
Gulliver first sets eyes on the Lilliputians he tells us that they are six
inches tall. We assume Gulliver to be of normal height. Later, in chapter
3, we learn he is six feet tall when his tiny hosts are trying to figure out
how much he will need to eat. They use a quadrant to determine his
height and find it "to exceed theirs in the Proportion of Twelve to One"
(27). And the six-foot measurement is later confirmed in Brobdingnag.
So the scale (here in Lilliput at least) is 1:12.

It is not necessary to do an exhaustive inventory of every instance of
scale relations in the two voyages, but a sampling shows us that Gulliver
(and Swift) gets things right more often than not. When Gulliver arrives,
for example, he is hungry, and one of the first things the little ones do is
bring him food – baskets of meat, shoulders and legs of mutton that appear to Gulliver to be "smaller than the Wings of a Lark"(7). Does the

comparison hold? Hoopoes or shore larks – in fact ground larks in general – were easy to net in Swift's day, and they made popular eating in England and Italy in the eighteenth century. They are relatively small birds, at best seven inches from tip to tail. A cooked wing might measure two inches. At scale, that would be the equivalent of two feet in Gulliver's world, not too much of an exaggeration for a leg of mutton.

Gulliver says he ate what they brought him, "Shoulders, Legs, and Loins shaped like those of Mutton" and that he ate them "by two or three at a Mouthful" (7) which again seems reasonable, especially since he is hungry, although one wonders about the bones. Did people in Swift's day order lark wings, for example, and crunch up bones and all? Gulliver later dispatches a steak he is served in three bites, "Bones and all, as in our Country we do the Leg of a Lark" (45). Later in Brobdingnag the Queen herself "would craunch the wing of a lark, bones and all, between her teeth" (84). The Lilliputians also bring him loaves of bread that Gulliver says are "about the bigness of Musket Bullets" (7). Later, when they search him they find some of those bullets in his pocket and tell us they were the size of their heads. So they are bringing him loaves of bread that are the size of their heads. Gulliver's head, like one of ours, might be about seven inches in diameter. On a six-inch Lilliputian that would convert to a head of a little over half an inch in diameter, just the size of a musket bullet of the sort fired by an eighteenth-century flintlock. As for a loaf of bread in Gulliver's world, one the size of his head would be normal.

Man Mountain also requires liquid refreshment so his hosts roll out a keg of their best small wine. Gulliver is not impressed. "One of their largest Hogsheads," he says, "hardly held half a Pint" (7). Half a pint, or ten fluid ounces, would fill a Lilli-keg slightly smaller than a can of Coke. Say three inches high – or a little under since the barrel shape swells at the waist – with a diameter of about two inches. That would equate in Gulliver's world to a cask slightly under three feet high. A hogshead held fifty-two Imperial gallons. To hold that much a three-foot-high keg would need to have a diameter of about seventeen inches, which is just about right. The Lilliputians seem to be happy drinkers. When Gulliver tosses off his half-pint they give a shout of joy, and another when he throws down his empty, as if this were also a drinking practice among them. "Hekinah degul!" (8) everyone shouts. Clearly, they would be at home in many English towns of Swift's time.

The Lilliputians are in fact a precise group whose temperament, customs, and mathematical prowess are reminiscent of the ancient Persians.

When Gulliver makes his pact with the Emperor and promises to be good they grant him freedom of movement and an allowance of food sufficient for one thousand seven hundred and twenty-eight Lilliputians. They arrive at this number using his height and by doing a volume calculation. They conclude, Gulliver says, "from the similarity of their bodies, that mine must contain at least 1728 of theirs, and consequently would require as much Food as was necessary to support that Number of Lilliputians" (27). Is Swift making fun of them? No, he is not. Volume (for a cylinder) varies according to the radius and height by the formula $V = \pi r^2 \times h$. If we assume the body of a normal six-foot-tall man to be a cylinder with a torso diameter of a foot, radius six inches, this would work out to $V = 8140$. If that is 1728 times the volume of a Lilliputian, the latter's smaller body volume would be about five. If he is six inches tall that would give him a torso radius of one half an inch. The proportions and scale are once again exact. Gulliver is not wrong to say: "By which the Reader may conceive an idea of the Ingenuity of that People" (27).

But there is also a problem here. If the volume differential is 1728 to 1, that should hold for the aforementioned hogsheads as well as the Man Mountain's body volume. Gulliver's fifty-two-gallon keg, in other words, should hold 1728 times as much as the Lilli-keg of ten ounces. But 1728 Lilli-kegs comes to over a hundred gallons. This is the only serious miscalculation in the book, but perhaps it is mine, not Swift's.

In Brobdingnag things are more interesting because Gulliver is a kind of Lilliputian himself now, and much more able to interact with his surroundings. Newton might have pointed out that the gravity of the situation back there would have prevented him from even moving. Or, we might add today, even breathing. By contrast, in a land where he is the small one and his hosts are sixty feet tall, he would feel as light as a lark. His respiration would really be mouse-like. The precision in Brobdingnag is as good as it was in Lilliput. The labourer in the field who finds Gulliver holds him up to within three feet of his eyes to have a look at him, and Gulliver tells us that he is above sixty feet from the ground. Later he is compared in size to a "*Splacknuck* (an Animal in that Country very finely shaped, about six Foot long)" (76). So the scale here will be 1:10 – a little less extreme than the difference in Lilliput. The more important difference is that Gulliver is in more danger here than he was in Lilliput, so his descriptions might sometimes be exaggerated. A good example of precision and imprecision in this regard comes right away when Gulliver first sees the giant labourer. He says "He appeared as Tall as an ordinary Spire-steeple, and took about ten Yards at every

Stride" (65). Church steeples in England certainly rose much higher than sixty feet. Swift himself lived within sight of the Salisbury steeple, which he mentions a bit later, and which is ordinary enough at four hundred and four feet. In terms of the giant's stride, though, Gulliver has it right. A six-foot-tall man would have a stride of something under a yard, or roughly half his height, so a sixty-foot man might well be expected to take one of about ten yards.

Later, Gulliver visits a Brob-temple in much calmer circumstances and tells us that the height from the ground to the pinnacle of the steeple was about three thousand feet, "which, allowing for the Difference between the Size of those People and us in *Europe*, is no great matter for Admiration, nor at all equal in Proportion (if I rightly remember) to *Salisbury* Steeple" (91). At a 1:10 scale, the four-hundred-foot Salisbury steeple would be four thousand Brob-feet high, significantly more than this one. So Gulliver is right in finding it less than impressive.

The great majority of scale relations in the tale are in order. Before the giant labourer even comes on the scene, for example, Gulliver notes that the grass is twenty feet high; that a stand of corn is forty feet high; that a hedge is a hundred and twenty feet high. He tells us that a stile between two fields has a bottom stone step that is six feet high with a top stone of over twenty feet. That would equate to grass two feet tall; corn standing at about four feet; and the hedge at twelve feet. That is tall for what we think of today as a hedge. The stone step would be something more than six inches, and the top one at two feet or so, which seems about right.

A serving dish for his hosts, Gulliver says, is twenty-four feet in diameter. At scale that would convert in his world to a dish of about twenty-eight inches or so in diameter. That is big for us, but not that extraordinary in the eighteenth century, when you might order a pig's head at the Upton Inn, for example, with Tom Jones, on that size of platter. The table is also to scale – thirty feet high, about half the height of a Brobdingnagian, or about three feet in a normal world. At one point Gulliver does battle with a linnet, a small bird about five inches from tip to tail, which would make it about four feet long for him. He says it was "somewhat larger than an English Swan." Close enough. He has a run-in with a monkey "as large as an Elephant." And a mastiff that is "equal in Bulk to four Elephants" (95, 99, 70). Does all this add up? A mastiff is a big dog. It can stand up to thirty inches at the shoulder, which in Brobdingnag would be twenty-five feet. Two rats that are also the size of mastiffs attack him. A black rat in eighteenth-century London could measure eight inches in length, but most were not that big. Let us put them at six inches; the Brob-rat then would be sixty inches, or five feet long. That is considerably larger, at least in length, than a mastiff. Gulliver kills one when it puts its forefeet up on his shoulders, and afterward measures the tail. He "found it to be two Yards long wanting an Inch" (72), or about six feet. The proportions here seem a little exaggerated, but we might overstate the case too if we were attacked by a couple of giant rats. There is also a frog that jumps over him, which works, and wasps "as large as Partridges" with stings "an Inch and a half long" (87). A male partridge is about a foot long and weighs about a pound. If one turned into a wasp it would indeed make a formidable foe, and have a sting about the length Gulliver mentions. Or if we looked at it through the other end of the telescope: if a six-foot man were one-tenth his size, or seven inches tall, would a wasp look as big as a partridge? It would.

Gulliver wonders himself whether he might be exaggerating – "at least a severe Critic would be apt to think I enlarged a little, as Travelers are often suspected to do." If this is the worst he can be accused of it is not much, although even this much is too much for him. To avoid such censure, he says, "I fear I have run too much into the other Extream" (92), so that if his hosts ever read his account he fears they will be insulted by seeing things too small.

But there are also places where neither exaggeration nor overcompensation for it can account for the scale disproportion. There are those hailstones, for example, that come down and batter him, he says, like tennis balls. He says that "Nature in that Country observing the same Proportion through all her Operations, a Hail-stone is near Eighteen Hundred Times as large as one in *Europe*; which I can assert upon Experience, having been so curious to weigh and measure them" (93). He makes no rash comparison, in other words, in the cold of the battle, but takes a measured, calm approach. But all the weighing and measuring in the world cannot fit eighteen hundred hailstones into a tennis ball.

Volume measurement is also an issue again in Brobdingnag, as it was in Lilliput. Gulliver is given what is a Brob-dram of small beer. For him, it is two gallons. The Lilliputians calculated Man Mountain's volume to be about 1728 times larger than a Lilliputian's. The scale here is a bit less extreme, so we might estimate that Brob-volume is more in the order of 1500 times Gulliver's. A dram is one-sixteenth of a fluid ounce so 1500 drams is about ninety four ounces, or almost five pints. That is just over half a gallon, but far from two. What if Gulliver is using an apothecary's measure? That might be, since he is a surgeon. An apothecary's dram is larger – one-eighth of a fluid ounce – so 1500 of those would be just over nine pints. That is a little more than a gallon, but still a distance from two. What if a dram were about what it is today when we order one – a "tot," as we say, of some good single-malt Scotch? In other words, about a quarter of an ounce. Fifteen hundred of those would add up to almost nineteen pints, or over two gallons. In the end, Swift is not far off. And who knows if the Brob-dram might be a dram unto itself that would make the proportion exact?

In any case, what goes in, as Gulliver himself learned in Lilliput, must come out, and if he is a little vague on one end, he is more precise at the other. Especially where women are concerned. When it came to women, Swift liked the scatological details. After the Queen's maids of honour drink they must logically "discharge what they had drunk," as Gulliver puts it, and the quantity, he informs us, comes to "at least two Hogsheads" (95). Does this measure up? Two hogsheads would be over a hundred and four Imperial gallons. If that is roughly 1500 times what a normal person, of either sex, would discharge, then the latter amount comes to a little over half a pint, perfectly normal. In this, at least, Swift was not unfair to women. To see the difference in spatial proportions, compare Rabelais's account of Gargantua urinating from the top of Notre Dame, aforementioned, in such volume that it drowns two hundred and sixty thousand people. Compared to Rabelais, Swift is a veritable Newtonian.

Granted, things are a little less exact with the maids when one of them puts Gulliver "astride upon one of her Nipples" (96). This carries the sense that he is smaller than he is, as if the nipple has for him something of the girth of a horse. Let us assume for a moment that the maids are tall for their time – say, five-foot-five or 65 inches. Using the 1:10 scale of things in Brobdingnag, Gulliver would be about six and a half inches in height. That is too big to be sitting astride even a large woman's nipple like a horse. That would only make spatial sense if he were two or three inches tall. In the earlier description of the nurse breastfeeding, Gulliver says the nurse's breast "stood prominent six Foot, and could not be less than sixteen in Circumference." These proportions are more reasonable. Reduced in scale by a tenth that would translate to a breast seven inches "prominent." It is slightly odd that Gulliver would give an estimate of its circumference rather than, say, its diameter, which would be more immediately calculable, but if $C = \pi d$, then the diameter of the breast is five feet. Reduced by scale, that would be six inches, which again is perfectly reasonable. "The Nipple," he adds, "was about half the Bigness of my Head" (71). That also seems about right, given the scale. Perhaps the exaggerated nipple size in the later description with the maids has something to do with the sexual stress he feels at being stripped naked, placed inside their clothes, and so on. In such circumstances, even Newton might get a little rattled.

All things considered, the doctor in Swift is more conflicted in his attitude to "enframing" than Rabelais. The Royal Society was something Rabelais did not have to deal with. The spatial distortions in *Gulliver's Travels* are therefore nothing like what we find in Rabelais, the Mannerists, El Greco, or the baroque poets. There is much in the bawdy and bodily functions and fluids in *Gulliver's Travels* that recalls Rabelais, but spatially, Swift is a Vermeer where Rabelais is a Mannerist.

In Horace Walpole's *The Castle of Otranto* (1764), young Conrad, the prince, is to be married on his birthday to Isabella. The guests are assembled in the chapel of the castle and everyone awaits the arrival of the groom. Time goes by but Conrad does not appear. Finally a servant is sent off to look for him. A minute later he comes staggering back in with a look of horror on his face and points speechlessly towards the courtyard. The company rushes out and sees in the middle of the courtyard "an enormous helmet, a hundred times more large than a casque ever made for human being, and shaded with a proportionable quantity of black feathers." The crowd approaches and finds Conrad "dashed to pieces" beneath it.[18] But the helmet that crushes Conrad is an anomaly. Spatial disproportion is not on display in Gothic fiction of the sort Walpole's novel initiated in the eighteenth century. Later works in the genre like Ann Radcliffe's *The Mysteries of Udolpho* or Matthew Lewis's *The Monk*, written in the 1790s, feature crypts, dungeons, evil protagonists, and even supernatural events, but they are all the right size.

Across the channel in France the same rule of just proportion generally holds in Enlightenment fiction by Prévost, Diderot, and others, although there is one interesting exception: Voltaire's *Micromégas*. Written in 1752, it is both a giant in its field, and a bagatelle, both very small (microscopes play a part) and mega-big. A Mannerist work in Voltaire's *oeuvre*, it is remarkable for being an explosion of fungible space in the otherwise rational scenery of his fiction. As unique in its way as *Gulliver's Travels*, which it resembles in many ways, it nonetheless is different in many more, beginning with its Rabelaisian delight in incommensurability. Where Swift surrounds his one violation of just proportion with an otherwise rational space, Voltaire gives us a Rabelaisian world of cosmic distortions and disproportion. What struck Voltaire about Newton's theory of gravity was the equilibrium of forces that allowed bodies to float freely in space."[19] And it is this anti-gravity effect that becomes the central trope in his *Micromégas*.

Micromégas tells the story of a visitor from Sirius, who is not just big, as in perhaps sixty feet tall, but several miles tall. He stops to pick up a slightly smaller friend on Saturn, then together they visit Earth, where they comment on how very little and trivial everything is. The idea of satirizing present-day life by bringing in a stranger from a strange land inverts Swift's conceit, but it was not new: Montesquieu, for example, had done it most recently in 1721 with his *Persian Letters*. And there had been other stories of interplanetary travel before. But where Swift and Montesquieu look down, Voltaire is up in the sky with the ceiling painters. And up there the laws of *commensuratio* do not hold. In *Micromégas* it is as if all measure, and all measurement is out of measure, and scale itself a mere device.[20] Voltaire's protagonist, for example, is Gargantuan:

> He was eight leagues tall, and by eight leagues I mean twenty-four thousand geometrical paces each measuring five feet. Certain algebraists, persons ever useful to the public, will at once reach for their pen and find that since Mr Micromegas, inhabitant of the land of Sirius, measures twenty-four thousand paces from head to toe, which is the equivalent of one hundred and twenty thousand French feet, and since we, the citizens of the earth, measure barely five, and since our globe has a circumference of nine thousand leagues, will find, I say, that it necessarily follows that the globe which produced him must be exactly twenty-one million, six hundred thousand times greater in circumference than our little Earth. In nature, nothing could be simpler or more commonplace.[21]

The "algebraists" do not need to "reach for their pen." It will not do them any good. The height calculation is not too far off: a league is about three miles, so eight leagues would be twenty-four miles, or roughly 127,000 feet. Using the author's own 120,000 feet measurement, and his five-foot man, the scale is then 24,000-to-1.[22] In that case, "the globe which produced" Monseiur Micromégas should be 24,000 times greater in circumference than the earth, since circumference is directly proportional to diameter, not "twenty-one million, six hundred thousand times." It is interesting that Voltaire should make fun of science like this, given his admiration for Newton. But then Swift mocks the Royal Society in his Laputa while elsewhere abiding by strict Euclidean laws of geometry.

Monseiur Micromégas is therefore about twenty-four miles tall. He would be fine floating in the zero-gravity conditions of outer space. But on earth Voltaire might have known that Newton's equations meant gravity would make it impossible for him to move. His head is up in the stratosphere where he will of course be breathing ozone and wearing sunglasses if he is wise. Time is proportionally larger for him as well. Around "the age of four hundred and fifty," we are told, he was getting "towards the end of his childhood" (102). As for his smaller Saturnian friend, he is only six thousand feet, or a little over a mile tall, which makes him small indeed compared to the Sirian, roughly 1/24th his size. For us, that would be like hanging around with someone three inches tall. Apparently Voltaire had Fontenelle in mind here, a little man he disliked, and who was also interested in interplanetary space. The little Saturnian complains of the brevity of life: "'Alas,' said the Saturnian, 'we only live for five hundred entire revolutions of the sun. (The equivalent by human reckoning, of fifteen thousand years or thereabouts.) Which is, as you can see, to die almost the moment one is born; our existence is a point in time, our span is but an instant, our globe a mere atom ... I feel like a drop of water in an immense ocean'" (105).

Fontenelle says something very like this in *The Plurality of Worlds*. Voltaire's satirical intention may have been to make fun of both the author and the sentiment – the new feeling of insignificance people felt in front of the vast expanse of space opened up by Copernicus, and explained by Newton – but if so, it wasn't something that struck anyone as particularly funny. And no one laughed at Fontenelle. The Sirian, we are told, covers thirty thousand feet, or a bit under six miles, in a stride. That is roughly a quarter of his height. This is proportionally incorrect. He should cover about half his height, as we do, or twelve miles. For his part, the Saturnian, Voltaire tells us, has to take twelve steps to each one of the Sirian's. If he is a mile in height, he would cover roughly half a mile in a step. Twelve steps would take him six miles. So that proportion, at least, is right. But the combination means that while Micromégas is moving ahead with what for him are small, mincing strides, his sidekick must be sprinting to keep up. Imagine walking along taking half steps, while your three-inch friend tries to keep up.

Microscopes also play a part in the action. Using microscopes (the diamonds of a necklace) proportional to their own size, the two visitors scour the planet for life. The Saturnian's "lens" has a diameter of a hundred and sixty feet, while his larger friend's is two thousand five hundred feet (111). Again, proportions are distorted. If Micromégas is twenty-four times the size of his small friend, it is fair to estimate he would need an instrument larger in the same proportion; that would mean a diamond-microscope with a diameter of something less than four thousand feet. In point of fact, the lens of the first so-called micro-scope was Galileo's "little eye," which probably had a lens of about an inch in diameter, or about 1/65th the height of a man five feet, five inch-es tall. For the Saturnian, his little diamond-stone microscope should therefore be roughly 1/65th of his height, or about eighty feet in diam-eter, not a hundred and sixty.

   With it he spots a whale, picks it up "with his little finger," and places it on his thumbnail for the Sirian to look at. Assuming a whale of eighty or so feet, or roughly 15/1000th the height of the Saturnian, that would correspond for us to finding a small sea creature about an inch long: much too large for the description, which tells of the Saturnian putting it on his thumbnail to show Micromégas. And finally, they spot a ship. Micromégas picks it up "without squeezing too hard for fear of crush-ing it" (112) and puts it on his nail the same way the Saturnian had put the whale on his. But even if the ship is three times the size of a whale it would be too small for this twenty-four-mile-high Sirian to do such a thing. The proportions are not close. So indeed, the algebraists need not worry. With *Micromégas* we are in a world of incommensurabilities more like Gargantua's than Gulliver's.

Part Two

Pathologies of Deformation:
Jonson, Sade, Pynchon

3 Narcissism: Jonson and the Disfigured Self

The "Elizabethan world picture" may not have been quite as stable as E.M. Tillyard's 1942 book implied, but it is certainly free of the kind of spatial anxieties that defined the Mannerist art of Rabelais's day.[1] Nor do Jonson's plays exhibit anything remotely similar to the spatial incommensurabilities we find in either Rabelais or Swift, with their fantastical measurements of big and small. Jonson's deformation is one of mind, as it is in Sade and Pynchon, and I would like to discuss it as such – in clinical terms (in Jonson's case), as narcissism, through the lens of a psychological spatial analysis (object relations theory).

To begin with a spatial metaphor, Jonson was a man who did not "fit" well in the Elizabethan frame. And this was something that he felt keenly. Jonson was an outsider, and in this chapter I would like to suggest that his particular inside/outside psychology can best be understood using a theoretical paradigm that is itself uniquely spatial. Object relations theory, moreover, is an approach that works well for a playwright, whose ideas are always literally "bodied forth" in real space as real objects.

This post-Freudian school of psychoanalytic thought was pioneered by Melanie Klein, and I would suggest that her treatment of narcissism makes a surprisingly good companion (when it comes to Jonson) to what might seem at first a completely antipodal approach to writing in the period – the one taken by the New Historicist critic Stephen Greenblatt. The reason for this surprising companionship is that Greenblatt's groundbreaking work on "self-fashioning" in the period is itself spatial in conception. Jonson does not figure in the study, which focuses on what Greenblatt calls the "profound mobility" of the writers he looks at. His spatial metaphor is determinant as he examines the "upward" mobility that applies to his self-made authors – those who rose in class from humble beginnings. This kind of mobility always remained unachievable for Jonson.[2] Spenser (Greenblatt reminds us) was the son of a tailor; Marlowe the son of a shoemaker; Shakespeare the son of a glover. Spenser became a large landowner; Marlowe went to Cambridge; Shakespeare owned a large house in Stratford. Another Greenblatt choice, Sir Thomas More, was the son of a lawyer and rose to the heights of power before achieving the ultimate in upward mobility by losing his head. Jonson, by comparison, could only relieve others of theirs, of their mobility at least, which he did twice; and convert to Catholicism, which he did once. That at least got him moving, since it (probably) saved his life in prison. But mobility also means something more material when it comes to Jonson. Greenblatt's self-made men are "intellectuals," men of ink and the quill, whose art gave them wings, while Jonson was a man of blood and the sword, stone-like in his determination, obdurate in his art. And it is this very obduracy in Jonson that fits well with an object relations approach to what "self-fashioning" meant for him.

This is because Jonson was, figuratively speaking, "cut from the stone." His first act of "self formation" in this regard came with the changing of his name in 1604. In that year, Benjamin Johnson, stepson of a Westminster bricklayer, dropped the "h" in his name to become Ben Jonson, son of no John. Jonson later told Drummond that he was related to the Johnstones of Dumfries, just across the Scottish border, and that his grandfather was a gentleman who had served Henry VIII.[3] The Johnstones were a rocky quarry of lowland Scots ("a band of butchers and cut-throats," as Rosalind Miles puts it) who would have made colourful ancestors for Jonson, and perhaps did. The nominal refashioning carries over into Jonson's plays, which can be read as an attempt to reconfigure and refurnish himself out of his Dumfries inheritance in more than name alone. The results, in the life as much as the art, were violent and bloody.[4]

Self-fashioning for Jonson began with this carving out of a new name for himself, free of the past. The "t" in "Johnstone" had been dropped long before, eliminating masonry in the name, and any connection to the "band of butchers." Dropping the "h" completed the job, eliminating the filial note altogether and allowing the author to spring forth into the footlights parthogenetically, like Athena, from his own mind.[5] Unfortunately, the once-repressed masonry had returned prior to this, when Johnson's mother took the bricklayer, Robert Brett, for her second husband. And one might argue that the loss of the aspirated "h" makes no material difference. Indeed, by the time he dropped it, Jo(h)nson was already well known, if not the poet and gentleman he envisioned. It was also about this time that he followed the vogue in Renaissance self-fashioning and purchased a coat of arms. He was by now on the way to a full makeover.

Mobility in the social sense depends on our understanding it in a material, spatial way. Jonson worried all his life about the first, about getting up the social ladder. But the very material transpositions of the letters in his name are, in a way, the rock he wants to found his church on. What does it mean, after all, to drop letters from one's name? In Jonson's case, that old "t" was perhaps the Scottish heritage, the link to the quarry, the stoneworks, and the "butchers" that returns in his own literary brickbats of violence, the contempt, envy, deceit, and excremental excess that Jonson wields like weapons in his plays. Those are pieces of his past he wants to dominate and get rid of, and he does so by casting them forth on the stage. He thought they had been eliminated before his time, but the arrival of Brett the bricklayer as his new father figure feels like the return of the repressed. Dropping the filial "h" was only the next (Oedipal) step.

In other words, if we are looking for a model of self-fashioning that might do justice to Jonson, a material approach seems promising. The scatological and excremental defines much of his comedy, and his anal and alimentary obsessions have been amply commented upon. But the picture of Jonson-the-composite can be better understood by considering disfigurement in his work through the lens of object relations theory, and (especially) narcissism.[6] From what we know of Jonson the man, narcissism in its general form defined him. He had an inflated ego and an overblown sense of his own value and importance, combined with a low opinion of others. He railed against courtiers, and yet yearned to be one himself. He saw things in stark black and white, and tended either to praise or blame. As for the emotional ability to connect with others that is called love, it is not much in evidence in the man or his work. Narcissistic personalities display "grandiosity, extreme self-centredness, and a remarkable absence of interest in and empathy for others in spite of the fact that they are so very eager to obtain admiration and approval from other people. [Narcissists] experience a remarkably intense envy of other people who seem to have things they do not have or who simply seem to enjoy their lives. [They] lack emotional depth and fail to understand complex emotions in other people, but their own feelings lack differentiation."[7]

Clinically, diagnostic criteria point to someone who "exaggerates achievement ... expects to be recognized as superior ... is preoccupied with fantasies of unlimited success ... requires excessive admiration ... has a sense of entitlement ...is interpersonally exploitative."[8] In Shakespeare's "Sinne of selfe love," narcissism and "self" are parts of a single multifold articulation. When we talk about ourselves, we are narcissistically engaged with "them." But the "self" is an ontological shadow that always takes a step back when we try to get a look at it – a kind of necessary fiction, as Nietzsche says about "truth," that we have merely forgotten is one. Perhaps there is some self-structure that comes to us genetically, a template. In any case, given the uncertainty, we should not be too sure we know what Shakespeare means by "selfe" when he writes about the "Sinne of selfe love" in Sonnet 62. We think we do because we still use the phrase "self-love" in the same way and sense he does. But how did Shakespeare's contemporaries understand the word? The meaning of "self" seems too often self-evident, as self-evident to us as what we mean by "self-evident" itself, for that matter, not to mention "self-regard," "selfish," or even "itself" itself – as self-evident as narcissism.

But the "self" is a chain of signifiers at best that migrates through language, reproducing, mutating, dividing, and playing itself out in a kind of semanto-cellular long division along the multiplying and signifying channels of its own oneiric devising, without ever reaching a moment of full presence – meaning one thing in a phrase like "self-evident" where it means, paradoxically and abysmally, evident to itself, and another in a phrase like "self-love" where it means the love one has for oneself. And this is not a motionless mirroring, getting us absolutely nowhere further towards knowing what the "self" is, for no good reason. The good reason might seem at first to be that this is just the nature of language, which is a play of differences only, as Saussure said, with no positive terms. But the infinite regress built into the ubiquitous word "self" and its multiple family couplings goes deeper than that and tells us something true about its ostensible signified – about the endlessly deferred and protean nature of what we are trying to nail down and coffin with that word. The self is itself a mutant deformation.

The "self" partakes of the differential and always differentiating nature of Hegelian "spirit," showing its face in self-making only as an endlessly vanishing point where every mark, every trace, every scar is only capable of significance or meaning, and hence of contributing to one's "identity," insofar as it is overcome, no longer present, as it vanishes (like the "h"), but not without a trace, into the penumbra of the kind of active "entanglement" [*Verflechtung*] that Husserl names as the true nature of signifying relations. Derrida notes that these relations must be understood as purely functional, grammatical, temporal, and free of what Heidegger called any "ontico-theological" presence. Thus, the self. The linguistic turn or language game that the self is so adept at playing comes as a result of its inability to signify in any other way than by reflecting upon itself in the equally self-perpetuating, self-referential way language does, as a function without substance. The fact that "identity" is self-composed, like language or a poem, of equally and exclusively functional qualities is no surprise; that one can succeed in self-fashioning means only that one can hypostatize the process and forget who (how) one is and becomes. To fail means leaving the process in view, the stage littered with body parts.

The relationship of material and corporal factors to "self-fashioning" was as important for Jonson as it is for any of us. The scars and memory traces that outrageous fortune leaves as its calling cards on our personalities are only understandable, after all, as taking place in space and time. They are both psychic and spatial, producing a "psychophysiological self." The self (and, by extension, its representation) is "the *whole* person of an individual, including his body and body parts as well as his psychic organization and its parts."[9] The self is less an entity than a dynamic, more a narrative than a snapshot. As such, its constituents are always in flux, interacting with one another, producing tensions and resolutions, but also activities and physiological changes, not unlike the experience of a character in a novel.

How does this dynamic apply to a playwright like Jonson? Object relations theory provides a helpful frame. We often use the phrase "bodied forth" when it comes to describing the writer's transformation of an idea into a character in a novel, but the phrase is even more apt for the playwright whose ideas become actual characters in real space. In a panel on "creativity" at the 1971 Psycho-Analytical Congress, Leon Grinberg stated that the object relations theorist works from the supposition that the artist experiences his product as part of himself and himself as part of the work. The anxiety of seeing the work "bodied forth" is both a physical and psychological trial that can produce monsters as easily as formed works, depending on the artist's mental stability and strength. In the case of a playwright, the physical bodies on the stage are psychically connected to the author, but are also felt viscerally as a part of the self, birthed and expelled out into the world. Every such birth produces anxiety and a sense of loss, although the partial self-object "bodied forth" is at the same time expelled by necessity, as a "bad" part one needs to be rid of.[10] A stage character written by an author with Jonson's self-fashioning issues is, from this perspective, going to be special and partial – less than an allegorical figure because less singular; less a provisional composite of the self, a "tryout" so to speak in the process of self-fashioning, for the same reason; and more like a body part, a partial object that embodies something (material) the author wants to drop, to set loose from his body, and yet hold onto at the same time.[11]

Narcissism is the operative dynamic for this sort of transaction between the object world and the ego, and this is where we see Jonson taking shape. Freud and Melanie Klein both accorded a high degree of importance to the object world in narcissism. Freud distinguished between primary and secondary narcissism, where primary narcissism is a healthy libidinal support to one's ego instinct for survival, while secondary or clinical narcissism is an aggravated state where libido is called in from external objects.[12]

Klein agrees with Freud on the constructive and developmental aspect of "primary narcissism" – like the Oedipal conflict, it is a necessary phase the child must go through, and even be encouraged to go through. But following her own ideas, she posits in the first months of a child's life the existence of a world of undifferentiated "partial objects" in which the infant is not aware of external phenomena as integral and other, but rather feels them as part of its own body, as "selfobjects" that are sources of both pleasure and pain. Without differentiating between ego and self, Klein calls this the "paranoid-schizoid position." In this position the infant harbours alternately beneficent and sadistic feelings towards these external "part-objects," depending upon whether it is feeling gratified or deprived of gratification. Klein presupposes the existence of a pre-verbal ego/self – one that is essentially moral and reacts to aggression by separating good and bad. When comfortable, the infant goes through "introjective identification," identifying the good feeling with an external object, which it sees as part of its own body – taking in the mother's breast for instance and identifying it with the thumb. When hungry or hurt, "projective identification" takes place, identifying the bad feelings, or as Klein calls them, the "bad parts," and projecting them onto an external object, which it also still feels to be its self, in this case its bad self.[13] We will see in a moment how Jonson tries to distance these "bad parts" from his better self.

His desire to do so is typical of one "position" the maturing child occupies, according to Klein. As the child matures, he or she slowly learns to see external objects as whole, and as "other" or not-self. At first, the infant is its surrounding world; then it has to deal with differentiation inside that unity.[14] Klein refers to this as the "depressive position." Here the child no longer sees "part-objects" that are either good or bad but whole objects that are *both* good and bad. One might argue that Jonson never achieved this resolution. Characteristic of the position is the realization that feelings of love and hate are directed at the same object. Symbolic thought and creativity are linked to this phase as a way of dealing with the anxiety created by the love/hate conflation.[15] One characteristic in patients with a successfully resolved depressive position is humour, the ability to laugh at oneself. Another is love, as reparation is made to the object for having harboured aggressive feelings towards it. The ability to deal with ambiguities and ambivalence implies a predominance of love over hate in this relation to whole objects.[16]

While Freud talks of stages, moving from primary narcissism towards healthy object relations, Klein calls the "paranoid-schizoid" and "depressive" states positions that subjects can occupy at different times in life. Anxiety and psychosis in the self-fashioning adult is characterized by a narcissistic malfunction that stalls the subject in the paranoid-schizoid position. And this is Jonson. Here exterior objects are seen as partial objects or "selfobjects," good or bad, fantasized as part of the body and the causes of sensations. Narcissism still retains its ambivalent quality. It remains in one respect a healthy self-defence mechanism where withdrawal of libido to the internalized part-object takes place.[17] Only when that libido is exclusively cathected to the internal part-object does the condition take on the familiar clinical symptoms of self-importance and omnipotence. But Klein insists that the central narcissistic (infantile) activity in the paranoid-schizoid position is not the self-cathecting of libido, but the sorting of objects into good and bad, and the acts of introjection and projection. Everything is part of the body, not just the good parts. This is what allows her to claim that relating to another person on the basis of projecting bad parts of the self into or onto him is [also] typical of a narcissistic personality.[18]

Kleinians assert that creativity is germane to the mature "depressive position." In Jonson, however, it appears to spring from the "paranoid-schizoid position," which Klein sees as a kind of fantasy fiction-making where the object created is a symptom. Projective identification, or a negative casting out, even in an infant, is obviously only a metaphor, a fantasy act, not a material one.[19] It can be likened to a primitive form of thinking, or organizing of internal and external experience. It is this early act of "fiction-making" that constitutes a child's first contact with the external world as she gradually learns to separate internal and external from the original unified experience.[20] This casting out of the "bad parts," and their projection into external objects, is easily understandable from a literary perspective, especially when the external objects as such are actors in a play. It is a creative act, purely mental, and a fantasy. In Jonson it was a way of sculpting himself, of self-fashioning, of trying to hold onto the good and chip away the bad. What we see in his plays are the chips, the bits that are cast off, the expelled "t" and the expelled "h" in all their material guises – the masonry. They are his self-projections, the bad "parts" of that self that appear on the stage – partial "self-objects," as Klein might say, in Jonson's drama of self-composition. The "depressive position," by contrast, is not in evidence. That would have obliged the playmaker to see how good and bad exist together in the same external part-object, adding complexity and dimension to characters. Jonson critics generally agree this rarely happens in his plays.[21]

Instead, Jonson's victims usually "embody" a fault he sees in himself and wants to expel and triumph over. They are his narcissistic creations. In *Every Man out of His Humour* he embodies a host of them. Many are themselves narcissistic traits – there is the man who wants to buy a coat of arms (Sogliardo), which was something Jonson himself had done;[22] there are those who need praise (Puntarvolo, Fastidius Briske); those who see themselves as unappreciated and owed a higher life (Fallace); or are self-absorbed (Saviolina). We also get a "prophane Jester" (Buffone), ready to "transforme any person into deformity" who is Jonson himself – those "whom he studies most to reproach" are those who "stand highest in his respect"; and most interesting of all, a "Presenter," Asper, who is also Jonson, and who goes off and returns literally transformed into Envy (Macilente), thus staging within the play the same projective identification that characterizes the play as a whole.[23] "Ile prodigally spend my selfe," Asper says, and as Macilente, he does so.[24]

This kind of exponential meta-staging of the "selfobject" – a kind of Jonsonian double-clutch – occurs again in the play with Macilente. Primary envy is a bitterness at the realization that the source of life and goodness lies without.[25] In the "paranoid-schizoid position," the subject identifies the source of pain with a part of its body that it tries to expel or project. In the play, the bitterness of envy is Macilente, "your envious man." When he sees others who are "great ... mighty and fear'd ... lov'd and highly favour'd ... wise ... learn'd ... [and] rich," his reaction is to identify them with his eyes.

When I see these (I say) and view my selfe,
I wish the organs of my sight were crackt;
And that the engine of my griefe could cast
Mine eye-balls, like two globes of wild-fire, forth.   (I.i.24–7)

Thus, Asper is the principal Jonsonian "selfobject," from which Macilente emerges as a partial object himself – "a Man well parted," Jonson calls him, to say the least – and Macilente in turn does his own casting out. This is the material form Jonson's type of psychological deformation takes. His theatre is a like a workshop where he himself is his own great sculpture.

There are other chips on the floor. Criticizing courtiers while desiring to be one of them is a form of hypocrisy, another "bad part," and one that "comes out," for example, in *Bartholomew Fair*. There it shows up as the reformers Adam Overdo, Zeal-of-the-Land Busy, and Humphrey Wasp. It may seem a bit harsh to accuse these three of hypocrisy, but the fact is that none are able to maintain any objective distance from the targets of their opprobrium. And all are brought down.[26] A chastened Wasp in the end states: "he that will correct another, must want fault in himselfe" (V.iv.99–100). He realizes too late that this prerequisite has not been met in his own case. Jonson wrote the play after his famous debauch in France, and he may have felt particularly guilty about preaching what he himself could not practice. So the "purge" here feels almost medicinal.

Self-satire can be seen in just this way, as a form of *exomologesis* or expulsion of sins. In the Middle Ages the word *repraesentatio* meant actual presence, not an artistic copy, and this is the concept of embodiment that defines *exomologesis* as the penitential disclosure and expulsion of one's sins. The Greek word for the purgative expulsion of sin from the body, as used by the early Latin fathers, meant "recognition of a fact." It was not a confession but a ritual display – in hair shirt and ashes – a spatial bodying forth of the penitent's guilt. It was, as Foucault writes, "the *dramatic* recognition of one's status as a penitent." The Roman Stoics called it *publicatio sui*. One renders the self public, or publishes it, although the Stoics' self-examination was a private affair. For Christians, however, the practice was public, and designed to expel sin from the body – another spatial metaphor. Like the Kleinian subject in the "paranoid-schizoid position," the penitent identifies the "bad part" and attempts to purge it. This "theatrical" act is a break-up of the self or identity from the perspective of the Church – a form of self-destruction that entails a necessary and deeply felt sense of self-loathing.[27] But it is also narcissistic in nature and characteristic of the "paranoid-schizoid position" that Klein outlines.

Volpone contains another variation of the Jonsonian double-clutch. Just as Macilente issues forth from Asper in *Every Man out of His Humor*, so are Corbaccio, Corvino, and Voltore, with their vulturous and taloned names, orthno-versions of Volpone himself, birds of avarice perched above his door that "peck for carrion" (V.ii.66). They are Volpone times three, his "selfobjects." The fox does not see this. Volpone sees himself rather in the shiny objects he has collected: the linen and carpets, damask, pearl and ebony that he calls his "substance." Jonson, however, knows we know they are not Volpone – that they are just acquisitions; that Volpone is essentially empty – since this is how he leaves at the end.[28] Jonson comments profoundly, unconsciously, and wishfully on his own "substance," on where the "h" should be (out) – the sly fox and its three clones – and what should be in: all the fine objects.

Germane to the "paranoid-schizoid position" is the subject's paradoxical need to maintain a strict moral division between good and bad partial objects, while subsuming both in the self. On one hand the narcissist projects and isolates, distinguishing good from bad parts, while at the same time striving like Narcissus to collapse boundaries and plunge into a self-destructive sameness. The world is spatially divided into objects that mean pleasure and those that mean pain. Jonson's life was similarly polarized, a mix of wild aggressiveness and reasoned self-restrictions. On stage the disunity is apparent. It is an either-or world of blame or praise, as Jonson was himself.[29] Inigo Jones called him "the worst of men," but Jonson called his mind "great and free," above censure, as he says in "An Ode. To himselfe," "high and aloofe, / safe from the wolves black jaw, and the dull Asses hoofe."[30] Holding onto all these walls, boundaries, and distinctions between good and bad objects, both of which make up the self, is of the utmost importance in the "paranoid-schizoid position." The collapse of this spatial stability is more than symbolic; it is physical (self-obliteration), with direct consequences for the psychic mechanism.

Jonson's reaction to the world he saw across the sewage ditch in front of his house – the back lanes of the upper-class world of Westminster – was both to yearn for it and resent it. The boundary itself has a special quality in Jonson, perhaps because subconsciously he recognized its psychological importance. The sewage ditch, for example, furnishes Jonson with material. Urine, faeces, and general ordure feature prominently in the plays and provide him with fecund weapons for abuse. He was not anal-retentive.[31] But his character was doubly marked by the ditch: it was an important boundary, and boundaries are important in the "paranoid-schizoid position," but the narcissist also yearns to collapse those boundaries and fold everything into himself. Sewage is the ultimate dissolution of boundaries. For Freud, the fear of a return to an undifferentiated state, and a yearning for it, is at the bottom of the repetition compulsion – both a death wish and a yearning to return to the oceanic.[32] Faeces and ashes: the cradle and the grave – these are the pure states of de-differentiation, and the bookends of identity that frame Jonson's workshop of the self.

The dissolution of spatial boundaries, for example, is an issue in several plays, in the circulatory obsession with intake and output in *Bartholomew Fair*, but also in *Sejanus*, *The Case is Altered*, and *The Alchemist*. A transgressor of boundaries like Sejanus, who forgets his place and believes that it is place and not blood that should matter in life, becomes geography, ending up distributed over the landscape like Pentheus. Arruntius says that he was "rais'd, from excrement" (IV.i.406) by Tiberius, and in the end he returns to a fertilizer-like condition. In *The Case is Altered*, Jaques de Prie hides gold under dung in his backyard, where the principle is the absolute difference and distance between these two "products." Where there is dung no one will ever think to look for gold.[33] And in *The Alchemist* the concern with boundaries and differentiation is "staged" almost literally – we are told that the transformation of metals into gold is nonsense, a ploy on the part of Subtle, Face, and Doll to gull their victim. Maintaining spatial boundaries is integral to the self-fashioning process, and Jonson appears to have felt it in good earnest. They are not only thematic in many of the plays, but meant a lot in his own personal life, as he strove to get across that ditch and into better society.

The absence of humour and love in Jonson's self-struggle is striking. The narcissistic personality displays a particular brand of humour that is self-defensive, never self-deprecatory, and often contains a sadistic kind of sarcasm.[34] The appearance of a capacity for genuine humour – laughter without sarcasm – is a sign that a resolution of the narcissistic cathexes is taking place. The clinician looks for evidence that the patient's devotion to his values and ideals is not that of a fanatic but demonstrates a sense of proportion by being open to humour.[35] In Jonson's plays, however, laughter never bleeds over into the celebratory or self-deprecatory. It is always at someone's expense, confined in the ring of sarcasm, and never an expression of delight. The accusation of "railing" made so often against him voices this complaint. There was little joy or merriment in Hartshorn Lane.

The predominance of love over hate is a sign of the dissolution of the narcissistic boundaries. Jonson's plays never break out into the tender emotion – there are "no women one feels mad to kiss," as Keats said, no Orlandos or Romeos. With Volpone, Celia would still be alone. This is not to say the plays never treat of love. Echo loves her lost Narcissus, Thorello loves and marries Biancha, Ovid loves Julia. One might say that love is to narcissism what the open country is to a closed room, or what humour is to sarcasm. A certain expansiveness or expansion of the self is required to pass from the "paranoid-schizoid position" to the "depressive position," where whole objects and love exist. This is not in the cards for the narcissistic personality. In *The Poetaster* love is vulgarized, and in Ovid's case it appears as a dangerous self-dissolution. When he waxes lovelorn over Julia, Tibullus warns him: "thou'lt lose thy selfe." Ovid answers: "O, in no labyrinth, can I safelier erre, / Then when I lose my selfe in praysing her" (I.iii.46–50).[36] This sounds Shakespearean, but Ovid's words are not the Sonnets; they are empty, and he is a "shallow libertine" who leads the Emperor's daughter into low company and is banished for his trouble.[37]

There is little love lost in *Cynthias Revels, or The Fountayne of Selfe-Love*. The play is the most direct expression of Jonson's narcissistic pathology as it relates to love that he produced – the lack of the heart of the problem. The characters who drink the water from the "fountain of self-love" in the play are immune to Cupid's arrows. No one is in love. As if in recognition that Narcissus is the embodiment of the problem, the character of Narcissus is himself cast out from the cast. He is displaced and put aside. Echo's love for him is purely posthumous. Jonson treats the emotion with a stonecutter's hands. The lyrical passages surrounding Echo's arrival and her opening lament for Narcissus are as warm as he gets in this regard. Echo knows the consequence of her love will be identical to the fate of Narcissus: the collapse of the boundary of self into the "other." But she doesn't care: "His name revives, and lifts me up from earth. / O, which ways shall I first convert my selfe?" (I.ii.18–19). Echo, however, now runs into Mercury, who is immediately curt with her and tells her to "be brief" (I.ii.54). Echo asks for and receives his permission to "sing some mourning straine / Over [Narcissus's] watrie hearse" (I.ii.58–9), but her song, "Slow, slow, fresh fount," is received by an increasingly impatient Mercury with scorn. "Now, ha' you done?" he hallows like a fishmonger (I.ii.76). Echo begs him to be patient, to "bide a little," but he replies by telling her ominously to "Foregoe thy use and libertie of tongue" (I.ii.80).

Depending on the direction, sympathy could be with either character at this point. Echo could be pretentious and melodramatic, or Mercury an unfeeling boor. The text directs us towards the first choice. Echo goes on talking, turning steadily into a parody, a domestic chatterbox. When she continues with "Here yong Acteon fell" (I.ii.82), one can almost hear the guffaws. Mercury, increasingly exasperated, interrupts her: "Nay, but heare," and when she again continues, he says brusquely, "Stint thy babling tongue!" (I.ii.92). Echo and the discourse of love are first vulgarized, then banished. They are cast out, cast forth like Narcissus. The Jonsonian stage comes with bins clearly labelled for triage. There is always an inside/outside dynamic at work where the spatial boundaries are so hard and fast they often become the unacknowledged subject of the plays.

Cupid in Jonson's masques, for example, always clearly represents danger, the Ovid problem of love as the loss of self in the other. The narcissist sees love as a betrayal of himself, a kind of infidelity, not a fulfilment; it feels like self-annihilation, a dissolution of boundaries. Cupid in the masques threatens boundaries, and his irrational temper produces discord. Traditionally viewed as a convention of the Renaissance ideal of concord from discord, or the coincidence of opposites, Jonson's treatment of Cupid and the dangers of *cupiditas* feels nonetheless more personal and material than artistic, aesthetic, or philosophical. Cupid means betrayal, and a collapse of boundaries. He wants discipline. And in masques like *Lovers Made Men* and the *Balet Comique* it is Mercury who again supplies it. On love, Jonson was always clear that one must love God first, and then the king. It is hard to imagine that this rigidity could have any remainder.

With respect to his own domestic relations, Jonson seems to have had just as fine an appreciation for the importance of spatial boundaries. We do not know why, when the plague struck in 1603, he took himself off to Robert Cotton's manor house in Huntingdonshire and left his family behind, trapped in the plague-ridden city. He had been separated from his wife for a year. Perhaps his house had been quarantined. In any case, he did not make Orpheus's mistake, or risk his life like Aeneas going back for his Creusa. Or for his seven-year-old Ascanius. The death of Jonson's son caused him great pain, but the poem that he wrote about the boy blurs the distinction between father and son in predictable ways, and has a marked narcissistic quality.[38] In Kleinian terms, one might say that the boy was Jonson's one material projection that was non-theatrical, a good part of himself (appropriately Ben times two) that he cast forth as his "best piece of *poetrie*." Dropping the "h" from his name the next year cut the filial thread in the other direction. With no more connections to either father or son, Jonson was at last a fully self-contained man, alone in a space of his own.

4 Sade and the Deformed Body

The idea of deformation in Sade is usually understood in psychological terms that are normative in nature, referring to his mind and morals, and those of his libertine characters. That is, Sade's psychology, or what we loosely call sadomasochism, is judged a perversion of normal, healthy sexuality, and this forms the basis for our understanding of his fiction, which we then read as a symptom of this abnormality – much the way we looked at narcissism in Jonson and how it is "bodied forth" in the object world of his stage. In this chapter, by contrast, I would like to examine a particular spatial obsession in Sade's prison fiction (tunnelling and blockage) in terms of the medical condition he suffered from, which appears to have been a deformity in his urological tract.

In general, Sade's spatial settings and his handling of proportion are as conventional as Jonson's and as rational as Swift's. Like Gulliver (and Rabelais for that matter), Sade was a man of science, not to say an outright materialist, and his descriptions of buildings and rooms, bodies, geography, architecture, and so on are always spatially coherent and precise, not to say (very often) overdetermined. Of course, Sade's narrators are monomaniacal monsters compared to Gulliver, and display nothing like Gulliver's quiet interest in scientific accuracy as he rationalizes scale differences, but that does not mean that the geometry of Sade's characters and settings are any less coherent or rational. They are just as well thought out as Swift's. Spatial laws, in other words, are not violated in Sade as they are in Rabelais and Mannerist painting. He occasionally brings "giants" onto the stage, but they behave with the kind of geometrical propriety that Gulliver displays in Lilliput. His libertines may be implausibly endowed, for example, but once that one incommensurability is accepted, what follows, in terms of spatial logic, always makes good Newtonian sense. There are no twisted horizons in Sade's fiction. His spatial eccentricities instead have to do with the way he handles underground passages leading to and from the scenes of his atrocities, and these, I would argue, have their basis in the physical deformity he complained about while he was in the Bastille.

Given the preponderance of psychological readings of Sade's work, it might be helpful to begin by pointing out how even perversion has a physical basis. The word "algolagnia" is often used to describe Sade's mental aberration. It means the obtaining of sexual pleasure from the infliction and experience of pain: sadomasochism. It has come to denote a psychological abnormality, and its use in Sade studies implies that Sade was simply a pervert, in today's usage, with a mental condition like the one described by Krafft-Ebing in his *Pychopathia sexualis*. Simone de Beauvoir's comment, in her famous 1951 essay "Must We Burn Sade?" is typical. She recognizes that there was probably some physical basis for Sade's obsessions – sexual impotence, for example – but feels there must be some deeper psychological explanation for the Sade phenomenon. This leads her finally to forego the physical altogether and assert that "Sade's sexuality is not a biological matter. It is a social fact."[1]

But in Sade the two are hard to differentiate. Troubled with painful and difficult ejaculations in prison, Sade invented characters like Minsky in *Juliette*, who tells Juliette that when he ejaculates, "the jets of sperm thereupon released mount to the ceiling, often fifteen or twenty ... my tenth ejaculation is just as tumultuous, just as abundant, as the first."[2] The passage is typical of one kind of spatial disproportion we find in Sade's fiction, and it is directly (and obviously) related to his physical confinement. The idea that the physical trumps the psychological in Sade is not new.[3] Sade himself insisted on it. His explanations are always in line with the materialism of Julien Offray de La Mettrie and Baron d'Holbach. He often reminds his readers that "*sensibilité*," for example, is a physical state that has no conscience, correcting Rousseau's Julie in this regard with his own Juliette, exchanging Rousseau's benign "nature" for his own jungle law.

Krafft-Ebing was clear on the distinction between physical and mental ailments. He distinguished between "perversion," which he called a disease, and "perversity," which he called a vice: "Perversion of the sexual instinct ... is not to be confounded with perversity in the sexual act."[4] He treats sadism in section 3 of his work, under the heading of "General Pathology," rather in the section devoted to psychology. It is a medical condition. The association of lust and cruelty, pain and plea-sure, is a physiological matter, Krafft-Ebing insists, since it exists among animals, where the female is passive, pursued, and finally subjugated, often violently, by the male (59). For Krafft-Ebing, the moral feeling is inhibitory, but the drive itself is physiological: "Sadism is thus nothing else than an excessive and monstrous pathological intensification of phenomena – possible too, in normal conditions in rudimental forms – which accompany the psychical *vita sexualis*, particularly in males" (60).

This includes another aspect of Sade's "perversion" – the tendency of characters like Minsky in *Juliette* to eat their victims. Krafft-Ebing cites numerous examples of anthropophagy, where the male predator liter-ally cuts out parts of the female victim's anatomy and eats them, includ-ing a contemporary one where the killer is at large as he writes. The Whitechapel murder victims, for example, were all missing their uterus, ovaries, and labia, which Krafft-Ebing presumes the killer is eating (64). These grisly examples are cited by Krafft-Ebing with all the horror that a scientific treatise like his will allow, but it is clear that he sees them in strictly medical terms, where the individuals are suffering from a physi-cal ailment. He discusses them as tied to different forms of illness, atro-phy of the frontal lobe of the brain, and genetic factors. He does not deny they must necessarily also have a psychological aspect, but often is content to leave this part of things to the inhibitory function of the moral feeling. When it fails, a simple suggestion can spark the atavistic instinct. He cites a nineteenth-century work, P.L. Jacob's *Curiosités de l'histoire de France*, which includes the case of Gilles de Rais, executed in 1440 for the murder and mutilation of some eight hundred children over a period of eight years, and who confessed that his acts gave him "inexpressible pleasure." Lacking the necessary psychological inhibi-tors, his act was sparked, in his own account, by reading Suetonius on the orgies of Tiberius.[5]

Flagellation was another of Sade's algolagnic addictions whose aetiol-ogy even in his day was known to be purely physiological. It had been an accepted fact that the "English vice" was linked to sexual pleasure in some, albeit mysterious, physical way, for hundreds of years. Krafft-Ebing cites Paullini's 1698 *Flagellum Salutis*, which includes the 1580 case of a Carmelite nun from Florence called Maria Magdalena, a "heroine of flagellation" who had been whipped "from her earliest youth" and en-joyed it. Krafft-Ebing writes: "she frequently cried, 'Enough! Fan no lon-ger the flame that consumes me. This is not the death I long for; it comes with all too much pleasure and delight'" (28–30).[6] Paullini goes so far as to claim that it has always been a well-known fact that Persian and Russian women in particular are easily aroused by beating, and often demand it of their husbands as a part of their conjugal duties, without the slightest sense that there is anything perverse about it. Krafft-Ebing discusses flagellation in section 2, under "Physiological Facts," rather than in the first section on psychology. There is no moral stigma involved since sexual arousal from whipping is purely an autonomous physical response. Flagellants' societies and bordellos were of course common in the eighteenth century, in both England and France, and had a ready-made clientele accustomed to the pleasures of the whip from an early age. In school, in the military, at home: there was plenty of opportunity for the sort of initiation and addiction to the pleasure that Rousseau describes in his *Confessions*. Krafft-Ebing writes: "This should be remembered by those who have the care of children" (28).

Judging by the books on anatomy and medicine in Sade's library at La Coste, his claim that he was driven in his sexual tastes by material and physical considerations must be taken as sincere. His 1776 library, for example, contained a copy of Jacques Boileau's 1700 *Histoire des Flagellants* in which the materialist approach to whipping is again implicit in the scientific attempt Boileau makes to distinguish between the proper and improper uses of flagellation; and a treatise called *Aphrodisiaque externe*, written in 1788 by François Amédée Doppet, that takes the same scientific approach.[7] Boileau's treatise is less a history than a cry of warning. He discusses the history of self-flagellation in the Church orders and admits its usefulness when accompanied, and only if it is accompanied by other mortifications of the flesh. He reminds his readers that in ancient law flagellation was used only to punish crime and was never self-inflicted or inflicted by someone else for pleasure. Whipping was a pagan practice that in Augustine's day was reserved for heretics and criminals; it first appears, Boileau writes, among religious orders in the form of self-flagellation around 1047. A sect of flagellants existed in 1260, and Boileau places its beginnings in Boulogne.[8] In that year, according to a monk of the Abbey of Sainte Justine of Padua, "toute l'Italie … étoit plongée dans toute sorte de vices et de crimes" [all of Italy was plunged in all kinds of vice and crimes] when suddenly the fear of God took hold of them and processions of people, "nobles et roturiers, jeunes et vieux, et les enfans même de cinq ans" [nobles and commoners, young and old, and even children of five years of age] formed a procession and marched in pairs whipping themselves as they went (255–7). Boileau believed that whipping on the shoulders caused damage to the eyes (303), and he cites the Capuchins' decision to change from the shoulders to the buttocks as a definitive moment in the history of the practice. "Mais il faut prendre garde," Boileau writes laconically, "que pour fuir un mal, ils ne courent imprudemment vers celui qui est opposé" [But one must be careful, when fleeing from one evil, not to run imprudently into one that is its opposite" (306). In medical terms, Boileau describes the situation as follows:

les esprits animaux soient repoussés avec violence vers l'os pubis, et qu'ils excitent des mouvements impudiques à cause de la proximité des parties génitales; ces impressions pasent d'abord au cerveau, et y peignent de vives images des plaisirs défendus, qui fascinent l'esprit par leurs charmes trompeurs, et reduisent la chasteté aux derniers abois.

[the animal spirits being violently propelled against the pubic bone excite lewd movements because of the proximity of the genitals; these pressures are conveyed first to the brain, and paint there vivid images of forbidden pleasures, which fascinate the spirit with their delusionary charms and press chastity to its limits.] (307)

Boileau then goes on to cite some cases of "ces criminelles délices" [these criminal delights] (308) that resemble Krafft-Ebing's. He tells us that Coelius Rhodiginus in 1560 recounts the story of a man who had the "criminal delight" "enracinée dans son coeur des l'enfance" [rooted in his heart from childhood] (312) and lists two other instances: one mentioned in an entry in the *Onomasticon de Medicine* of Othon Brunsfled under the heading of "coitus" where a man is mentioned who could not carry out his conjugal duties unless whipped; and another from Jean Henri Meibomius, Bishop of Lubeck, who mentions in his *Christien Cassius* a butter and cheese merchant afflicted in the same way, as well as a merchant caught with "une femmelete qu'il entretenoit" [a little woman he kept] who testified that her lover had to be whipped to be sexually aroused. Since public flagellation seemed to authorize the "delight," it was finally condemned by both the Church and the University of Paris and banned by the Parliament of Paris in 1601.

Sade also had Tissot's 1766 *De la santé des gens de lettres* (*On the Health of Men of Letters*) in his library. This work, by a doctor, brings together medicine and the humanities. Tissot claims that sitting for long periods of time, as Sade certainly did in prison, harms the circulation in the lower part of the male body. Being bent at the waist, late hours, bad air, and reading after meals are among the factors Tissot cites as damaging to the male urological tract, a combination of which can produce in men poor digestion, haemorrhoids, and stones. Sade's mechanistic philosophy was shared by Tissot, who discusses the body strictly as a machine. A disturbance in one part is transferred through nerve impulsions to other locations. Stones most commonly developed in the kidneys, bladder, and urethra, but Tissot adds, they can also occur in the seminal canal, a comment that must have caught Sade's attention. What Tissot calls "la liqueur séminale" in the male is negatively affected by the same factors and "loses much of its activity" in writers. Boisseau notes that for this reason great male writers seldom have "sons worthy of them." It is common to see the son of a soldier distinguish himself, he says, but uncommon to see the son of a great writer do so. But there is nothing in Tissot that is more specific on the kind of illness from which Sade suffered.[9] Krafft-Ebing also talks about the "sedentary life" and says it is a cause of sexual dysfunction in the male. Poor posture is the principal culprit since the nerve tract from the genitals to the brain travels along the spinal cord. Observations of hanged men, for example, show that the spine rather than the brain is the physical centre for erections, while the ejaculatory centre according to Krafft-Ebing is located in the fourth lumbar vertebra of the back (25; 33). But again, the sort of sexual dysfunction Tissot and Krafft-Ebing associate with spinal injuries does not correspond to Sade's complaint.

Sade makes the complaint explicit in the famous "Vanilla and Manilla" letter, written to his wife from the Bastille at the end of 1784. His illness might be described as a kind of spatial disarticulation of the seminal vessels. Sade was adamant that there was to be no autopsy performed on his body, so the only account we have of his ailment comes from this letter. In it, as in all of Sade's fiction, pain and sexual/textual release go together. He is in a cell, so the physical realities of confinement and the impossibility of release were before him every waking minute. It is therefore no surprise that much of the prison fiction should feature different fictional treatments of restriction, constriction, release, and other spatial "enlargements." All these scenes echo and reconfigure his physical malady. In the letter, he uses the code words "vanilla" and "manilla" to refer to the different methods of masturbation and self-sodomy he uses to try for a sexual release that is both slow in coming and abnormal when it does. He first uses a bow and arrow metaphor to describe the situation, then switches to a different military image that seems more apt: "[N]or is it because the bow is not taut – oh, don't worry, on that score it is everything you could hope for as far as rigidity goes – but the arrow refuses to leave the bow and that is the most exasperating part – because one wants it to leave – lacking an object, one goes slightly crazy – and that doesn't help matters in the least – and 'tis for this reason I tell you that prison is bad, because solitude gives added strength only to ideas."[10] Lacking an object in prison, Sade says he goes slightly crazy and requires an inordinately long time to reach what are consistently violent and painful orgasms. Lacking objects, preferably male objects, who will arouse him, he has only "ideas," only his imagined scenarios, which he proceeds to invent at a furious pace, repetitively reproducing through hundreds of pages the violence, pain, and release generic to his condition. The second image draws attention to the problem as one of disproportion:

> But I've already made up my mind about the stubborn refusal of this arrow to leave the bow, all the more so because when, ultimately, it does cleave the air – 'tis veritably an attack of epilepsy – and no matter what precautions I may take I am quite certain that these convulsions and spasms, not to mention the physical pain, can be heard as far as the Faubourg St. Antoine … I wanted to analyze the cause of this fainting spell, and believe that 'tis because of the extreme thickness – as if one tried to force cream out of the very narrow neck of a bottle or flask. That thickness inflates the vessels and tears them … Imagine in your mind a rifle, and in its firing chamber is a bullet, the nature of which is that the longer it remains in the gun the larger it grows; if you fire the rifle within a couple of days, the explosion will be relatively light; but if you leave the bullet there for some time, then it will burst the barrel as it exits.

The lack of an object of desire in prison was not compensated for by masturbation or self-sodomy, which Sade practiced relentlessly and furiously, since this auto-eroticism did not succeed in bringing him to orgasm as often or as easily as he needed. His self-diagnosis takes the form of the bullet-in-the-gun metaphor, where expansion and constriction are the forces in conflict: "If I had those other means which I utilize when I am free, the arrow being less recalcitrant and flying more frequently, the crisis of its departure would be neither as violent or as dangerous – for its danger can be explained by the difficulty of departure … if the arrow were to fly more frequently, 'twould be *more fluid*; and consequently there would be fewer [violent] episodes."

Fewer episodes perhaps, and fewer complaints, but the condition remained. In the Bastille letter Sade asks his wife to go see a doctor, describe his symptoms and find out what the problem is; and he says that as soon as he gets out he is going to do that himself, "car il est très sûr qu'il faut que j'aie un défaut de conformation que n'ont certainement point les autres hommes" [because I definitely have some kind of congenital defect that no other man has].[11] Sade thinks this congenital defect may even worsen as he gets older: "cette idée," he writes, "me désespère" [this idea makes me despair].[12]

As to the nature of the dysfunction itself – which Sade calls "physical or congenital" – speculation today on its nature has usually settled on the notion that he might have had some kind of venereal disease.[13] But the symptoms Sade describes, especially as they seem to decrease in severity when the frequency of his ejaculations increases, are hard to reconcile with any of our known sexually transmitted diseases. Even if there were strains in Sade's day that we no longer know about, he certainly would have known about them; so when he says he is "quite certain" the problem is congenital we can probably believe him. In the letter of 1784 Sade refers to "convulsions, spasms and pains." The illness is not new: sixteen years earlier Rose Keller had reported that Sade's orgasm after whipping her was accompanied by "des cris 'très hauts et très effrayants'" [cries that were "sharp and very frightening"]. And Sade writes to his wife: "tu en a[s] vu des echantillons a la Coste" [you've seen examples at la Coste], although the problem, he says, has gotten twice as bad since he has been in prison.[14]

Sade's fiction is riddled with tortuous underground passages whose spaces are analogous to the vision he has of his own internal vesicles. They are inevitably made up of tortuous windings and filled with blockages. Stones are always being removed, often starting in a church, to facilitate the passage of the characters to some site of sexual release. The sex haven of Delbène in *Juliette* is below the church and accessed through a tunnel blocked first by a tombstone and then halfway along by another stone that must be swung aside before the travellers can, so to speak, come out. The chambers at the end of these passages are always low-ceilinged, dank, and vaguely gastroenterological in nature.[15] Sade refers to them as located in the "bowels" of the earth, or deep in the "earth's entrails." In *The 120 Days* there is a "fatal stone" blocking the entry to a passage, again in a church. From there we descend into "a very narrow" passageway, "into the bowels of the earth," and so on.[16]

Sade's one self-diagnosis, using the bullet-in-the-gun imagery, may be more helpful in tracking down the "blockage" problem than any of the speculation on venereal disease. The literature on urology, for example, provides several alternatives. Sade may have had some kind of seminal vesicle cysts, for example, that caused him pain when he was sexually aroused for long periods of time.[17] The seminal vesicles are single tubes four to five inches long that are coiled upon themselves, so any blockage would be serious. Or he may have had some kind of ejaculatory duct obstruction – an irregularity or stricture in the ejaculatory duct, for example, at the junction of the proximal portion of the seminal vesicle and the vas deferens that caused him pain. Cysts in the Müllerian duct can, as a result of the duct's extrinsic compression, also lead to blockage of the ejaculatory ducts, although (again) this does not seem to produce symptoms today of the sort Sade describes.

The imagery and figures in the literature change, however, if one looks back into the world of nineteenth-century urology. The Victorians suffered from a number of sexually related illnesses and neuroses that are no longer with us, so it seems reasonable to think the same applied to Sade's century. In the nineteenth century paroxysms of the sort Sade experienced with orgasm were quite common. Hospital records were full of them. They were viewed as closely related to epileptic seizures, and some concluded in good Victorian fashion that epilepsy was really where all masturbators and libertines were headed.[18] The Victorians in any case seem to have thought a lot about blockages, not only in the urethra but elsewhere in the male genito-urinary tract, and acknowledged that the complicated nature of this tract in the male made locating the blockages difficult. The testis, for example, contains more than 250 lobules containing the *tubuli seminiferi* – five hundred tubes per testicle that if stretched out would reach to about sixteen feet; 250 lobules would come to about 480 feet. Strictures or blockages in the tract are rare but not unknown.

Sade's libertines are naturally secretive, so many of their outrages take place in underground hideaways. Sade always devotes a lot of attention to describing the arteries leading to and from these sites. In *Justine*, for one of many possible examples, Roland's sex haven is underground. He leads Justine into a darkened passage that winds about, is blocked by a door, descends a hundred paces, is blocked by another door, becomes "a narrow passage … filled with sinuosities," whose air contains "a terrible humidity," and finally is blocked by yet another door that must be laboriously unlocked and swung back. Only then are the travellers released upward into the site of sexual release.[19] Of course, the feeling Sade had of "blockage," while easy to understand, given his symptoms, could just as easily be wrong or misleading. The pain might have had a completely different aetiology. For example, a cyst or defect somewhere can cause pain during the muscular contractions of the perineal striated muscle. Contractions during emission are produced by sympathetic input to the genitalia and involve contraction of the seminal vesicles, prostate, vas deferens, bulbourethral glands, and ampulla, which pushes seminal fluid into the proximal urethra and produces the feeling of ejaculatory inevitability.[20] There appears to be no evidence that men, at least today, suffer from blockages that would make these contractions painful. Instead, male sexual dysfunction today, aside from erectile disorders, is for the most part related to impotence or idiopathic anejaculation – having no bullet in the gun, or power behind it, to borrow Sade's image, rather than the bullet being too large. One form of impotence involves the innervation of the bulbocavernosus and ischiocavernosus muscles, and it is possible that Sade had some congenital defect in one of these muscles that made prolonged stimulation painful.

But the sheer length and complicated nature of the male genito-urinary tract makes Sade's imagery of blocked passages compelling. One very likely location would be the narrow convoluted tube called the epididymis, which is located on the posterior margin of each testis, and in which spermatozoa are stored before being conveyed along to the vas deferens. Eisendrath and Ralnick describe it as a single tubule that is "coiled and twisted upon itself … a number of coils of the tubule are grouped and bunched together … producing a compartment-like formation." A blockage here would be difficult to locate. The entire epididymis, if unwound, would stretch to about twenty feet, and is "blocked off into a continuous compartment of coils," where a cyst or congenital defect could have a serious effect on the passage of fluid. At the junction of the body and the tail, the tubule makes a number of acute angles upon itself, where a defect would again be serious, before becoming larger and thicker.[21] Nor is the interior passage of this tubule smooth; rather, it is irregular and broken by protrusions in the interior wall that stick out like room dividers. The vas deferens, which is the continuation of the epididymis, would also be a possible candidate for trouble. It is a small, thick-walled tube about two feet long, and joins the seminal canal at the duct. Strictures in any of these passages, although rare, might have caused Sade pain during long periods of stimulation.

Another diagnosis that would fit with Sade's spatial imagery is that he might have suffered from some form of amyloidosis. The seminal vesicles synthesize and secrete protein, and a disturbance in protein metabolism can result in starch-like or amyloid deposits in the seminal vesicles or urethra – deposits that form waxy translucent blockages. The condition is slightly more common with older men and is often a

secondary effect of tuberculosis, and we know that Sade had tuberculosis. Doctors in the nineteenth century, again, seem to use language that
gets closer to what Sade describes. G.M. Phillips, in 1898, described
blockages in the urethra as "partitions" and "apertures" that obstruct the
passage with deposits of "a hardened, inelastic tissue, through which the
canal may run as a narrow, irregular tortuous passage. This form of stricture is called tortuous."[22] Like other Victorians, Phillips saw excessive
venery as the culprit. "Prolonged and unrelieved congestion occurring
in young men whose minds are ever upon matters sexual," he writes,
"may cause stricture."[23] Sade does not complain of pain in passing water,
so any such strictures, deposits, or even cysts, if present, would have
been located anterior to the urethra. In any of these cases it would seem
possible that pain could either be associated with prolonged stimulation,
or aggravated by the build-up and discharge of seminal fluid.

Interestingly, similar descriptions in the literature of male urology in
the nineteenth and early twentieth centuries that focus on the vascular
passages leading from the testis to the urethra depend heavily on the
word "tortuous." Eisendrath and Ralnick describe the ejaculatory duct
at the outlet of the seminal vesicles, for example, as "a tortuous inelastic
duct." They call the "winding course" of the vas deferens "quite tortuous" and discuss the "tortuosity" of its various compartments and fold-
ing.[24] They could well be describing the route to Minsky's castle in
Juliette. Juliette, Sbrigani, and their servants visit this island keep at the
invitation of their host, the seven-foot-three giant Minsky. Sade's spatial geography manages to feel "tortuous" without being overtly expressionistic. The company first approaches Minsky's hideout by climbing
the slope of a high mountain. They come to a precipice from where they
gaze down into an "abyss a full two thousand fathoms deep." The climb
has taken only an hour and they did not encounter any obstacles. The
only incommensurability so far is not spatial but rather between the nature of the setting and the nature of the characters moving through it.
This is clearly a rugged landscape more suited to mountain goats than
Sade's libertine blue bloods.

The little troupe now descends into the "abyss," and their passage
becomes more arduous. They follow a "winding path" through a forest
so dense and dark that they can barely see their way. The climb down
takes three hours. At the bottom they come to the edge of a lake, where
they must take a boat to get out to Minsky's island. Only when they
move out from the shore and see the rim of surrounding mountains
looming up all round them do we realize that the group has come down

into the cone of an extinct volcano. Minsky's hideaway is on an island at the centre of a volcanic lake. Juliette describes the scene as "unearthly."

Once they are ashore on the island it is still two furlongs to Minsky's castle. And this is where words like "confinement" and "blockage" become operative. First they come to an iron gate set in a "thick outer wall." Then there is a moat twenty feet wide to cross. Then comes a second wall, and again they must pass through an iron gate. Next comes a forest with trees so close together they must force a passage through them. Then they come up against a third wall, this one ten feet thick, with no gate at all. Instead the entryway is blocked by a huge stone, which only Minsky can remove. At this point the necessity of security from unwanted visitors has been more than satisfied. But instead of coming out on the other side of the wall the entryway leads down into the "dank darkness" of an underground passageway. At the end of this one, like others Sade invents, lies the site of sexual release. The travellers move through this viscous dark vesicle until finally they come to some stairs leading up. And here, at the end of their voyage, is one more stone blocking their way. Minsky removes it and they emerge into the room, where the giant satisfies his larger-than-life sexual appetites.[25]

The underground twists and turns and blockages that are common in the spaces surrounding and sheltering Sade's hideouts not only lead usually to some form of sexual torture, as they do here, but are themselves tortuous and painful to pass through. Sade did not consciously write them as fictional analogues of his own painful medical condition, but they go so far beyond any rational need for safety, and are so obviously anatomical in their descriptions, that it is hard not to see them through the lens of his urological deformation.[26] The approach to Silling in *The 120 Days* also begins with climbing a mountain: this one requiring five hours of heavy labour. At the top, instead of looking down into a volcano, the travellers find a deep crevice that must be crossed. Once across, they come down into a plain but are again blocked by a wall; another moat has to be crossed, and another wall breached, before they finally are released into Durcet's chateau.

As if to confirm the material basis of his fictional spaces, Sade never tires of denying their psychological genesis. He cites Nature time and again to explain the pathology of his condition. This is usually understood as nothing more than Sade's attempt to rationalize his enormities, but he was a man of his age and a dogged materialist. He really did see cause and effect in strict empirical terms. His characters may not see the urology-fiction connection I am drawing out, but the explanations they offer for their behaviour are always material in nature. Minsky, for example, credits his diet of small boys for his excellent sexual constitution. He prowls about in his neighbourhood, kidnaps them, tortures them, sodomizes them until their flesh is tender, and then eats them. He tells Juliette that "such inordinate quantities of human flesh as I consume heavily contribute to the plentifulness and density of the seminal matter; whoever tries this diet is certain to triple his libidinous capacities, to say nothing of the strength, the health, the youthfulness such fare assures."[27] There is no evidence Sade had read Swift's "Modest Proposal."

Sade's constricted and "tortuous" fictional passageways are the correlative of his painful urological deformity. A similar relationship exists in the fiction of Defoe. The scenes of torture in his "criminal lives," for example, probably had a lot to do with his lithotomy surgery for bladder stones. He wrote that hanging was an easier way to die than the "Tortures of the Stone," and gives us a description of the corrective surgery in a 1725 Applebee's essay: "Here's a Man ... torn and mangled ... cut open alive, and bound Hand and Foot to force him to bear it; the very Apparatus is enough to chill the Blood, and sink a Man's soul within him."[28] The apparatus in question would have interested Sade. Hospitals in England used wooden pallets that the patient was strapped to, with his knees bent and his wrists tied to his ankles. Even this was not enough, and it took three or four strong men to keep the patient still and hold his legs apart.[29] In the sixty-fifth Criminal Passion in the *120 Days* the female victim is placed in an "armchair balanced on springs" so that her weight "releases a number of springs connected to iron rings which bind her tightly to the chair. Certain levers and gears advance twenty daggers," and so on.[30]

Defoe "reports" on the case of an eighteen-year-old cabin boy who was tortured and killed by his Captain on a journey home from South Carolina to Bristol. The boy was whipped several times "and after whipping, pickled ... in Brine." For "nine Days and Nights," Defoe writes, the Captain "tied him to the main Mast, his Arms and Legs being all the Time extended at full Length." "[N]ot content with this he had him unt'd, and laid along upon the Gangway, where he trod upon him, and would have had the Men do the same, which they refus'd." The Captain "kick'd him about as he lay ... stamp'd upon his Breast so violently, that his Excrement came involuntarily from him; which he took up, and with his own Hands forc'd it several Times down his Throat." It took eighteen days for the boy to die, during which the Captain fed him only enough to keep him alive. He whipped the boy every day, especially violently on the eighteenth day, on which the boy was given eighteen lashes. "When he was just expiring," Defoe writes, basing his information on testimony of other sailors at the Captain's trial, "he put his Finger to his mouth which was took for a Signal of desiring something to drink, when the Brute, to continue his Inhumanity to the last, went into the Cabbin for a Glass, which he pissed in, and then gave it him for a cordial." The boy swallowed a little, pushed the glass from him and died. The sailors testifying at the trial said that the body, when sown up in the hammock for burial at sea, "was of as many Colours as the Rainbow; that his Flesh was in many Places like Jelly, and his Head swollen as big as two Men's Heads of the largest Size."[31]

At his trial in the Old Bailey, Defoe's Captain Jeane, a twenty-nine-year-old native of Bristol, is asked to explain his behaviour. He replies that the boy stole some rum and had been insolent. When pressed further as to "what could induce him to so much Cruelty," the Captain says, "'Twas what he took Pleasure in; Words [Defoe adds], "'tis believed, never spoke before in a Court of Judicature!" Defoe does not suggest that the man might be ill, but is clearly amazed at his refusal to repent or regret his actions. Instead, the Captain, who turns out to be something of a gentleman with money enough to bring a lady friend to stay with him in prison, "insisted to the last, that he could not apprehend it criminal in him to punish the Boy; and that his dying under Correction, was the Lad's Misfortune, but not a Crime chargeable upon him."[32] In Defoe's description, the man does not seem to apprehend the seriousness of what he has done right to the last, and even on the scaffold cries out over the injustice of his punishment before finally lying down and putting his hat over his face. Captain Jeane's reply that "'Twas what he took Pleasure in" suggests that like so many of the cases Krafft-Ebing cites, his acts might well be considered the result of an "excessive and monstrous pathological intensification of phenomena."[33] The addict knows full well what he or she is about, but is helpless to do otherwise. We are willing to accept this when the addict is the victim, but less willing to do so when someone else is injured. Sade had the requisite inhibitory moral feeling, as Boileau puts it, and the requisite imagination to translate his pathological condition into fiction.

Krafft-Ebing's distinction between the medical nature of perversion and the psychological nature of perversity finds an interesting echo in Deleuze's discussion of sadomasochism and the difference between symptoms and syndromes: "les symptômes sont des signes spécifiquex d'une maladie, mais les syndromes sont des unités de rencontre ou de croisement, qui renvoient à des lignées causales très différentes; à des contextes variables" [symptoms are specific signs of illness, but syndromes are unities of meeting or intersection that have very different causal connections, and variable contexts].[34] Deleuze is in the business of pointing out how everything (from diagnosis on) is a kind of writing or fiction, but the distinction he makes between material symptoms and the more ethereal (psychological) world of syndromes applies well to what Krafft-Ebing had to say about perversions of the body like Sade's. Deleuze writes: "La symptomatologie est toujours affaire d'art" [Symptomatology is always the business of art]. To a degree this is of course always true. But like Krafft-Ebing, Deleuze accepts the medical nature of the two "perversions."[35]

Captain Jeane's final gesture of lying down and putting his hat over his face feels like a final act of frustration with people who do not see this – who see his actions as a kind of mental weakness that he should have been able to correct, rather than a condition with a medical pathology. As a gesture of shame, hiding the face acknowledges guilt, which was probably how the crowds who came out for the hanging saw the gesture. But given the young Captain's refusal to admit wrongdoing, it might also be read as another denial, as a refusal to face not his own guilt but that of his judges and executioner for what he saw as their misunderstanding of his case. It is not his shame he tries to hide, but theirs, just as we look away in embarrassment from a person who does not see his own culpability. The ambiguity of the gesture in the circumstances can be read as a representation of, and final comment on, his accusers' refusal to see the real relationship of body to mind.

Sade's relentless presentation of passageways and blockages surrounding and leading to and from the sites of his sexual release always has a material and (literally) bio-graphical feel. Deleuze is right that symptomatology is always a kind of construction, a matter of some "art." In the case of Sade, one might say that the obsession in his writing with "tortuous" underground passageways and blockages was just that kind of literary construction: his own attempt to "body forth" spatially on the page what he felt in his entrails.

5 Hysteria: Pynchon's Cartoon Space

The realization that space is not a fact but a necessary fiction (a form of perception, as Kant called it) dates back to the ancient Greeks. Like the heliocentric hypothesis, which has a similarly ancient pedigree, the idea had to wait until the early sixteenth-century Mannerist period for conditions to be right for it to be understood. From that moment, space and time in fiction became demonstrably fungible, and the notion of "form," in a Kantian sense, came alive for painters and writers, and the public at large. "Formalism" was born as an idea, both empirical and aesthetic (Mannerist space), and with it, the realization that space was Copernican in nature, infinitely expandable, infinitely malleable, and a matter of art as much as science.

In part 1 of this study I looked at two writers who deal overtly in their fiction with the kind of spatial incommensurabilities intrinsic to Mannerist art: Rabelais and Swift provided contrasting views of spatial deformation and disproportion in two ages when Copernican astronomy flourished. In part 2 the focus has been on the deformation of mind, body, and text, beginning with narcissism in Jonson, where I looked at what a spatial analysis (object relations theory) of the mind-text relationship in his plays might look like. In Sade, his particular and famous psychological deformation was indexed to a bodily one, and I looked at how a physical deformity is bodied forth in the narrow and constricted spaces surrounding his various sites of sexual release (the body-text relationship). In the third and last study of part 2, devoted to Thomas Pynchon, I want to return to a mind-text approach and look at how a psychological deformation (hysteria) is related to what might be called the battle between real space and cartoon space in his fiction.

Pynchon throws these two very distinct spatial systems – what might otherwise be called everyday space and the space of fantasy – against one another relentlessly and repetitively, without any self-evident plan or reason, leading one to suspect that the action is symptomatic of some deep pathological drive. An example will clarify what I mean by the running together of two kinds of space. In *The Crying of Lot 49*, Oedipa Maas and a character called Metzger are co-executors of the defunct Pierce Inverarity's will. Oedipa drives to San Narciso to confer with him and stays at a motel there, where Metzger comes to meet her. There is the usual craziness in the scene that marks Pynchon's fiction and that he gets (for example) by giving his characters impossible names like Oedipa Maas and, better yet, Mucho Maas, her husband, along with names like San Narciso and the motel she stays in called Echo Courts (narcissism). The manager of the motel plays in a group called the Paranoids – adding another pathology to the mix just to get the reader going in yet another wrong direction. The craziness is a steady refrain in Pynchon and succeeds in making the realism of his stories feel fragile to begin with. But this kind of semantic distortion is not accompanied by any particular scalar or spatial disproportion in the scene, or others like it. In that respect Pynchon's space feels as conventional as Jonson's. The motel room feels "normal."

Once she gets set up in her room at Echo Courts, Metzger shows up unannounced, and we roll into a long scene that includes the piece of spatial Mannerism I want to point out. They begin to watch *Cashiered* on television, the movie Metzger starred in as a child actor, named Baby Igor. The description Metzger provides of the movie action in a kind of running commentary makes it sound utterly implausible, a kind of Looney Tunes cartoon, to the point where Oedipa suspects that Metzger is playing a joke on her, or got the movie on her television as part of some plot or trick to seduce her. This rational response on her part is important because it provides a sane perspective, objectifying the nonsense as such. But the point of the television moment is to draw our attention to the difference between the real and unreal, and suggest that the membrane that holds them apart is fragile.

This point is underlined by Metzger, who points out that he is a lawyer who was once an actor. Raymond Burr, he says, was an actor who played a lawyer, who acted every time he faced a jury. He tells Oedipa a movie was made of his (Metzger's) life where the character who played him had been a lawyer: a lawyer become an actor playing an actor who became a lawyer. All this in preparation for the tableau that now follows. Oedipa is asking Metzger questions about the movie and he tells her that for each question she will have to take off an article of clothing. This is the "Strip Botticelli" sequence. She agrees, but before they begin she excuses herself and goes off to the bathroom. They are both drunk.

Up until now the reality / unreality issue has been strictly abstract, a semantic element in the novel. The action, as eccentric as it may be, has been taking place in a recognizable and realistic space. This all suddenly changes in the bathroom, where the spatial paradigm is suddenly converted to that of a cartoon.

Since she and Metzger are going to play a version of strip poker, Oedipa puts on six pairs of panties, a girdle, three pairs of nylons, three brassieres, two pairs of pants, four half-slips, a black sheath, two summer dresses, half a dozen skirts, three sweaters, two blouses, a quilted wrapper, a peignoir, a muumuu, and assorted jewellery. The action, in other words, takes us out of the everyday and into a Rabelaisian fantasy space where Oedipa's body is the representative object. She looks at it in the mirror, recognizes its absurdity, and bursts out laughing. So for a moment we feel pulled back from the edge, using Oedipa's self-aware reaction to hold onto the two-world vision, the possibility that the real and unreal can maintain some separation. But it is too late, because in the real space of the bathroom she has actually put on all those clothes, something that would be quite impossible.

As a result, the scene becomes a cartoon. Laughing, Oedipa knocks over a can of hair spray. The aerosol cap breaks and the depressurized can starts whizzing about in the small room. It bounces off one thing, then another, off the wall, then the toilet; Metzger comes in and falls to the floor with Oedipa as the can continues its "high-speed caroming" (CL 25).[1] The scene is funny and Pynchon milks its humour for almost a page. It is "expressionistic" in nature, if not surreal. The reason it is funny, however, is that real space and cartoon space do not mix. One cannot be folded into the other without producing the kind of incongruity that makes the scene comic. Pynchon seems to want to say that life really is a kind of cartoon; and that's fine, understandable. Many would agree. But that is only to speak figuratively. When real space and cartoon space are actually run together, the result is incongruity. And in Pynchon, it is more than comical, it is hysterical. He emphasizes the mutually exclusive nature of the two spatial modes when he ascribes an emotion to Oedipa, inside the cartoon bathroom, that comes from the other world: "She was scared but nowhere near sober" (CL 25). For that line not to be absurd it would have to be uttered in a different novel, a different room, a different ontological realm, one inhabited by Hemingway's Nick Adams, for example. Once Oedipa has entered the space of the cartoon "strip" it does not work. It is impossible to say of Yosemite Sam or Wile E. Coyote, "He was scared but nowhere near sober."

The passing reference to narcissism and paranoia in the sequence only diverts us from the real deformation of mind at work here, which is hysteria. So how is this connected to Pynchon's spatial Mannerism? To begin with, what sort of hysteria we are talking about? Once we know that we can look at how it is generated in the crux of the two spatial modes, and possibly get some inkling of why it happens.

Hysteria has not been a favourite mode when it comes to understanding Pynchon's fiction. To date, that honour goes to paranoia, which is mentioned so often in Pynchon's work that it is often thought of as his "great subject."[2] There are the Paranoids in *Lot 49*, certainly, but the real dose is Oedipa's as she wonders whether the mysterious postal system she is trying to track down really exists. If it does not, she says, she must be "assumed full circle into some paranoia" (*CL* 151). Many of Pynchon characters are paranoid; the author tells us they are, and they often enough bring it up themselves as explicitly as Oedipa does. *The Crying of Lot 49* has in fact been called a "textual avatar of paranoia," a case of "hyperparanoia."[3] Pynchon's central characters are often paranoiacs suffering under the same kind of delusions that Oedipa worries about.[4] In *Gravity's Rainbow* we are in "a great swamp of paranoia"; Slothrop is "a latent paranoiac" (*GR* 33, 90); the plot of *Lot 49* is "a joke on the paranoid, oedipal reader"; and so on.[5]

However, it is important to distinguish between diegetic content and register here. In *Lot 49*, for example, paranoia is not a function of the register or quality of the storytelling, it is a diegetic element in the story, like music, which is also a story element in many places. Oedipa may wonder if she is being paranoid, but it is an idle thought, a loose use of the word. She herself is no more paranoid than her namesake, Oedipus, or Philip Marlowe, another detective.[6] The principal characteristic of the paranoid style, of "suspicious thinking" in general, is that it is "remarkably and impressively rigid."[7] It is a buttoned-up, overstructured, anal style that is more in line with the language of analytic philosophy than the language of fiction (as Freud noted).[8] So while paranoia is omnipresent in the stories, it occurs only at the diegetic level of story; it does not define the register of Pynchon's writing. And it feels irrelevant to his figures and treatment of space.

By contrast, while there are no hysterics in Pynchon's fiction – at least none specifically labelled as such – hysteria defines the general register in which the stories are told. And it is a new brand of the malaise. Freud's hysteria, while still part of critical debate today on nineteenth-century literature, is no longer being diagnosed, and as such is not listed in the *Diagnostic and Statistical Manual of Mental Disorders* (*DSM*). The new hysteric is one "who faces the dissolution of the old unified self and the awful fact of his or her expendability. No one is special, everyone can be replaced, like a cog in a machine. We are lifeless and faceless in front of the 'system,' victims of a new functionalism."[9] Hysteria is a response to extreme situations, including death, and as we shall see, death has always been Pynchon's real subject. The postmodern strain of hysteria no longer has anything to do with conflicted sexuality. Today the disturbance is characterized by corporal manifestations that include manic laughter and zany behaviour – a new kind of "acting out." In the early sixties the only other book that does anything similar to Pynchon in this regard is Heller's *Catch-22* (1961), where war is the direct cause of the zaniness. In fact, the last significant group of people to suffer from hysteria in its earlier form were soldiers – veterans of the First World War.[10]

Today, however, hysteria in the *DSM* has been replaced with "histrionic personality disorder," which gives it a dramatic, literary identity. The hysterical "style" is impressionistic of cognition, averse to fact (history) and objective description, and has a love for histrionics.[11] The hysteric has little interest in factual information, and tends to distort and exaggerate. Such a person prefers fantasy to the real.[12] Hysteria is marked by a histrionic or dramatic state of mind.[13] It entails the enactment of stereotypes that can be "comic" and produce a "topsy-turvy world" where "mayhem" may temporarily reign as the result of the actions of the hysterical person's temporarily "daffy" actions.[14] This is utterly and completely Pynchon.

"Daffy's Elixir" in *Mason and Dixon* is opium, not marijuana, but it is just as easy to get hooked. At which point one practices "Daffyolatry" (*MD* 267). In *Vineland*, DL and the marshal, coming to get Frenesi, "strolled into the facility smooth as Daffy and Bugs" (*Vl* 255). In a scene reminiscent of the Upton Inn episode in Tony Richardson's film version of *Tom Jones*, where Tom is surprised in bed with a woman Fitzpatrick believes (wrongly) is his wife, and the action is speeded up in a Keystone Cops manner, the usually imperturbable Mason in *Mason and Dixon* is caught in bed with Vrou Vroom. "There is a sudden hammering upon the Door. Mason jumps up and runs 'round the Room twice before locating the Window, which, without looking back, he raises, climbs thro', and vanishes from with a receding wail and a thump somewhere below" (*MD* 88). This kind of scene, familiar in animated cartoons, is reminiscent of the shift to cartoon space we looked at in the "strip" scene in *Lot 49*. It is common in Pynchon's fiction and fully in the hysterical register.

The next question is: if a spatial incongruity has this kind of power, how is it generated? What are its mechanics? Once we answer that we may be able to answer the question of "why." What is behind it? What is the aetiology of the intensity driving it? In answering these questions we will be answering a couple of others that are central to this study as a whole, such as: Why is formalism important? What can it do? Why is Mannerist space so much more than just a random stylistic occurrence? The answer to these questions as they pertain to Pynchon's work can be obtained by anatomizing his hysterical intensity – by describing its mechanics and identifying its purpose.

As it happens, a clue to the right direction to take here can be found in the general critical use of terms like "paranoia" and "hysteria" in describing postmodernism. The latter term is not always easy to define, but it is generally the banner Pynchon's novels are ranged under. And other writers in this "category" like Robert Coover, Donald Barthelme, and Don DeLillo also juxtapose real and unreal spaces the way he does, so this may be a good place to start.[15]

Critics have had recourse to different pathologies in trying to describe the main qualities of postmodernism. Narcissism, of the kind we saw in Jonson, has had its place, alongside paranoia, hysteria, and schizophrenia. The last has emerged in recent years as a favourite heuristic. Frederic Jameson, for example, claimed in 1984 that schizophrenia was the right pathology for postmodernism. In a post-sixties world, alienation no longer works, he suggests, because it presupposes a unified (coherent) subject. Instead, identity today is fluid and fragmented – an idea that emerged from the sixties drug culture. This completely changed the intellectual paradigm, making schizophrenia the best approach, and relegating the hysteria and neuroses of Freud's day to the dustbin of history.[16] Baudrillard follows suit in claiming that hysteria and paranoia are anachronisms in the postmodern world. Hysteria looks like an obsession with the subject and an almost Romantic insistence on "expressivism," which is out of date in an age where the subject has become a kind of Jonsonian partial-object, a human shard, a commodity, and even come under erasure as a merely rhetorical (or grammatical) effect. And paranoia is part of the same staging – an obsession with the sort of organization and structure that is really just a figment of the imagination. Since there is no design beyond the design of language, paranoia can only refer to the benighted attempt to assert one – a plot designed to salvage the disappearing self. Both are exercises in futility for postmodern artists who no longer believe in structure as an a priori category, leaving (again) schizophrenia as the best approach.[17]

Pynchon's fiction is usually discussed in terms of "paranoia," as I mentioned above, but neither paranoia nor schizophrenia can account for the unique effects he creates. Jameson provides the clue I refer to when he talks about postmodern architecture and uses the phrase "the hysterical sublime."[18] Taking "postmodern" architecture as the example draws our attention to the kind of spatial incommensurabilities and deformations I am discussing. It might also remind us of the scientific spirit behind such deformations. Pynchon was a student of physics with an interest in entropy – another man of science, like Rabelais, Gulliver, and Sade; but his own Mannerist disproportions are sui generis. There are no giants like Gargantua, Gulliver, or Minsky in his work, and he shows no particular interest in the kind of spatial disproportions the Mannerist painters specialized in. Instead, the clue comes in Jameson's use of the word "sublime," because the sublime takes us directly to the kind of intensity Pynchon generates with his formal juxtapositions.

It is a word with a strong presence in late twentieth-century criticism, with articles in journals on the fugitive sublime, the gothic sublime, the melancholic and feminine sublime, the Romantic, revolutionary, and Republic sublime, the digital and wanton sublime, and even the ordinary sublime. By contrast, keyword searches for the "schizophrenic" or "schizoid" sublime, along with the "paranoid" or "narcissistic" sublime, return no results. The "hysterical sublime" appears once, applied to the work of Kathy Acker.[19] Hysteria on its own does better, and remains an important theoretical template for articles on medicine, women's studies, and nineteenth-century literature, where Freud continues as the defining referent.[20] Pynchon's novels, however, have introduced us to a post-Freudian understanding of hysteria, and they do the same for the sublime. The idea of the "hysterical sublime" is the key to understanding the mechanics of Pynchon's spatial intensities.

Two prerequisites for the sublime that are foundational in Pynchon's work, as they are in Sade's, are blockage and excess. These are negatives that were not originally part of the discussion when Boileau's 1674 translation of Longinus's "On the Sublime" appeared. At that time, the sublime referred to written or oral expression that creates the effect of "transport" [*ekstasis*] in the listener or reader. From there, however, it was only a few years until Addison, Dennis, and others introduced the key notion of negative pleasure: the fact that the feeling of the sublime is not necessarily a pure positive. Samuel Monk wrote in 1935 that Addison in the "Pleasures of the Imagination" essays of 1711 and 1712 already had a sense of the mind being thwarted in some special way by its encounter with the sublime object. The imagination is pulled up short and goes through several stations of anxiety that include a need to grasp the object, the inability to do so, and the resultant feeling of distress and bafflement, accompanied by awe and wonder.[21] By the time of Burke the sublime object has become principally although not exclusively a fearsome quantity – in particular, deriving from immensity and grandeur in the natural world, of the sort we see in the Romantic sublime. Here the anxiety of bafflement that Addison notes has darkened to feelings of fear and terror.[22]

Kant continues with quantity rather than quality as the spark that fires sublime feelings. With Kant, space enters the picture, along with excess. Like Burke, he focuses on the natural world, but reminds us that sublimity inheres in the mind, not the natural object. Blockage and bafflement are words that in Kant refer to what he calls an "unboundedness" that thwarts our understanding. We experience "a momentary inhibition of the vital forces followed immediately by an outpouring of them that is all the stronger," producing what can then rightfully be called a "negative pleasure."[23] While the "beautiful" is a matter of rational judgment, the sublime is "contrapurposive for our power of judgment" and "incommensurate with our power of exhibition."[24] Kant points to the incapacity of the human mind to give representation to such enormous forces.[25]

The only thing that has really changed over time is the nature of that excess, of those forces. Blockage and excess meant one thing in Sade, where we were part of the company striking into impenetrable forests and dark tunnels. In Pynchon things are more complicated, more conceptual in nature: a matter of mind rather than body. Here the barriers are more strictly formal. On one hand, there is the impossibility of the two mutually exclusive spaces (real and cartoon) to coexist; and on the other, the inability of the human mind to encompass or understand, in the way Kant mentions.

We have already gotten what I hope is a clear idea of what the first looks like. Blockage at a cognitive level, however, has more to do with the mind's inability to encompass or understand some mystery, and it is equally distinct in Pynchon's work. It always occurs at two levels: story and reception. At the diegetic or story level, characters in Pynchon's novels commonly find themselves brought up short in front of something that seems to go beyond the limits of cognition. Herbert Stencil, Oedipa Maas, Zoyd Wheeler, Mason and Dixon, and most recently, the Chums of Chance in *Against the Day*, all are thwarted in the pursuit of ends and explanations, solutions and villains, that they either do not see or understand, or that prove inconsequential or a sham – like Shambhala for the Chums of Chance, or the Mason-Dixon line, which is of no consequence in the novel by that name. What V. really is ultimately proves impossible to determine for anyone in the book, as does the nature of the mysterious underground postal system of the Tristero for Oedipa Maas in *The Crying of Lot 49*. Nothing comes into focus in these works for the characters when it comes to pursuing ends and explanations; they remain unimaginable. As Kant notes, the sublime does actual violence to our imagination, "and yet we judge it all the more sublime for that."[26]

Second, blockage and bafflement occur at the reception level in Pynchon's novels for the very reason that the reader is not told any more than the characters. The reader is not given any privileged look behind the scenes. We have no more sense than they do of what is "actually" going on in these stories. We observe the various objects being pursued through a glass darkly, as they do, moving with them across a flat narrative landscape with no learning curve, following a stochastic, associational progress that does not culminate or conclude because its "progress" is not progress but merely a Brownian motion. There are no reliable coordinates. The reader cannot imagine where things are heading, and once there, is still baffled. This is as true of Pynchon's early novels as it is of his last.

Blockage and excess were desperately empirical in Sade; in Pynchon they are as figurative as they were for Kant. Cognitive blockage in Pynchon is often the result of his excessive iteration of pseudo-scientific or (more recently) historical facts. In *Mason and Dixon* and *Against the Day* the reader is awash in a sea of ostensible scientific and historical realia. Facts and pseudo-facts abound in a display that is astonishing and even slightly frightening in its intensity and relentlessness, as if a kind of madness were on display. The idea has even been proposed that in Pynchon reality is not being erased at all, but rather pushed to its breaking point.[27] The point is not "the loss of the real, the light years of estrangement from the real, the pathos of distance and radical separation,

as is commonly said, but, very much to the contrary, the absolute proximity, the total instantaneity of the things, the feeling of no defense, no
retreat."[28] The excess of factual and historical detail in Pynchon surpass-
es the understanding, since it never enters the self-consciousness of either the characters or the novels that house them. If it did, the notion of
"excess" would be objectified, recognized as such the way Metzger's
craziness is momentarily for Oedipa. This would entail an attitude towards it that the reader would recognize, in the way "excess" in Rabelais,
for example, becomes an object of parody. This would short-circuit any
sublime effects. Or it might be passed through the self-consciousness of
a character, which would achieve the same result, as it is in Laurence
Sterne's *Tristram Shandy*, where a similar avalanche of factual detail
flows from Tristram, thus becoming nothing more than a quirky character trait. In Pynchon, however, the flood of such detail is not conceivable
or rationalized in any such way. Pynchon, one might add, is also a student of Sterne in his excess of digressions. And these have the same at-
omizing effect on the narrative in Pynchon as they do in Sterne. In Sterne,
the difference is that the narrator recognizes this; no such thing happens
in Pynchon.[29] In Pynchon's novels – with the exception of *Lot 49*, which
is the most linear of his fictions – we are treated to an accumulation of
narrative excursions: brilliant openings that proceed for a space, only to
be interrupted, restart, or transpose into parallel narratives. They are examples of unrationalized excess and narrative blockage.

In considering the hysterical sublime as Pynchon's special contribution to postmodernism, it is also important to understand that the relationship between the two words when they are applied to his writing is
not the usual one. When we think of the Romantic sublime, for example,
we accept that the first term stands in relation to the second as a qualifier. The sublime in Wordsworth is Romantic because it springs from
Romantic scenery: from towering cliffs and dizzying crags; from a
Kantian limitlessness of space. The sublime is generated from Romantic
imagery. The word "Romantic" qualifies the sublime in Wordsworth.
But in Pynchon the sublime is not itself an excess of hysteria, a leap into
the boundlessness of some hysterical abyss. To the contrary, in Pynchon
the hysteria is driven by the blockage and excess; it is a product of it and
a response to it. In Pynchon's view it is an actual antidote. So this is the
first thing that is new with Pynchon. And yet, as they accumulate in his
work, these hysterical responses themselves become a source of blockage and excess, so that the "hysterical" in the "hysterical sublime" does,
at the same time, follow conventional usage and become a generator

and source of its own sublime effects. This poison/cure dualism is what makes the hysterical sublime something new and different in Pynchon and his postmodern followers.

But if it is there as a "cure," what is it supposed to cure? What is the illness? What is behind Pynchon's hysterical intensity? What is its purpose? When we answer this last question we will be in a position to fully understand the point of his spatial games, and why formalism per se and Mannerist space in general are much more than stylistic ornaments. Again, the sublime shows us the path. What provokes the feeling of sublimity? In Pynchon it is obviously not a matter of mountain passes that stun us with their immensity, or storms at sea that terrorize us. If the Kantian sublime is about the limits of figuration and the mind's inability to give representation to some enormous force, what exactly is the enormous force in Pynchon that cannot be handled? What is the source of the blockage and bewilderment that Pynchon's novels so effectively stage in terms of puzzles and antithetical spatial modes? What is his big issue?

A number of them are scattered across his work: in *V.* (1961) the concerns are largely academic and writerly; in *Gravity's Rainbow* (1973) war and paranoia take centre stage; in *Vineland* (1990), family values; in *Mason and Dixon* (1997) it is American history and the Age of Reason; and in *Against the Day* (2006) it is Time and, again, writerly issues like genre that dominate. But these are merely thematic; the books are aware of them as such, and objectify them; they fall within the bounds of our understanding and are thus off limits as sites for the generation of sublime effects. And they feel generally irrelevant to the way Pynchon handles his two kinds of space.

One answer often proposed for postmodernism as a whole is technology. Technology and its discontents: this is the post-Einstein age's great new Simplon Pass – something that has gotten way beyond us, and our feeble ability to understand it. Or perhaps it is one facet of technology, related to "capitalism" or "consumerism" – a matter of what Marxists see as that mass of human labour poured into the bottomless well of the Metropolis: the defining feature of our dystopian horizon, for the individual and collective alike.[30] This in fact is close to Pynchon's sixties politics. But it also allows a solution, one that Marx might help us towards. It can be interpreted and understood, and is thus off limits as a source of the sublime. For Pynchon, the dystopian horizon is not so easily identified, or circumscribed. He is closer in spirit to Philip Roth's comment in 1961 on the incommensurability of event and mind, the inner and outer life, when Roth wrote that contemporary reality defies the writer's imagination; that it "stupefies, it sickens, it infuriates, and finally it is even a kind of embarrassment to one's own meager imagination."[31] Roth expresses a truly Kantian level of bafflement at the incommensurability of life on the ground and its idea, the ineluctable incongruence of mind and event. This was echoed in Don DeLillo's claim that postmodernism began with the assassination of President Kennedy in 1963 – "a natural disaster in the heartland of the real, the comprehensible, the plausible" that forced us "to question the basic suppositions we make about the world of light and shadow ... and to wonder further about our ability to measure such things."[32] But the incommensurability of mind and event in Pynchon feels more like a symptom than a cause: just another kind of Kantian blockage and bafflement. The stone blocking the door still needs to be identified.

Fortunately, Pynchon helps us out. "When we speak of 'seriousness' in fiction," he writes, "ultimately we are talking about an attitude toward death" (SL 5). And for Pynchon, as it was for Burroughs, the embodiment of death (at least in America) is "system" – the final great product of the Enlightenment. This is the real Simplon Pass in Pynchon: the system-as-Machine. This is the nexus of those Kantian "enormous forces" that cannot be encompassed. It is not a general problem of the incommensurability of mind and event, as Roth put it, but a particular instance of it. And Pynchon suggests that the way to respond is to alter the mind. His hysterical intensities are the antidote he offers. He answers "system" with a kind of fall into ecstasy and delirium that is antithetical to Enlightenment "reason." In Against the Day, Drave tells Lew Basnight: "Delirium literally means going out of a furrow you've been plowing" (AD 41). Pynchon uses the phrase "against the day" to mean "contrary to Reason" (MD 683), which is death, not life. In Against the Day, once the cosmic flash of light fades people revert to "orgasm, hallucination, stupor, sleep" as a way to arm themselves "against the day" (AD 805).[33]

So this is the issue, the problem and the solution. Systemic rationality leads to sameness and homogeneity, which is death. It is a matter of repetition. As Freud noted about the return of the repressed, it is not the nature of the repressed that matters as much as the fact that it keeps coming back. Sameness or a state of de-differentiation, he pointed out, may characterize the infantile "oceanic" feeling, but it is also the meaning of death. In this case, it is not the content of the digressions or particular collapsed narratives that matters in terms of excess; it is the fact of their repetition – the fact that the same thing occurs over and over.

Freud concluded that the repetition compulsion, rather than being related to the pleasure principle, was a death wish, since death is the ultimate state of sameness or de-differentiation, and repetition is the assertion of sameness. In one very real way, blockage means the victory of sameness.

Burroughs had his own machine metaphors to describe it. Pynchon's are different and come from his doctoral studies in physics. In a closed system particles tend towards maximum randomness, homogeneity, and heat death. In the early short story "Entropy," Callisto calls it "an adequate metaphor" for consumerism, which is moving us steadily "from the least to the most probable, from differentiation to sameness" (SL 88). This is the heart of the matter for Pynchon: his emphasis on what death-by-system looks like. It is sameness and de-differentiation. Downstairs at Meatball's party, in the same story, Saul says that his wife is "bugged" over the idea of "computers acting like people," but he says: "I made the mistake of saying you can just as well turn that around, and talk about human behavior like a program fed into an IBM machine ... it is sort of crucial to communication, not to mention information theory" (SL 90).

This is not a single occurrence in the story of a young writer that subsequently goes away; it is a constant. In "Under the Rose" – an early draft story for V. in the Slow Learner collection – we see it in the comment on the clockwork universe attached to the episode with the automaton, Bongo-Shaftesbury (SL 120–1). In V. the focus sharpens: "In the eighteenth century it was often convenient to regard man as a clockwork automaton" (V. 284). In that spirit, Yoyodyne has produced two such automatons, "SHROUD" and "SHOCK." The former tells Profane that automatons are "what you and everybody will be someday ... None of you have very far to go" (V. 286). In Gravity's Rainbow the symbol of system is the Ouroboros, the snake swallowing its own tail that tells Kekulé in the latter's dream that "'The World is a closed thing.' It's all about taking and not giving back, demanding that 'productivity' and 'earnings' keep on increasing with time, the System removing from the rest of the World these vast quantities of energy to keep its own tiny desperate fraction showing a profit: and not only most of humanity – most of the World, animal, vegetable and mineral, is laid waste in the process ... the System, which sooner or later must crash to its death" (GR 412).

The essence of system is reification, so Pynchon's concern with system has that much in common with a Marxian critique. But Pynchon's metaphors of heat death and entropy allow no possibility for a Marxian intervention. The sort of "mediation" that Pynchon sees the System producing, which insulates us from human experience, is more in line with Burroughs and McLuhan than with Marx and the alienation of labour. In *Vineland* (1990) Hector is a compilation tape of TV shows who has to check into Tubaldetox where the "house hymn" speaks the truth to media: "It's poi-soning your brain! / ... It's driving you insane ... Big fat computer jus' / Had you for lunch" (*Vl* 336–7). Isaiah Two Four tells Zoyd: "Minute the Tube got hold of you folks that was it, that whole alternative America, el deado meato" (*Vl* 373).

Mason and Dixon again targets the clockwork mathematics of the System by setting its action in the century that showed a fascination for automatons and science: The Age of Reason, where a talking dog calls "fantastick" elements like himself "Provisions for Survival" (*MD* 22); and Lord Huang tells the two astronomers, Hsi and Ho: "Your Emperor was answerable to Heaven, – here must we answer to the Market, day upon day unending, for 'tis the inscrutable Power we serve, an invisible-Handed god without Mercy" (*MD* 627). America rids itself of the Indians not for their land but out of fear of "dancing and drug-taking, that allow humans to be in touch with the powerful gods hiding in the landscape" (*AD* 777). This is the picture of "system" and its measurements that Pynchon sets up as the impossible force that cannot be mentally encompassed.

The only possible response is hysterical intensity, or "Daffyolatry" (*MD* 267). And not just a presentation of the same; the effect comes from a constant to and fro, back and forth between the spatial logic of the everyday and the spatial irrationality of the cartoon. The duck in question appears in the "Frankenduck Episode" in *Mason and Dixon*. The skit is based on the eighteenth-century fad for automata, which (although Pynchon does not notice this) was part of a larger questioning in the century of "soul" and its possible materialization. It was the century of La Mettrie's "L'Homme-machine," but also, for Pynchon in this skit, of Jacques de Vaucanson, who invented a mechanical digesting duck in 1738. The duck here, however, resembles Frankenstein's creation in wanting his creator to provide her with a mate. Vaucanson has a second duck and this one would like "permission, to take this very Duck out for the evening, – I have tickets to the Opera ... We could stop for a bite at L'Appeau, they have my table there" (*MD* 377), and so on. This is the Looney Tunes bird: the duck's "eye holding a certain gleam, [it] began to speak, in a curious Accent, inflected heavily with linguo-beccal

Fricatives, issuing in a fine Mist of some digestive Liquid" (*MD* 375). The narrative mode is "all theatre," just like the Evacuation that begins *Gravity's Rainbow* (*GR* 3). History (and *historia*) collapse into hysteria.

Early victims of hysteria often suffered from glossolalia, speaking in tongues like Vonnegut's island Bokononists in *Cat's Cradle* (1963). They speak in tongues, sometimes the tongues of others; they go out of themselves and play roles. The hysteria-histrionics connection emphasizes the artistic, writerly component of the deformation. The histrionic patient is always playing a part, performing, or choosing a number of different parts to suit the environment.[34] The literary connection is not new. Flaubert called himself an "old hysteric," and Freud noted the connection of hysteria to art, as did the Dadaists and surrealists.[35] Its antisocial statement has also been noticed. It has been suggested that hysteria can be read as a cry of protest against social conditions.[36] In another parafiction that came out the same year as *Lot 49*, the author puts in a questionnaire where Question 7 is: "Do you feel that the creation of new modes of hysteria is a viable undertaking for the artist of today? Yes ( ) No ( )."[37]

The reason Jameson finds "hysteria" a fitting qualifier in his "hysterical sublime" is that, like the sublime, it deals in moments of transport (euphoria, *ekstasis*). And these "intensities" are what postmodernists like Bartheleme and Pynchon specialize in, rather than the older plot epiphanies of "realistic" fiction.[38] Pynchon does not address the issue of hysteria explicitly, but the transitions between real and cartoon space that generate it in his writing are everywhere. They are what he calls his "brisking." He sees it all as a kind of "marijuana humor" (*SL* 8). Indeed, many of the transitions involve characters "under the influence" of one drug or another. Mason and Dixon, for example, seem to be constantly on their way to drinking establishments – where the spatial transition will occur and we will be shoved from the real into the cartoon world. George Washington gets stoned in one of them, at which point Martha comes in, bringing food: "Smell'd that Smoak," she says, "figur'd you'd be needing something to nibble on" (*MD* 280). Andrew Gordon smoked pot with Pynchon in the sixties and says "he was a heavy doper ... Thus his sympathy with an aging, beleaguered head like Zoyd Wheeler" in *Vineland*.[39] Pynchon's hysteria may have its origin in the altered, stoned consciousness of the pot smoker. Reality prevails only so long in its dull conventional form before it turns into an episode of *The Simpsons* (a show Pynchon's voice once did a guest appearance on) or a Bugs Bunny cartoon. Charles Tart writes: "An aspect of the positive emotional tone characteristically associated with marijuana intoxication is ' … I am silly, even though the situation is not that funny.' This is a very common effect." Tart's study indicates that the effect is directly proportional to the amount smoked but that older smokers begin laughing at lower levels than younger ones. One of his informants reports that a characteristic effect of marijuana intoxication is the ability to both appreciate and produce very subtle humour. When stoned, things can appear incredibly humorous.[40]

Pynchon's remark on "marijuana humor" is in the introduction to *Slow Learner*, whose stories also give us an early indication of the "enormous forces" his hysterical effects are designed to counter. Etienne, the boy in "The Secret Integration" whose "obsession" is "practical jokes" (*SL* 149), says: "My father says everything's going to be machines when we grow up. He says the only jobs open will be in junkyards for busted machines. The only thing a machine *can't* do is play jokes" (*SL* 150). Or we might recall Porpentine in "Under the Rose": "At regular intervals he found need to play the buffoon. 'A bit of skylarking,' he called it. It made him, he believed, more human" (*SL* 105). This is Pynchon's (humanist and hysterical) response to the "enormous forces" of de-differentiation he associates with system.[41]

But buffoonery alone is an inadequate description of Pynchon's comic "brisking." It always involves the running together of two distinctive spatial systems – cartoon and realism. The essence of comedy is incongruity, usually of high and low. Pynchon's version involves beginning in real space (verisimilitude) and then shifting to cartoon space. The effect is the equivalent of watching someone pretentious slip on a banana peel: the "real" world is brought low and made to look ridiculous. And while this may be "brisking," it is also (obviously) a political statement.[42] A baseline of verisimilitude that reaffirms the status quo is established, then subverted. And what is remarkable in Pynchon is how quickly this happens. In *Vineland* we are only four pages into the story when we are told that the birds have eaten so much of the dog's food they now think they are dogs and chase cars and bite people (*Vl* 4). Sylvester and Tweety appear a few pages later (*Vl* 22). In *V.* we get ten pages into the story before Ploy, having had his teeth removed, is swinging through the rigging "like an orangutan, trying to kick officers in the teeth" (*V.* 11); and on the next page we learn that Beatrice, who is barmaid at the Sailor's Grave, has "had custom beer taps installed made of foam rubber in the shape of large breasts" (*V.* 12–13). In *Gravity's Rainbow* the giant "Adenoid" goes on its rampage on page fourteen.[43] Cartoon animals enter sooner as the novels progress. In *Gravity's Rainbow* we only get to the dog in the pram saying, "You vere eckshpeckting maybe *Lessie*" on page 44; in *Mason and Dixon* the singing and dancing Norfolk Terrier enters on page 18; in *Against the Day* we are only three pages in before Pugnax the dog is introduced, reading Henry James (*AD* 5), and later Eugene Sue, in French (*AD* 125). Paranoia ceases to play much of a role in *Mason and Dixon* or *Against the Day*, but the hysterical juxtaposition of the two spatial modes remains a constant. In 1965 a character thinks he is a volleyball (*CL* 9); in 1997 a character thinks he is a beaver (*MD* 619 ff); in 2006 a character thinks he is a jelly doughnut (*AD* 626).

The novel that best exemplifies what I have been discussing so far, from Pynchon's spatial deformations to their hysterical pathology, is *The Crying of Lot 49* (1965), with its mysterious underground postal system, the Tristero. A postal service is a good choice for what Pynchon wants in terms of "system" because it is all about non-human functionality and sameness. Like the empty tower in Bentham's Panopticon, there is no single central intelligence driving it. It is an information highway that has the same randomness as a real one, a degree of the same kind of unpredictability, and even some of its chaos. No one can predict how many cars or envelopes will come down the street at one time, so to speak, or which will turn here, which there. Snarls and blockages occur; density waves move and swell and dissipate. Order and patterns will emerge from the chaos, driven by some invisible force, some "strange attractor" as chaos theorists say, but there will be no way to "rationalize" it. Entropy is at work in such systems, involving expansion and the dissipation of energy. Oedipa cannot get a picture or fix on it, on the pattern she is after. The Tristero cannot be mapped. Fluidity in the mails, as in traffic, makes it impossible to predict where or when a piece of symmetry will appear.

The sound of the system is a telegraphic clicking, machine-like, a type of white noise, like the sound of traffic or the sorting of letters. The post office is a closed system whose epigone is the stamp, and it exists in a hierarchical relationship to the subsystem of exchange principles for information, which is what the letters contain, where information eliciting and producing more information is constantly flying all over the globe. But the focus is not on communication; it is about the system of roads down which the envelopes travel. Information theory has no bearing on the dynamic because the information is inaudible, as invisible as the contents of the envelopes to the postman, overwritten by the telegraphic clicking of the sorting machinery Oedipa tries to interpret.

The machine sorts, but the white noise erases distinctions.[44] The postal system may be devoted at the micro level to enforcing distinctions through sorting, but at the macro level it is entropic, striving towards stasis and equilibrium. Oedipa tumbles around lost in its space.

Matter near equilibrium behaves in a "repetitive" way.[45] The universe is expanding and heading towards just this kind of final equilibrium, called heat death. So while the Tristero may look like a Romantic option, the irruption of some possibly salvational fourth dimension or sur-reality, it is as a postal system invested in just this kind of stasis. Oedipa wonders "how had it ever happened here, with the chances once so good for diversity" (CL 150)? Instead we get binary code, "zeros and ones ... thick, maybe endless." The Tristero promises that if we listen, like Oedipa, to "the roar of relays," that the "brute repetitions" might "someday call into being the trigger for the unnamable act, the recognition, the Word" (CL 149). But in the end we are left in the dark and the lock snaps shut. At the end of The Crying of Lot 49, nothing is revealed, nothing is visible. Space is not infinite but closed down, snapped shut, like a coffin. Oedipa remains lost.

Pynchon's obsession with the two kinds of space has been read in different ways. Critics have talked about how Stencil's "double vision" in V. structures all Pynchon's work.[46] There is the "ontological instability" in Gravity's Rainbow.[47] Neither realism nor cartoon is stable or defining in Pynchon's use of space; we swing unpredictably between them and our feet never touch the ground. Pynchon writes that surrealism was important to him when he was working on "Under the Rose." He says he missed the point about the importance of dreams (he was too young), but became fascinated with the idea "that one could combine inside the same frame elements not normally found together to produce illogical and startling effects" (SL 20). The most "startling effects" involve running together the two ontologically incongruous spatial modes.

The sudden arrival in Pynchon's work of real historical space in the "persons" of Mason and Dixon encouraged many reviewers to think a change was in the offing with respect to the author's habitual disrespect for the non-cartoon world.[48] But the book only makes the collision of real and cartoon space more poignant by giving us a realistic one that is so fully historical and American. To introduce cartoon space into this context only accentuates its (political) effect.[49] The result is most noticeable whenever the "characters" in the book say or do anything "political" – criticizing the country, attempting to free a group of slaves – all of which feels like so much familiar sixties politics that the author does indeed want to cheer for, but that can only fall into bathos when promoted by someone called Reverend Cherrycoke.

In *Mason and Dixon* the die is cast as soon as we learn this is our narrator's name (Cherrycoke is recycled from *Gravity's Rainbow*). Pynchon's skills in this area seem only to be improving. In *Against the Day* we get the likes of Vaseline the maid (161), Dodge Flannelette (131), and the Uckenfays (225) – who seem to be related both to Lieutenant Unchleigh from *Mason and Dixon* (36) and Lord and Lady Overlunch, who own "the sumptuous Oxfordshire manor" called "Bananas" (*AD* 900). Pynchon's two-world view of cartoon space confronting realism remains constant throughout his work.

This is where Freud's repetition compulsion returns with a vengeance in Pynchon's aesthetic. The compulsive (excessive) repetition of hystericism in his novels finishes by sending a different message from the one Pynchon wants to send. If hysteria is his response to the blockage one feels in front of the death-by-sameness of system and the planar field of homogeneity, producing Pynchon's "hysterical sublime," we can only wonder why these effects themselves demonstrate such a compulsive repetitiveness. Freud, as previously noted, thought that the repetition compulsion was a kind of death wish in its drive towards sameness. And jokes are involved in the same levelling. In *Jokes and Their Relation to the Unconscious* (1905) Freud is in synch with Porpentine in "Under the Rose" in insisting that laughter is essentially restorative and refreshing to the ego. Weber, however, notes that a joke's purpose, like the banana peel, is to bring down the high, to humiliate, to reduce difference, much as a rhyme does. Doubly so, one might say, if the joke is endlessly repeated. Humour de-differentiates.

Thus we reach the unfortunate irony of Pynchon's hysterical dualism. If the fatal element of "system" is the way it "does the same," taking us "from differentiation to sameness" (*SL* 88), then it would be sad to think that Pynchon's "brisking," designed to save us from that, in fact ends up taking us to the same place – that his cure might be only another dose of the poison, his hysteria more symptom than solution. Weber argues that jokes are a form of narcissism "bent on reducing alterity to a variation of identity" (*SL* 98). It is surely not Pynchon's conscious intention to go down the same road Jonson travelled, into some form of narcissism, but it is hard not to notice the lack of modulation in his storytelling. At the end of *Lot 49* it crosses Oedipa's mind that the Tristero is a kind of "death wish" that "it would be lovely beyond dreams simply to submit to" (*CL* 95). So this is something Pynchon has thought of. In the end, whether the intensities of his "hysterical sub-lime" are submission or subversion may be a question only the individual reader can answer. But the fact remains that his juxtaposition of different spatial coordinates is what generates those intensities. In Pynchon, deformation is psychological, aesthetic, and political.

Part Three

Back to the Future:
From Picasso to Aristotle

6 Modernism and Mannerism

For the last twenty years neither matter nor space nor time has been what it was from time immemorial.

Paul Valéry

The bi-spatial nature of Pynchon's writing is its main feature. Postmodernists in general are more interested in deformations of space than time. And in that regard they seem to bear out William Burroughs's contention that "the future of writing is in space, not time" (quoted in the epigraph to the introduction to this volume). In the earlier modernist period, by contrast, the more traditional division of powers still held, where writers dealt in time, and painters in space. But this was the age of Einstein, and his claim about space and time being a single continuum is reflected in the fact that many chafed under the limitations that such a division of powers seemed to impose on them. Painters worried about depicting motion, and writers about representing space. It is also reflected in the fact that many of the deformations we find in the art and writing of the period have to do with both space and time: that is, with motion.

Consider, for example, the opening scene in William Faulkner's *As I Lay Dying* (1930). It is Darl's description of the cottonhouse that he and Jewel come upon as they cross the field. Darl, it should be remembered, is the "seer" in the family who describes things and events that he has not witnessed and therefore could not know about. It is worth quoting his "narrative" in order to see what this sort of deformation looks like.

Jewel and I come up from the field, following the path in single file. Although I am fifteen feet ahead of him, anyone watching us from the cottonhouse can see Jewel's frayed and broken straw hat a full head above my own.

The path runs straight as a plumb-line, worn smooth by feet and baked brick-hard by July, between the green rows of laidby cotton, to the cotton-house in the center of the field, where it turns and circles the cottonhouse at four soft right angles and goes on across the field again, worn so by feet in fading precision.

The cottonhouse is of rough logs, from between which the chinking has long fallen. Square, with a broken roof set at a single pitch, it leans in emp-ty and shimmering dilapidation in the sunlight, a single broad window in two opposite walls giving onto the approaches of the path. When we reach it I turn and follow the path which circles the house. Jewel, fifteen feet behind me, looking straight ahead, steps in a single stride through the window. Still staring straight ahead, his pale eyes like wood set into his wooden face, he crosses the floor in four strides with the rigid gravity of a cigar store Indian dressed in patched overalls and endued with life from the hips down, and steps in a single stride through the opposite window and into the path again just as I come around the corner. In single file and five feet apart and Jewel now in front, we go on up the path toward the foot of the bluff.[1]

Faulkner gives us enough details here to easily "frame" the represen-tation. Since Jewel ends up five feet ahead of Darl and comes out the window just as Darl rounds the corner, and given that we are told the windows are in the respective centres of the two opposite walls and that the cottonhouse is square, it follows that the distance from the cor-ner to the window where Jewel appears is five feet, and hence, that the width of the full wall is ten feet and that the cottonhouse must be ten feet square. But if that is the case, and Darl is fifteen feet ahead of Jewel to begin with, he (Darl) will have gone five feet to the first corner, then turned and travelled ten more feet along the side wall to the corner (fifteen feet), where he will be at the point when Jewel is only first step-ping through the window into the cottonhouse, not when he is step-ping out through the opposite window as per the text.

The deformation here is not particularly spatial in nature, at least in the way we have been discussing it, nor is it temporal. The cottonhouse is what it is, and time is continuous and conventional as the action un-folds. But when space and time meet to produce motion, the scene loses definition. One might reply that since this is the narrative of Darl (the seer), not Cash (the carpenter), the skewed description should not surprise us. Darl cannot see Jewel inside the cottonhouse, crossing the floor, and yet he describes the action as if he could. But Darl is never wrong anywhere else. There is never any indication in the novel that his "vision" is impaired, and none here to indicate that he has gotten his numbers wrong. Nor is it likely that this was mere inadvertence on Faulkner's part. He was much too careful a writer for that, and the scene's geometrical specifications and measurements make it read almost like a kind of high-school geometry problem. It is a problem with a wrong answer.

An even more vivid, and visual, example comes with the river crossing. The high water has washed out the bridge, so the Bundrens have to find a way to get the wagon with Addie's coffin on it across by fording the torrent. It is a problem in engineering and hydraulics, rather than geometry, so time is much more important in narrating the action. Cash, Darl, and Jewel are the main players. The others have crossed on a footbridge and look on from the opposite bank. Cash is the carpenter with the toolbox, the planner who tries to think the problem through. He proposes that they tie one end of the rope to the wagon, then have Jewel walk the other end across the footbridge and secure it on the other side. It seems like a good plan. Darl agrees: "'Let Jewel take the end of the rope and cross upstream of us and brace it,' I say. 'Will you do that, Jewel?'" (146).

But then something different happens. With Cash driving the wagon, pulled by two mules, and Darl on with him, Jewel precedes them into the river, with his end of the rope wound round his saddle horn. There is no explanation for the change of plans, almost as if some text were missing. It creates anxiety as one struggles to visualize the dangerous undertaking. Darl narrates the first part, and begins by trying to give us a spatial description of the scene: how wide the river is, and where the others are across on the other bank, relative to their position. He notes how small they look over there ("dwarfed"), so far away. And then, as if he had just been reading Einstein on the space-time continuum, he says: "It is as though the space between us were time: an irrevocable quality. It is as though time, no longer running straight before us in a diminishing line, now runs parallel between us like a looping string, the distance being the doubling accretion of the thread and not the interval between" (146).

The scene then enters a kind of otherworldly time zone characterized by freeze-frames. A log is suddenly spewed up out of the foam, rises in the air, and comes down on the wagon. A moment in time; but if time is more Bergsonian "duration" than clock time, a moment can last forever. As the log comes up out of the water, Faulkner stops the narrative clock. Darl sees the log and says: "It surged up out of the water and stood for an instant upright" (148). This moment will recur three times while the rest of the action continues. A passage of dialogue between Darl and Cash now takes place, while the log is (apparently) standing upright in the water: "*Get out and let the current take you down to the bend, Cash said, You can make it all right. No, I said, I'd get just as wet that way as this*" (148).

Faulkner may have wanted this to strike us as comic: talking of getting wet one way or another while seconds away from possible death. That would fit with other similar moments of black comedy in the novel. But the principal effect is one of temporal disfigurement: in the time it takes, or took, to speak these words, all would be over. Instead, we get another description of the log appearing. This time it "appears suddenly between two hills, as if it had rocketed suddenly from the bottom of the river" (148). This is close to what narratologists like Gérard Genette call "repeating narrative," where something that happens once is narrated several times.[2] In such cases, in the film *Rashomon*, for example, or in epistolary fiction, the idea is to provide another perspective, or several of them, on one event. That is not the point here, where Darl is the only narrator. He has time to describe a gout of foam that hangs from the end of the log, as if it is still poised in the air; and he says that while Cash has been speaking to him, "he [Cash] has been watching it all the time, watching it and watching Jewel ten feet ahead of us" (148). At this point real time and the time of narration have parted ways and the scene starts to feel hallucinatory.

Fearing that if the log hits them, or comes down on the rope, they will all be pulled under, Cash tells Jewel to let the rope go, then reaches down and unfastens it from their end on the wagon. This too takes place while the log and river remain frozen in time. Cash then says something inexplicable: "'Ride on, Jewel,' he says, 'see if you can pull us ahead of the log'" (148). The confusion, in other words, is spatial, temporal, and logical. Jewel urges the horse forward. Freed of the wagon, it pulls itself half out of the water and lunges up the bank. Jewel realizes Cash has unfastened the rope and tries to pull the horse around. This all happens as the log's motion is described for a third time: it "rears in a long sluggish lunge between us, bearing down upon the team" (148).

The mules see it coming too, Darl says. How they get out of their traces we don't know, but they appear to do so on their own, quickly and easily. Unfortunately, like Cash, they can't swim, and quickly vanish downstream. Time is momentarily released, just long enough for the mules to go, and for the wagon to shear around in line with the current and get hung up on its centre on the ford, before, finally, the log hits it. But it does no apparent damage and passes on, leaving Darl and Cash still in their places. They now have another talk. Cash tells Darl to jump and Darl tells Cash he should jump too. By now, given the speed of the current, one would expect the mules to be somewhere down around Biloxi. But no, one remains close by: a head appears, "its eyes wide; it looks back at us for an instant, making a sound almost human. The head vanishes again" (149). As the scene goes on, one begins to suspect that Faulkner's vision of the scene may be close to caricature. Cash shouts to Jewel and leans his weight against the wagon. And then the log is back yet again. "I see the bearded head of the rearing log strike up again," Darl says (149). He jumps off the wagon into the water. And then the mules are also back. "Between two hills I see the mules once more. They roll up out of the water in succession, turning completely over" (149). We are in the river of eternal recurrence.

What Faulkner's motives were for carrying out this experiment in stuttered temporality we do not know, but it is tempting to think back to Darl's comment at the beginning of the scene about space being time (146). In any case, what it does is act as a kind of rough emetic on conventional approaches to time and space in narrative descriptions. The cottonhouse scene was relatively static, given that it was about numbers; here there is action and movement. It is not so much that things do not add up; rather, what they add up to here is visually disfigured. The picture loses definition; it becomes Mannerist space. I mentioned (in the introduction) Heidegger's understanding of the motives for this type of "dis-figurement" in modernist art. He read it as an attempt to point out the dangers, if not the impossibility, of "enframing" or (better) representing (*das Gestell*) when it comes to knowledge. The "freeze-frame" removes time from the picture, emphasizing the act of "enframing." The result (the new image) is what that looks like; what it looks like when Being itself disappears. What is inside the frame is deformed and misleading.[3]

This is the kind of deformation we see in the Einstein period. One can understand how tempting it is to see the modernist moment, as so many art and literary critics do, as the birthplace of formalism. A look back at a painting by Pontormo (ca 1550), however, is all it takes to show us that space and time were already under revision in the age of Copernicus.

Without getting into the business of intellectual or literary history, it seems safe to say that writers themselves often noticed the family affiliations, with Joyce looking back to Sterne, and both of them looking back to Rabelais.[4] *Ut Copernicus, Einstein*. But to say that Copernicus provided the conditions for the possibility of Newton and Einstein is not to say he caused them, any more than one would want to say that Pontormo somehow led to Picasso, or that printing and mapmaking made the "Copernican revolution" inevitable. Direct causal links are difficult, if not impossible, to establish.

Likewise, there is no way to prove that Einstein's theories led to the formalist experiments of modernist art.[5] Much of it was either underway or completed by the time Einstein's theories became known. That is not to say that when the theory of relativity and the space-time continuum (which are not really distinguishable in any meaningful way) became known they did not influence artists; they did, although not as much as one might expect. And there were plenty of artistic productions that showed no evidence of Einstein's influence at all. So in terms of connections, it is enough to notice the family resemblances. Einstein himself said he was just completing what Copernicus and Newton had started. He feels very recent and vivid to us, as do the striking paintings of Picasso and Klee, and this makes it tempting to lose sight of those affiliations and think of modernism as a kind of island of invention. With Einstein, for example, many spoke of how his general theory of relativity demolished the status quo, as if it had existed as such "from time immemorial," as even Valéry puts it in the epigraph to this chapter. But space and time had not been that way "from time immemorial"; they had been revised at least twice before Einstein came along.[6]

A more persuasive argument about "influence" when it comes to modernism can be made for Darwin and Marx (and later, Freud). It is interesting to see how their contributions stand in relation to the spatial and temporal dislocations we are discussing. Without worrying about a chain of events, it is not hard to see the connections here. The question centres around perspective and subjectivity. Darwin and Marx, for example, are often cited as providing the pre-conditions for modernism because of what they did to the idea of human agency and subjectivity. The decentring of the subject that their work set in motion (we are products of our heredity or class, or, when Freud arrives, childhood traumas) has been linked, first, to the writing produced by Zola and Hardy and the "naturalist" school, where human agents are helpless in front of forces they cannot control, and then to painting. In Impressionistic and expressionistic art the traditional "subject" and subject-view disappear, either refused entry to the representation by surface effects or simply replaced with a multiplicity of superimposed "views." The all-seeing, all-knowing "I" that had been dear to the Victorians (especially in the large panoramic novels of the nineteenth century) suddenly became a thing of the past. In painting, so in prose. The author retreated up into the clouds to sit paring his fingernails (Joyce), leaving the storytelling to a character: a narrator who is just another one of the puppets on the stage, struggling against the mysterious odds and ends of an absurd existence (Kafka, Beckett).

Perspectivism – a philosophical term tied to another giant of nineteenth-century thought (Nietzsche) – is yet one more way of describing the new "view": the loss of the privileged, all-knowing gaze and its replacement by a collection of perspectives. Reality is that collection, so truth becomes a construction, or as Nietzsche said, an illusion we have simply decided to forget is one. Perspectivism, or relativism, is a version of scepticism, and might be called the philosophical core of Mannerism. Perspectivism as such defines the temporal and spatial disproportions of cubism and its clones, which look very much like an illustration of its discontents. Indeed, it is part of an older sceptical tradition that goes back to Protagoras and his claim that "Man is the measure of all things," with all that implies about the hopeless quest of the individual for transcendental truth and certainty.

Einstein's own "perspectivism" – as "relativity" theory – did not appear on the scene until 1916. Nonetheless, Ortega y Gasset was already using it in 1910 to explain why there was no absolute reality anymore, why everything had become just a version. He put it in manifesto form in the first issue of *El Espectador* in 1916, so that Einstein only seemed to confirm his views. And with the First World War, he turned the tables on Einstein, grandfathering him in as the culpable instigator, in *The Modern Theme*, as the muse of "perspectivism," and as such, the real cause of the war. In the art world, Picasso painted *Les Demoiselles d'Avignon* in 1907, well before he had ever heard of Einstein.[7] Virginia Woolf denied that Einstein made any difference to her.[8] And Proust's first two novels in his *Remembrance of Things Past* (to use the old title translation)[9] were out by the time Einstein's theories became known.

Proust's treatment of time reminds us of the magnitude of what was happening to the space-time paradigm in his day. His thoughts on the matter, however, had nothing to do with Einstein, but drew instead on Bergson, whose *Matter and Memory* (1896), *Time and Free Will* (1889), and

Creative Evolution (1907) pre-date Einstein by a number of years. Bergson is a figure of importance, and I will have more to say about him in my last chapter, but since he is sometimes seen as Proust's muse when it comes to temporality, it is worth noting that what he did to time also had much to do with space, since he pointed out that our conception of time is really spatial in nature, following the Greek model. That allows it to be quantified and easily conceptualized, but also leads us to misunderstand its true nature. Bergson argued instead for an understanding of time as duration (*durée*), a fungible and fluid thing, as fungible as it looks in Dali's 1931 classic, *The Persistence of Memory*, with its melting timepiece, or in the river-crossing scene in *As I Lay Dying*. Proust's use of Bergsonian "*durée*" has of course been much discussed. And Bergson even appears in disguise in *Swann's Way*, begun in 1909, where much is said about time, and where it behaves in a decidedly Bergsonian way.[10] Proust follows Bergson in believing that real time has nothing to do with hours and minutes, the rags of time as Donne might say, or material for surveyors as Augustine said (i.e., spatial in nature), but instead is a purely subjective, fluid, intuitive experience. As such it feels like ripe material for the poet or artist, and has been taken as such. Bergson's 1896 *Matter and Memory* was a major work, and Proust's *Remembrance* goes a long way towards actualizing its ideas.[11]

Heidegger's major work, *Sein und Zeit* (*Being and Time*), is really about space and time, or the relationship of ontological being-in-space to Being-in-time. He struggles with the interrelation of the two modes in ways that rival Einstein in originality. His concept of *Lichtung* or "lighting" as the space where Being must "appear" to achieve meaning is part of a larger space-time concept he locates in relation to Bergson's thought.

Time must be brought to light – and genuinely conceived – as the horizon for all understanding of Being and for any way of interpreting it. In order for us to discern this, time needs to be explicated primordially as the horizon for the understanding of Being, and in terms of temporality as the Being of Dasein, which understands Being. This task as a whole requires that the conception of time thus obtained shall be distinguished from the way in which it is ordinarily understood. This ordinary way of understanding it has become explicit in an interpretation precipitated in the traditional concept of time, which has persisted from Aristotle to Bergson and even later. Here we must make clear that this conception of time and, in general, the ordinary way of understanding it, have sprung from temporality, and we must show how this has come about. We shall thereby restore to the ordinary conception the autonomy which is its rightful due, as against Bergson's thesis that the time one has in mind in this conception is space."[12]

I will come back to this in my final chapter. Despite Heidegger's demurral, his claim for temporality as the basis of being is decidedly Bergsonian. Both men accepted that our usual (and mistaken) sense of time was not really temporal, but spatial. Bergson was content to leave it at that while Heidegger set out to prove that even our ordinary (spatial) sense of time had a temporal quality. Suffice it to say here that the pre-eminent phenomenologist of the century was preceded on the topic by Bergson, and that Proust, arguably the pre-eminent modernist writer of his time, had Bergson as his muse.

Einstein's theory of space and time as a single continuum was part of the same subject field, but on its own it did not produce, cause, or lead to the Mannerist concerns with temporal and spatial territorialism we see in the painting and writing of the day. If anything, it was itself more a part of the "Copernicus" effect than a cause. The same could be said for the notion of synaesthesia in the arts that gained traction at the time. This is the overlapping of spatial and temporal effects, and it too was just one more manifestation of the general anxiety over the space-time relationship. Can painting not have a narrative quality, reflecting the passage of time? Can writing not be painterly, with a sense of space? We might recall Gertrude Stein's comment that she used words like paint. None of this came about because people had been reading Einstein. The Renaissance concept of *ut pictura poesis* (as in painting, so in poetry) that originated with Horace was one expression of this idea of synaesthesia, so it was not new. It returned as an issue in Newton's age, in the writing of Lessing, who argued for a division of labour as far as space and time and the sister arts went. "Painting," he wrote in 1766, "makes use of entirely different means and signs from those which poetry employs: the former employing figures and colors in space, the latter articulate sounds in time ... It follows that bodies, with their visible properties, are the proper objects of painting ... actions are the proper object of poetry."[13] Pontormo, the Mannerist painter, puts different time-events in one painting in his *Joseph in Egypt*, although medieval art did so as well. The debate over the similarities and differences between the "sister arts" of visual and textual expression was ongoing through the sixteenth century. Of course Horace's point had not been the more technical one that both arts deal equally in space and/or time, but only that both should imitate nature and be about the expression of passion. No one worried much about the technical aspect of the intersection or overlay of space and time in either painting or poetry until the seventeenth century, when the question of the unity of time and action in painting became an issue. In 1637 Franciscus Junius in *De pictura veterum* pointed out that the absence of time in painting (since motion could not be depicted) was what distinguished it from poetry. The painter picks his moment, aiming at one that will be the most eloquent, and will somehow recapitulate the larger situation or context. And since the subjects of the best paintings were historical, biblical, or mythological stories, the belief was that choosing the right moment (the famous *punctum temporalis*, or "point in time") would set the entire narrative in motion in the viewer's imagination. So the temporal or narrative component of painting (space) was a given.

When Charles LeBrun came along in French history painting of the seventeenth century it became even more important. LeBrun was one of a group of history painters in France who enjoyed the patronage of the court in the seventeenth century. He founded the Académie in 1648 on the belief that history paintings should be faithful to their textual sources. Such paintings, according to the LeBrun dogma, had to accurately depict events from the Bible or mythology, stories whose existence was textual and therefore temporal in nature. This was the age of the great French history painter Nicholas Poussin, who was not particularly interested in having painting indentured to narrative in this way, but who was in Rome during much of the period so not part of the debate. Poussin agreed that his paintings needed to be "read." But LeBrun went further, literally checking off elements in paintings against their textual counterparts to see that nothing was left out or added by the painter in a fit of uncontrolled creativity. LeBrun, a bad painter himself, succeeded in defining the direction of history painting for the next two hundred years. Academy art became completely discursive and text-oriented.[14] Temporality (as narrative) ruled this painting.

By late in the seventeenth century art critics were insisting that painting should observe the same three unities as drama: time, place, and action. Henry Testelin, a member of the French academy, insisted on it in 1675.[15] Like a play, Testelin said, a painting should deal with one event, taking place in one place, at one moment in time. What was important was not just space, or the narrative moment, but the right combination of the two. So by the time Lessing was writing his essay on "the proper objects of painting" and "the proper object of poetry" in 1766, the notion of synaesthesia as the interrelation of space and time (in painting at least) already had a long history. Given this, it is interesting that Lessing's argument on the separation of powers of painting and poetry was generally accepted in the eighteenth and nineteenth centuries. Painting was principally a spatial art, literature a temporal one. And this was the state of the union around 1900, before Einstein's space-time continuum was known, when the synaesthesia notion nonetheless again came up with the modernists. In painting, artists began trying to introduce a temporal element; in writing, authors strove for spatiality.[16] For the most part, *pace* Einstein, neither initiative succeeded.

Klee, for example, tries to disprove Lessing's claim that painting is not able to render the time element by making it the subject of his 1921 *Runner at the Goal*. The overlapping and staggered patterns around the shoulders, especially, but also around the legs, are like time-lapse snapshots of limbs in motion.[17] An even more dramatic attempt is Marcel Duchamp's famous 1912 *Nude Descending a Staircase*, where we get an explicit series of time-lapse images of a woman coming down a staircase, all superimposed on one another. The question is whether either of these works succeeds in refuting Lessing by getting temporality into the picture. Duchamp's painting almost seems to dramatize Bergson's argument on how wrong it is to think of time spatially. In a superimposed series of stop-action images time is frozen instead of flowing, and so is no longer time. And the same would hold for Klee's attempt. One might even say that temporality is the subject of these paintings. But there is no meld of space and time into anything like an Einsteinian continuum.

In writing the case is more complicated, since spatial concerns are more prominent there, one might argue, than temporal ones in painting. What is surprising is that despite this the writers are no more successful than the painters in refuting Lessing. Perhaps for this reason, time (and its discontents) remains the central issue with modernist writers. Gertrude Stein writes: "There must be *time* ... This is the thing that is at present the most troubling and if there is the time that is at present the most troublesome the time-sense that is at present the most troubling is the thing that makes the present the most troubling."[18] The shake-up in the spatio-temporal modes makes present, past, and future equally troubling, although Bergson would argue that they would be less so if we stopped thinking of time spatially. Space is not a conscious consideration of Stein's. Wyndham Lewis writes in 1927: "He who understands fully what Miss Stein means by 'time' ... will possess the key to the 'transitional' chaos."[19] It is interesting that Lewis sees it as "transitional chaos." But the "chaos" seems limited to temporality in Stein.

The worries about synaesthesia in the arts carried on through into the fifties with the New Critics. Joseph Frank's 1945 essay, "Spatial Form in Modern Literature," tried to "synthesize" the aesthetics of painting and writing. Frank argued that Proust and Joyce wanted the reader to see their work spatially, in a moment of time, rather than as part of a temporal sequence. He claimed that form in painting and form in writing in the period were basically the same, and that each art was in the business of trying to overcome the temporality in their structure.[20] And Wylie Sypher, writing in 1960 from the same perspective, argued that cubism defined the novels of Gide, the theatre of Pirandello, and the music of Schoenberg.[21] In the twenties much the same was said of Joyce's work.[22] Gertrude Stein said that her writing was all about juxtaposing words in space the way painters juxtaposed colours. Sherwood Anderson said he tried for the same effect, and quoted Stein on the topic. Anderson was heavily influenced by the 1913 Armory Show in New York, where Americans first had a chance to look at the work of Picasso and the cubists. One might say that Faulkner, who claimed Anderson as his main influence, breaks up the traditional story line in his novels just as Anderson does in *Winesburg, Ohio* into narrative parcels that are juxtaposed like patches of paint on a canvas, or a collage. But this is about as far as the experiments go. Today some critics still try to apply the rules of one art to the other, but the exercise has largely been abandoned.[23] The suggestion that both painting and writing in the period struggle against the temporal tapeworm is interesting. It would mean that in abstract art when the painter destroys conventional space he or she is really out to destroy the constraints of temporality. Time is the central concern. Modernism as a whole, some have suggested, was a revolt against measurable time along Bergsonian lines, and an attempt to replace it with a more cosmic, cyclical, or even infinite variety. In this sense, the work of Picasso as much as Proust can be understood as an attempt to destroy temporality.[24]

The work of the Swiss writer Robert Walser is pertinent here. Susan Sontag was largely responsible for bringing Walser to the attention of American critics, and she writes that Walser "spent much of his life obsessively turning time into space: his walks."[25] By this she means that the obsession Walser had with nothing happening, as he goes on his walks (his story "The Walk" is the best example), produces a kind of hallucinatory stasis that becomes object-like in its heaviness, like endlessness materialized. Walser ended his life in a lunatic asylum, but Sontag's point is a sane one, and a good description of what Walser's work accomplishes. Time, however, remains the central issue. Walser refers in the story to his belief that life treads water, moves in place, getting nowhere, only re-peating itself in an endless present: "I consider nature and human life to be a lovely and charming flow of fleeting repetitions."[26] Gertrude Stein said something similar about repetition. The repetition compulsion for Freud was a death wish, and it can feel like that in both Walser and Stein. Walser wrote that the notion implicit in normal storytelling is that time flows, giving us motion and actions. But that is for "sensation-hungry novelty hunters" looking for diversion and is "a sign of pettiness, lack of inner life, of estrangement from nature." In Walser time passes but doesn't go anywhere.[27] It is spatially non-existent.

Sontag nonetheless likes the spatial angle. Echoing Frank's synaes-theticism, she refers to Walser as "a Paul Klee in prose." There is some-thing childlike in both artists, which may be what Sontag is thinking of.[28] But in reading Walser, Stein, Anderson, and Faulkner, one does not really get the sense of words being used as paint. Such a claim remains merely a manner of speaking, a metaphor. Nor does space appear to be of any particular concern to them per se. As for Walser's "turning time into space," as Sontag says, this too is a kind of abstract thought. Walser's concern was with time. Spatially, "The Walk" is quite conventional. Streets, sights, and encounters "take place" according to the laws of na-ture. So again Lessing's policy of the segregation of modes remains to all intents and purposes intact.

By 1919 Einstein's theories were well known. They had an effect on both Joyce and Thomas Mann. Joyce made corrections to *Ulysses*, for ex-ample, based on astronomical information.[29] When Bloom bids Stephen Dedalus goodbye, to take just one reference, he looks up and ponders the "heaventree of stars." What follows is a Rabelaisian parody of the dis-course of astronomy. Bloom thinks of "the infinite lattiginous scintillat-ing uncondensed milky way" and

of Sirius (alpha in Canis Maior) 10 lightyears (57,000,000,000,000 miles) distant and in volume 900 times the dimension of our planet: of Arcturus: of the precession of equinoxes: of Orion with belt and sextuple sun theta and nebula in which 100 of our solar systems could be contained: of mori-bund and of nascent new stars such as nova in 1901: of our system plung-ing towards the constellation of Hercules: of the parallax or parallactic drift of socalled fixed stars, in reality evermoving wanderers from immea-surably remote eons to infinitely remote futures in comparison with which the years threescore and ten, of allotted human life formed a parenthesis of infinitesimal brevity. [30]

Despite the aeronautics – the takeoff and send-up and put-down – we learn a lot from this, including the fact that talk about the stars must have been in the air to get into Joyce's ear at the time. It is one thing to accept that people might well have been discussing things like light years and parallax and the precession of orbits at the time, but Joyce also seems to have been aware of Einstein's comeuppance, so to speak – the new information that the universe was not static, as Einstein had believed, but was everywhere in motion. Galaxies are "plunging" off into space. Those "socalled fixed stars" are "in reality evermoving wanderers" (698). Einstein thought nothing was moving, so he puzzled over why gravity did not make it all collapse into itself. To explain why it did not he came up with a fudging number he called the "cosmological constant," which he added to his equations to hold the whole fabric up. Gifford suggests that by 1900 it was assumed that all stars moved. Evidence for this, however, only came later.

The passage above shows that Joyce was attuned to the discussion. It also reveals his awareness of another cosmological discovery that was even more significant than the work of Einstein. This was the discovery in 1915 by Harlow Shapley that the sun was not the centre of the galaxy, which it had been presumed to be since the time of Newton. The idea came to Shapley when he noticed that most of the giant globular clusters of metal-poor stars in the galaxy were located in one particular area of the night sky in Sagittarius. It is possible to know the chemical make-up of stars through spectroscopy – that is, by looking at the spectrum of light they deliver as broken through a prism and captured on a photographic plate. One can thus tell if the light source is mostly hydrogen and helium, for example, or if it has a high percentage of the heavier metals. The first stars, the oldest in the sky, are mostly hydrogen and helium, since those were the first elements to form in the first moments after the Big Bang. Stars in the big globular clusters that Shapley saw in Sagittarius were old stars, dating from the early moments after the Big Bang, almost all hydrogen and helium – the oldest in the sky, the oldest in the galaxy, he thought. The only explanation was that they must (he thought) be close to the centre of the galaxy. All other stars, along with the more open, less dense star clusters, are distributed fairly evenly throughout the galaxy; but these huge, dense globular clusters – Shapley identified ninety-three of them and determined their distance as about thirty thousand light years away – are all centred in this one spot in Sagittarius, which, he rightly concluded, therefore had to be the true centre of the galaxy.

The sun, as we now know, is roughly thirty thousand light years out from the hub; about three-fifths of the way to the edge of the galaxy, in other words. What Copernicus did to the earth, Shapley now did to the sun. In Shapley's time the universe had not yet separated itself from the galaxy. No one thought they were different. Joyce mentions "lightyears" – 10 to Sirius (actually 8.7) – but it is not clear whether he (or Bloom) believes this puts it outside the galaxy. It seems not, since the picture we get in the passage is intra-galactic, of other solar systems careening around, but not of our galaxy itself careening around. In 1923 Edwin Hubble put an end to that mistake, doing to the galaxy what Shapley had done to the sun. Hubble discovered there were other galaxies besides our own, that the sky is in fact full of them, that they are all moving away from us, and that, since we cannot see any end of them, or anything that might be called the edge of the universe, we cannot say our own galaxy is any more the centre of the universe than any other. Without any known edge the notion of centre loses its meaning.

Kant appears to have had some intuition that this was the case with his idea of "island universes." He had looked at the distant fuzzy nebulae people later thought were gas clouds inside the confines of the galaxy and wondered whether they might not in fact be distant stars. In fact, he was so bold as to suggest out loud that they were far-off galaxies like our own. This was in 1755 and Kant referred to them as "island universes." He argued that the so-called Andromeda nebula was really just such a giant system of billions of rotating stars, just like our own galaxy, which of course it turned out to be. It is fitting that Kant's contribution to the philosophy of knowledge in his three *Critiques* should be called his "Copernican revolution," although his intuition about "island universes" was much more literally so.

Hubble proved that Kant had been right: that the "island universe" of Andromeda really was a giant galaxy like our own, located far away in space – two and one-quarter million light years away, as it turned out – and one of many in the heavens. The diameter of our own Milky Way galaxy is only one hundred thousand light years, so Hubble's discovery settled the debate once and for all. These historical moments of cosmological decentring – Copernicus, Newton, Einstein, followed by Shapley and Hubble – are profound in ways that are not easy to understand in relation to art. There is something of the Kantian (mathematical) sublime about the sheer spatial and temporal immensities they represent. The reaction in the room on 30 December 1924 at the meeting of the American Astronomical Society, where Hubble presented his findings, must have been interesting. A few years later he raised the stakes again by discovering that the further away galaxies are, the faster they are "plunging" off into space away from us. These changes to the spatial map have proven even more shattering than Einstein's space-time continuum.

Decentring is the central dynamic of the Copernican revolution. And in each of its two successive instalments space itself has undergone revision and gotten a little more fungible. The sense that we are not where we thought we were, that we are neither on a flat world nor at the centre of the solar system; that the sun is no more the centre of the galaxy than the galaxy is the centre of the universe; and that space is infinite and has no centre at all – all these radical revisions of our sense of space have their analogue in art and the concern with form. In the deformations of Mannerism boundaries disappear and space "often appears extended into infinity."[31] We see it perhaps most vividly in Einstein's day, with modernism, and even more in postmodernism. But it has its precursors.

Inversion is another spatial twist that is part of the decentring enterprise. From hierarchy and the elite to pluralism and pop culture, from depth to flatness, gravity to anti-gravity, from the infinitely great to the infinitely small. Joyce is full of this. Given the immensity of the universe and of time, life can only appear as "a parenthesis of infinitesimal brevity." Time is compressed, expanded. In *Ulysses*, immediately after we hear about Sirius and outer space, Joyce gives us some "obverse meditations of involution increasingly less vast":

> Of the eons of geological periods recorded in the stratifications of the earth: of the myriad minute entomological organic existences concealed in cavities of the earth, beneath removable stones, in hives and mounds, of microbes, germs, bacteria, bacilli, spermatozoa: of the incalculable trillions of billions of millions of imperceptible molecules contained by cohesion of molecular affinity in a single pinhead: of the universe of human serum constellated with red and white bodies, themselves universes of void space constellated with other bodies, each, in continuity, its universe of divisible component bodies of which each was again divisible in divisions of redivisible component bodies, dividends and divisors ever diminishing without actual division till, if the progress were carried far enough, nought nowhere was never reached. (699)

Despite the parodic tone (echoes of both Sterne and Rabelais) the issue is one of proportion: from macro to micro. The difficulty with Einstein's theory turned out to be that it did not hold at both ends, big and small – at the cosmological level as well as the quantum level of particle physics. Joyce saw that the "transitional chaos" was located in the heavens, but again time and time alone seems to have been his concern. There is nothing particularly dream-like or distorted about the space of his Dublin streets.

Thomas Mann shows signs of feeling the space-time shift in his ruminations on inversion in *The Magic Mountain*, written in 1924, two years after *Ulysses*. The protagonist, Hans Castorp, reflects as follows on macro and micro: "But confronted with the statement that atoms were 'so small they were no longer small,' one lost all sense of proportion, because 'no longer small' was tantamount to 'immense,' and that last step to the atom ultimately proved, without exaggeration, to be a fateful one. For at the moment of the final division, the final miniaturization of matter, suddenly the whole cosmos opened up."[32] Astronomy is at the heart of Mann's reflections. His language prefigures the discourse of string theory, which is an attempt to bring macro and micro together in one Grand Unified Theory (GUT). The possibility of other dimensions that it proposes – not just a fourth, but many more – may eventually break us out of the present paradigm and give us a new model of space where words like "decentring" and "inversion" no longer signify. Castorp continues:

> The atom was an energy-laden cosmic system, in which planets rotated frantically around a sunlike center, while comets raced through its ether at the speed of light, held in their eccentric orbits by the gravity of the core ... the innermost recesses of nature were repeated, mirrored on a vast scale, in the macrocosmic world of stars ... Once the cosmic character of the "smallest" bits of matter became apparent, any objection about the "smallness" of these stars in the inner world would have been quite irrelevant – and concepts like inner and outer had now lost their foundation as well. The world of the atom was an outer world, just as it was highly probable that the earthly star on which we lived was a profoundly inner world when regarded organically ... [A]t the very moment when one thought one had reached the outermost edge, everything began all over again. (279–80)

Mann, like Joyce, has astronomy on his mind and is straining to find a way to give the "effect" an imaginative outlet in his writing. In the novel, Settembrini's friend, Naphta, the flammable Jesuit, inveighs against the "degradation" of man "beginning with modern astronomy – which turned the focal point of the universe, that sublime arena where God and Satan struggled to possess the creature whom they both ardently coveted, into an unimportant little planet, and, for now at least, has put an end to man's grand position in the cosmos, upon which astrology was likewise based" (389). Here we have inversion in its most painful form – one that Mann's precursors back in the 1500s would have understood. The "great unmooring," as Greenblatt called the first instalment, is really an ongoing phenomenon. When Settembrini asks what he means by "for now," Naphta replies blithely that the whole theory of heliocentrism will soon be proven mistaken and "Copernicus will be routed by Ptolemy" (389).

Mann's transpositions back and forth between time and space in the novel have a distinctly Einsteinian feel: he describes Hans' trip up to the sanitarium as follows:

> Space, as it rolls and tumbles away between him and his native soil, proves to have powers normally ascribed only to time; from hour to hour, space brings about changes very like those time produces, yet surpassing them in certain ways. Space, like time, gives birth to forgetfulness, but does so by removing an individual from all relationships and placing him in a free and pristine state – indeed, in but a moment it can turn a pedant and philistine into something like a vagabond. Time, they say, is water from the river Lethe, but alien air is a similar drink; and if its effects are less profound, it works all the more quickly. (4)

One might conclude from this that Mann sees the issue of space and time in an Einsteinian way, but the fact is that *The Magic Mountain* is almost all about time. Castorp comes up the "mountain" in the Alps to a tuberculosis sanitarium to visit his friend, discovers the essentially "timeless" nature of life there, and falls under the spell of this timelessness as if it were a drug. Time itself behaves in a distinctly Bergsonian way and Castorp loses track of it. Days become weeks, weeks become months. And Mann never loses an opportunity to emphasize how different real time is from clock time. Clock time, calendar time is a comfort prison that we yearn to break out of. Castorp reflects on this as follows:

> And what is the cause of the enervation and apathy that arise when the rules of life are not abrogated from time to time? It is not so much the physical and mental exhaustion and abrasion that come with the challenges of life (for there, in fact, simply rest would be the best medicine); the cause is, rather, something psychological, our very sense of time itself – which, if it flows with uninterrupted regularity, threatens to elude us

and which is so closely related to and bound up with our sense of life that the one sense cannot be weakened without the second's experiencing pain and injury. (102)

The prison of time causes "enervation and apathy," and this must be broken up. What, Mann asks, is the cause of this enervation and apathy? He answers that it is more than just the day-in and day-out grind of the Time Prison. A little rest would solve that. It is that our "sense of time" does not really correspond to that sort of imprisoned time: the two do not match. One of them is wrong. Clearly, it is the day-in and day-out "regularity." That is the one that is killing our sense of real time, of who we are, so that we feel our real life is eluding us. He goes on:

A great many false ideas have been spread about the nature of boredom. It is generally believed that by filling time with things new and interesting we can make it "pass," by which we mean "shorten" it; monotony and emptiness, however, are said to weigh down and hinder its passage. This is not true under all conditions. Emptiness and monotony may stretch a moment or even an hour and make it "boring," but they can likewise abbreviate and dissolve large, indeed, the largest units of time, until they seem nothing at all. (102)

The important thing here is not so much the familiar idea that when we are bored time seems to pass slowly, but that under certain "conditions" the opposite can also happen: boredom and monotony can make large chunks of time pass quickly. On the "magic mountain" of the sanitarium this is what happens as Castorp is amazed at how quickly time passes under conditions of extreme monotony. When every day is the same, as it is in prison, the days run together. Time is as fungible, as space. Mann writes:

Conversely, rich and interesting events are capable of filling time, until hours, even days, are shortened and speed past on wings; whereas on a larger scale, interest lends the passage of time breadth, solidity, and weight, so that years rich in events pass much more slowly than do paltry, bare, featherweight years that are blown before the wind and are gone. What people call boredom is actually an abnormal compression of time caused by monotony – uninterrupted uniformity can shrink large spaces of time until the heart falters, terrified to death. (102)

The book is full of Bergsonian reflections like this on the time problem. Mann shows no awareness that spatializing it the way he does is what Bergson warned about. His objective is to show that it is just as plastic as space. In the foreword, he refers to "the problematic and uniquely double nature of that mysterious element" that is time. By which he means, its clock life, and its real life: very much in keeping with Bergson's ideas. Castorp says, "There is nothing 'actual' about time. If it seems long to you, then it is long, and if it seems to pass quickly, then it's short." And when Joachim, his friend, replies that a minute is "as long as it takes a second hand to complete a circle," Hans points out: "that's a matter of motion, of motion in space ... so we measure time with space." He adds: "for it to be measurable, it would have to flow *evenly*, but where is it written that it does that?" (63–4)? This is Bergson's *durée* talking.

In Mann's novel, Joachim is the scientist and no-nonsense military man, for whom time *does* flow evenly. He understands it spatially and measures it on the face of a clock as a portion of a circle, like pie. This is Mann engaging (and agreeing with) Bergson, not Einstein, that time is other than its measure, as Augustine might say. It is a testimony to Mann's skill as a novelist that he can conduct a fictionalized debate on the issue without turning his work into a dissertation. But a question remains even here with respect to the larger shift in the spatio-temporal paradigm in the age, and whether it succeeds in confounding Lessing's categories. Joyce and Mann are indeed thinking about space as well as time, and are aware of the turbulence in the space-time paradigm, but their stories nonetheless contain only temporal instabilities. On the magic mountain the laws of everyday space are observed to the letter. There is no battle of different spaces as we saw in Pynchon, nor any of the psychological deformations of the sort we looked at in Sade and Jonson. In *Ulysses* time is fungible and compressed so that we can hardly imagine how so much can have happened to Bloom in one day. But the Dublin setting itself has an almost depressing facticity. Joyce's imagination unfolds in the temporal precincts of his linguistic eloquence, but leaves space in a conventional condition not that different from what it is in George Eliot or Balzac. The laws of gravity, volume, and geometry are observed to the Euclidean letter.

The same can be said for Proust's world, and those Virginia Woolf gives us in her novels. Their fictional spaces are stable and realistic. They feature "perspectivism" in so far as the focus of the narrative shifts between characters and times, as it does in Faulkner's *The Sound and the Fury* and *As I Lay Dying*. But in Proust, as in Faulkner, the houses and mansions of Paris and Combray and Balbec all obey the laws of scale and just proportion. Church steeples throw Marcel's mind into gear in a marvellous way and spark reflections that exceed both place and time, but those steeples, like Marcel himself, exist in Euclidean space with a tenacity and inexorability that is unquestioned. Space is not an issue. In Virginia Woolf the temporal tapeworm turns and winds on itself in *Mrs. Dalloway* and *To the Lighthouse*, and almost swallows itself whole in *The Waves*, but London and the seashore and the flowerbeds and restaurants of *The Waves* are all delivered according to the rules of everyday space. Perspectivism, in other words, is rampant as a destabilizing device in these modernists, but it is an exclusively temporal perspectivism. The formalist impulse in these works is limited to the temporal sphere.

All this would seem to confirm Lessing's territorial imperative even more: space is the province of painting; time, the stuff of narrative. And in general it is true that one must wait for literary postmodernists like Pynchon and Barthelme and the magical realists for Mannerist space to make an appearance in narrative. But while it is true that modernists like Joyce, Mann, Proust, and Woolf show the effects of the Copernican revolution exclusively in terms of temporal disjunctions and dispro-portions, the spatial dynamic of the space-time shift nonetheless does show up in certain other literary works.

Kafka is a literary Mannerist. In his *Amerika* (1913) young Karl Rossman finds himself in a house at night outside New York where he becomes disoriented and loses all sense of direction. One might ascribe this to a problem of perception, but it is the house itself that is spatially incoherent with "great stretches of blank wall devoid of doors" (29) and inexplicable vaults and hallways cropping up at every turn.[33] In *The Castle* (1926) the protagonist K is actually a land surveyor who is unable to get from A to B. Making him a land surveyor stresses his rationality. His job is measuring space. His perceptions are not in question; it is the terrain itself that is irrational. In the Herrenhof inn, where castle func-tionaries stay when they are in town, K is caught in a nightmarish cor-ridor, lined with closed doors hiding the people he needs to contact. He talks about "his struggle with these stubborn little rooms" and says that for him "it often seemed to be a struggle with the rooms, since he scarce-ly ever caught a glimpse of the occupants." *The Castle* is full of these spatial incommensurabilities.[34]

A similar thing happens in other Kafka stories. In "The Burrow" we enter the mind of a subterranean mole-like creature who begins to pan-ic in his underground maze when he hears what sounds like some large animal burrowing slowly towards him underground. Time is an issue, but in an underground burrow, space is primal. In *The Trial*, written in 1914, K is again trapped in various nightmare spaces, including his own room, which is only accessible through his neighbour's. People that he visits, such as lawyers and painters, live in attics, crushed up against the roof in stuffy windowless spaces. The courtroom where he is summoned has a gallery under the roof where the ceilings are so low the people in them have to stand "in a bent posture with their heads and backs knocking against the ceiling" from which they protect themselves by putting cushions on their heads. And there are more panic attacks in hallways.[35] What happens to space in Kafka is analogous to what happens to time in Joyce: it shrinks. There are no giants, as in Swift or Rabelais (although when Gregor Samsa turns into a beetle in "Metamorphosis" we get something like this kind of spatial inversion), but space becomes constrictive, nightmarish, and otherworldly. In Kafka space falls out of all proportion. "My stories," Kafka said, "are a kind of closing one's eyes."[36]

Another modern Mannerist is Louis-Ferdinand Céline, author of *Voyage to the End of Night* and *Death on the Installment Plan*, both published in France in the 1930s. Céline is not well known in North America, although he was lionized by Henry Miller and the Beats. In Céline space neither shrinks nor expands, it just loses its authority. Laws of proportion and gravity disappear. His *Voyage* demonstrates a lack of proportion and has a manneristic quality in its descriptions.[37] "Delerium writing," as Céline called it, demonstrates the same kind of spatial "effect" we see in Mannerist painting. Consider, for example, *Death on the Installment Plan*. Céline begins at a normal temperature, so to speak, where the laws of nature apply, but then gets in a fever, or "delerium," at which point the rules of proper geometry are broken. Ferdinand, the narrator, tells us that the office of the journal *Génitron*, where he works for Courtial, is rather messy. But the disorder increases exponentially, until it is "monstrous, in a class by itself." Céline uses his famous three dots to drift us into this space:

> ... the place was a junk shop, absolute chaos ... From the door of the shop to the ceiling of the second floor, every step of the stairs, every ledge, every piece of furniture, the chairs, the cupboards, were buried under papers, pamphlets, piles of returns, all topsy-turvy, a desperate hodgepodge, creviced and lacerated, the complete works of Courtial helter-skelter, in pyramids, a fallow field. [ ] You'd dig in at random, groping your way ...

sinking into garbage, a leaking bilge … a teetering cliff … Suddenly it would cave in … you were caught in a cataract … a landslide of printed matter would fall on your face … That would start new avalanches, a frothing torrent of paper … a dust storm … a volcano of stinking filth …[38]

As "delerium" takes over, the laws of just proportion are abrogated. When the contestants in the diving bell scheme finally lose their patience with Courtial and storm the office of the *Génitron* they are "a horde of haggard maniacs, roaring frothing brutes." They start demolishing everything in their path … they uproot the fence "at one blow" … "They smash both arcades … Blocks of stone are falling like marbles … crashing, collapsing, bursting into smithereens right and left." They charge the office. Verdunat, the inventor of one of the diving bells, who hasn't been getting any satisfaction from Courtial, appears "half-naked … Riding his monster … He's climbed up on top of it! He's shouting! … mustering his lousy troops …" The scene ends with the diving bell being propelled into the office and the whole place going up in smoke and dust … "the end of the world! Thunder all the way up to the sky!" (448–51) Thus, space in Céline. Time, on the other hand, in both Kafka's and Céline's works, behaves rather tamely.

In sum, while the effects in modernist novels usually divide along the lines set down by Lessing, there are interesting deviations where painters introduce temporal disjunctions into their works, and writers give us spatial incoherence. Heidegger and Bergson remain the most influential thinkers of the period on these space-time instabilities, and I will devote my last chapter more exclusively to their contribution.

7 Space and Time for the Ancients

As a result of this plan and purpose of god for the birth of time, the sun and moon and the five planets as they are called came into being to define and preserve the measures of time.

Plato, *Timaeus*

And God said, "Let there be lights in the dome of the sky to separate the day from the night; and let them be for signs and for seasons and for days and years ..."

Genesis 1.14

Hebraism and Hellenism – between these two points of influence moves our world.

Matthew Arnold

Formalism as praxis (rather than theory) in the life of the mind, body, and text has been a steady baseline in the preceding chapters, from the time of Copernicus through Newton to the age of Einstein and Picasso. The modernist moment in this long history was not the first, but it is the one closest to us, and so the one we are most familiar with. It is the moment of Heidegger and Bergson, whose work on time and temporality is central to an understanding of the formalist practices of writers like Faulkner, Joyce, Woolf, and Mann in the twenties. Heidegger's *Being and Time*, however, was itself a product of the decade, and thus more a symptom of the Einstein moment in this history than a cause. His work helps us make sense of its temporality in retrospect, so to speak, while Einstein and Bergson were part of it, contemporaneous with it. Of these two it was Bergson who had the greatest influence. He was active in the first two decades of the century, and a friend and relative of Proust, whose *Swann's Way* came out in 1913. He is generally acknowledged as the true grey eminence behind modernist experiments with time, and especially as the philosophical *maître* of the one writer (Proust) who authored what many regard as the modernist masterpiece par excellence. Virginia Woolf, in turn, credited Proust with making her own work possible. Wyndham Lewis went so far as to say of Bergson: "It is he, more than any other single figure that is responsible for the main intellectual characteristics of the world we live in."[1] In what follows, I want to deal with Bergson's relation to Heidegger first, and then look to the past, back to where I think we find the roots of Bergsonian time.

Neither Bergson nor Heidegger seems to have noticed that the sort of temporality they had in mind was itself not new but had a lineage going back to antiquity. Heidegger, however, did notice Bergson, and knew what Bergson's theory of "duration" was about. The quote I included from Heidegger in my previous chapter, where he first mentions Bergson, comes early on in *Being and Time*. Heidegger writes that the task of his book will be to introduce a conception of time that is different from the ordinary understanding of that mysterious quantity. That is an exact description of what Bergson had been trying to do as well, a few years earlier. Our mistake, Bergson argued, is that we think of time spatially, in terms of a succession of moments, one coming after the other, the way clothes pegs are spaced on a clothesline or the way frames in a movie follow one another, one fixed state following the other. This was the basis of Zeno's "paradox of the arrow," which dates from around 400 BC. The paradox consists in the fact that motion logically cannot be said to exist since at any given instant during the flight of the arrow, it is immobile. The analogy with the flow of frames (motion) in a motion picture is clear. Bergson calls it the "cinematographical method" of looking at time, but writes in *Creative Evolution* that this sort of spatialization is only a metaphor (a linguistic trait) – a very important and necessary one for understanding and controlling our world, but also one that has misled us into taking its figurative truth for a literal one. There is no other way for us to conceive of action or movement, Bergson admits, or successfully undertake or begin a motion than to visualize it as a series of static states, like Zeno's series of stop-action snapshots of the arrow, moving from one state to another, through to its final state of rest. He calls it "a snapshot view of a transition" and follows in *Creative Evolution* with a lengthy analysis of Zeno's arrow paradox.[2]

The importance of this for historiography, or simply thinking about the past, becomes evident immediately, and its importance for Proust obvious. As I noted in my previous chapter, the title of Proust's work *À la recherche du temps perdu* was for years translated as *The Remembrance of Things Past*, but it is now being rendered as *In Search of Lost Time*, which is indeed a more faithful or literal, at least, translation of the French.[3] What the title change sacrifices in poetry it hopes to make up for in accuracy, and indeed it makes the book (and time itself) sound a bit more empirical than the French original. Proust meant by *temps perdu* those moments in the past, in childhood, buried in memory, that come floating to the surface of our adult consciousness, unbidden, like so many frozen pieces of the big jigsaw puzzle that we now are. But the new title translation puts his endeavour on a more Bergsonian footing. The time that has been "lost" can be seen as the sort of temporality Bergson also tells us has been lost, and Proust's work will be an attempt to bring it back to life as it bears on his own past. With respect to historiography, my point here is that while Bergson's concern was with the philosophical interpretation of time, his notion of how we spatialize temporal events applies to how we look back at the past, including our own personal one. We recall visuals more than events, snapshots rather than living history. Proust provides an example of just how apt Bergson's notion of living time is when applied to the past, to his own past, how justly it renders it.[4]

Eight years earlier in *Time and Free Will* Bergson had already made the case for his notion of "duration" as dynamic time – a Romantic, intuitional understanding that is more accurate than the model of motion as successive static states. He writes that the mind

> does not set them alongside its actual state as one point alongside another, but forms both the past and the present states into an organic whole, as happens when we recall the notes of a tune, melting so to speak into one another. Might it not be said that, even if these notes succeed one another, yet we perceive them in one another, and that their totality may be compared to a living being whose parts, although distinct, permeate one another just because they are so closely connected? ... We can thus conceive of succession without distinction, and think of it as a mutual penetration, an interconnexion and organization of elements, each one of which represents the whole, and cannot be distinguished or isolated from it except by abstract thought.[5]

But, says Bergson, we have fallen victims to our own metaphor for time as space, to the point where "we introduce it unwittingly into our feeling of pure succession; we set our states of consciousness side by side in such a way as to perceive them simultaneously no longer in one another, but alongside one another; in a word, we project time into space, we express duration in terms of extensity, and succession thus takes the form of a continuous line or a chain, the parts of which touch without penetrating one another."[6]

Heidegger gives short shrift to all this. He is nonetheless in Bergson's territory beginning with his introduction, where he says that his work will make temporality "the meaning of the Being of that entity which we call 'Dasein.'"[7] It is what his book is about; and yet, the attitude to time and temporality that he produces at length and elaborates over the course of his work is Bergsonian. His book, he writes, will be dedicated to showing that time, not space, is literally of the essence, the very beating heart of Being. And it is at this moment, in the same section, that he mentions Bergson. The last part of the section I quoted in the previous chapter bears repeating:

> This task as a whole requires that the conception of time thus obtained shall be distinguished from the way in which it is ordinarily understood. This ordinary way of understanding it has become explicit in an interpretation precipitated in the traditional concept of time, which has persisted from Aristotle to Bergson and even later. Here we must make clear that this conception of time and, in general, the ordinary way of understanding it, have sprung from temporality, and we must show how this has come about. We shall thereby restore to the ordinary conception the autonomy which is its rightful due, as against Bergson's thesis that the time one has in mind in this conception is space. (39; H. 18)

In other words, Heidegger does not disagree with Bergson that the "ordinary conception" of time we work with every day is a spatial conception. His only point is that it has "sprung from temporality," which is what (he feels) pits him "against" Bergson. His task therefore will be to restore to it that temporality; he calls it "the autonomy which is its rightful due." But it is not clear that Bergson would at all disagree with this, or even care too much about the point. From what Bergson says on the matter, in all of his work, it seems, to the contrary, that he would probably agree that Heidegger's way of putting it is a good one. In a way, he too was trying to restore temporality to its rightful place as the being of Being. So Heidegger essentially straw-mans Bergson in the passage, while founding his entire church, so to speak, on Bergson's *dureé*. This is not to diminish the importance of Heidegger's own thought and writing. It is monumental and has been vastly more important to us in the long run than what Bergson had to say. Nonetheless, the importance of temporality dealt with in *Being in Time* had already been stated by Bergson fourteen years earlier in *Creative Evolution*. Heidegger just thought Bergson had overlooked something. He saw the issue as more complex, and he was right. But Bergson would probably have shrugged, since the changes Heidegger rings on his coin do not make any real difference to his argument or the central perception in his work.

Bergsonian time, however, was not original to the modernist period. Its fluxual, intuitional nature, for example, is a feature of Romanticism. But it has an even more illustrious ancestor in the ancient Near East. In particular, scholars have noticed its similarity to the prophetic time of ancient Hebrew in the Old Testament. Nathan Söderblom had the opportunity of asking Bergson about the likeness: he writes that he asked him "a few years before the Great War" if he was "conscious of any underlying connexion between his doctrine of a creative evolution and the prophets of the Old Testament," to which Bergson answered in the negative, "that he did not know of this connection but the thought appealed to him." Söderblom goes on to say that he was later informed by a disciple of Bergson's in France (Jacques Chevalier) that a prominent French critic (unnamed) had noticed the similarity as well. Söderblom writes that this is not surprising since Bergson's conception of reality and being as dynamic rather than static "has its source in the religion of the prophets"[8] Many have noted this quality of ancient Hebrew. Even Herder commented on its dynamic nature. Herder was not a philologist, but in his work on Hebrew poetry he writes: "now with the Hebrew the verb is almost the whole of the language ... the nouns are derived from the verbs, and in a certain sense are still verbs. They are as it were living beings ... The language ... is an abyss of verbs, a sea of billows, where motion, action rolls on without end."[9]

Thorleif Boman is another scholar of the Old Testament who wrote about the Bergson connection.[10] Boman used a linguistic analysis of the aspectual and verb-based nature of ancient Hebrew to argue that the Israelites conceived of being and space temporally, whereas the Greeks conceived of being, and even time, spatially. Our tendency to spatialize time, as Bergson puts it, could therefore be seen less as a kind of rogue metaphor than as a legacy of Greek thought, whose obsession with essence Heidegger calls "the ontological malaise." Boman mentions, for instance, the way Indo-European languages conceive of the future as lying before us, while the past is behind us: spatial metaphors where "being" seems to be conceived of as a static state. In ancient Hebrew, by contrast, the future comes after us, which only really makes sense if being is conceived of not as a kind of "here" but as a "now."[11]

We need not be overly concerned with the sweeping conclusions about the contrasts between Hebrew and Greek thought that Boman draws from his linguistic evidence. While no one disputes that there is always going to be a connection between thought and language in a culture, the sort of direct correlation Boman tries to make between the two can be difficult to establish. In addition, his contrast between Hebrew and Greek does not include any linguistic analysis of Greek, and he seems to have carefully selected his examples in ancient Hebrew to support his hypothesis.[12] German is also largely a verb-based language, and ancient Hebrew has as many verbs that were probably derived from nouns as the other way around. An example in English would be the word "building." Does the static noun derive from the verb form, or vice versa? Nonetheless, there remains a large school of interpreters engaged in trying to establish the kind of correlations between language and thought that Boman is after, nor is there any real disagreement about the overall verb-based nature of ancient Hebrew. It will suffice to review some of the linguistic evidence for this in order to see how closely Bergson's (and Heidegger's) notion of "temporality" resembles it.

One example mentioned by Boman is the verb "to be" or *hayah*, used everywhere in the Hebrew Bible to mean "being" that is in the process of being, or rather, "becoming," not a static state in the way we might say, in English, "The house is old." In a statement like, "the altar was wood" (Ezek. 41:22), where the predicate inheres in the subject, the Hebrew Bible does not use a verb, the copulative "to be," the way we do, which seems to place the subject prior in time to the predicate, which is then attached to it like a quality; instead we get something like, "the altar wood" because the altar and its material coexist in the same moment.[13] In the Old Testament "days" are not forms filled with content; they are defined by that content, by events. Hence, they are not fixed the way they are for us. The Creation story is a case in point. God's first act is to create time, but it is not the kind we are familiar with. He begins by creating light, and separates it from the darkness, and calls the first "Day" and the second "Night." Time then begins as what seems like the succession of the two states: "And there was evening and there was morning, the first day" (Gen. 1:5). On the second day, He separates sky from earth; and on the third day, dry land from the waters. But on day four He returns to the time problem, creating "lights in the dome of the sky to separate the day from the night" since the sun and moon and stars are clearly necessary "for seasons and for days and years" and "to separate the light from the darkness" (Gen. 1:14–19), even though he had already separated them as his First Act. How are we to understand this? There are various explanations for the anomalies of the Creation story, but one is that we are simply facing a type of temporality unfamiliar to us.

Days and years in the Old Testament are different from what we think of them today, unfamiliar in their make-up. Events sometimes "occupy" time, hours and months, as they do for us, in our linguistic tradition, but not always. When they do not, we are unable to conceive of them. Our language obliges us to think of heavenly bodies, for example, in terms of static shapes occupying space, while the Hebrews, by contrast, defined them in terms of what they did. They shone. So they are lamps. In Nehemiah 7:3, for example, we read, "The gates of Jerusalem are not to be opened until the sun is hot," which strikes us as an odd way to say "at noon." Or "when the sun is high in the heavens." But it is merely to speak of "being" in dynamic terms, as becoming or "duration" as Bergson calls it, rather than in terms of space. The oddity of the Creation days goes away once we understand that light and dark, as qualities, were conceived of by the ancient Hebrews as primary, not as attributes or the content of some prior things called heavenly bodies. They do not need the heavenly bodies to be there. The light lights, the dark darks: those are their identifying qualities, not their spatial relationship, one to the other. God says, let them be separate and called day and night. But that is our language, our conception. Let them be separate: like two bodies. Something different was intended by the Old Testament writers.

Ancient Hebrew verbs that express static states of standing, sitting, lying, and dwelling have less of a spatial connotation than they do for us, and more of a dynamic sense of the beginning or ending of an action. A dwelling, for example, is not a place like a house, but means, "coming to a stop." Boman writes: "Motionless and fixed being is for the Hebrews a nonentity."[14] With the Ark, for example, we do not get a picture of what this structure looks like, only instructions on how to build it. The same occurs in the description in 1 Kings 6.:7 of how

Solomon had the temple in Jerusalem built. Again, as with the Ark, we get no clear picture of what this structure looks like, of its "image" fixed in time, only how it was built. In the Song of Solomon there are some strange comparisons – the bride's hair is "like a flock of goats"; her teeth are "like a flock of shorn ewes"; her "belly is a heap of wheat"; and both her neck and nose are compared to towers (4:1–4; 7:2–4). We find these comparisons odd because we are "seeing" them. They become understandable, however, once we realize that the comparison is not about looks but about function – the quality of the tower as a fortress and of nature as a living, fertile action.

Language expresses knowledge and always carries an implicit copulative: thus it is. Our own sense of "being," as both Bergson and Heidegger noted, is closer to the Greek obsession with "essence," a static state, and that makes language like that of the Song of Solomon hard to grasp. "Knowledge," Bergson writes in *Creative Evolution*, "bears on a state rather than on a change" (329); we must fix it in time to know it, to see it. That practice, however, in excluding temporality precludes us from grasping true being, or statements of fact like those in the Song that are based on change rather than a snapshot. Heidegger's concept of "thrownness" (*Geworfenheit*) and the "there" (*da*) in Dasein seeks to convey the dynamic quality of Being. True being is always being that is in the process of being disclosed. "The expression 'thrownness,'" Heidegger writes, "is meant to suggest *the facticity of its being delivered over*" (174: H. 135). The true nature of existence is in becoming, in its "clearing" as Heidegger says, or "lighting" (*lichtung*), in the sense of something cleared (*gelichtet*), passing from the dark into light, into a "clearing" where its being is itself the clearing. Heidegger's insistence on making his language itself disclose what he wants it to disclose can make it difficult for us to understand. And he tells us, as Bergson did, that the problem is that when we say, "I see," meaning, "I understand," we are revealing just how much we see, but do not understand.[15] We stand at gaze before being, as Heidegger says, and thus we miss it completely.

Words themselves in ancient Hebrew were less symbols and pointers than incarnations or instantiations of what they (for us) point to or symbolize or refer to. As Herder noticed, this makes Hebrew poetry special, since one might say that the words themselves are alive. The relationship of signifier to signified for us is a spatial one, visualized, an arrow pointing, one thing symbolizing another. Isaac Rabinowitz notes that in Hebrew the relationship is quite different, more iconic than symbolic. The thing and the word for the thing "were just different aspects of the same entity – the latter merely the concentrated essence of the former."[16] Thus, John 1:1: "In the beginning was the Word, and the Word was with God, and the Word was God." Words were "presumed to have the properties of material objects."[17] And a word read out loud to someone was "efficacious of a purpose that transcended the communicating of the content of that text."[18] In terms of modern language philosophy we might say that all utterance for the prophets was performative: words did things instead of saying things. Rabinowitz writes that much of the language has to be mistranslated into English to be understood.

Biblical scholars call "actualization" the bringing of the past into the present. Mircea Eliade writes that this is how festivals like Passover must be understood:

> The historical acts by which Jahweh founded the community of Israel were absolute. They did not share the same fate of all other events, which inevitably slip back into the past. They were actual for each subsequent generation ... when Israel ate the Passover, clad as for a journey, staff in hand, sandals on their feet, and in the haste of departure (Exodus 12:11) she was doing manifestly more than merely remembering the Exodus; she was entering into the saving event of the Exodus itself and participating in it in a quite "actual" way.[19]

The Sabbath, Jacques Doukhan tells us, in like manner actualizes the past event of Creation (Ex. 20:11); and wandering in the wilderness is actualized in the Feast of Tabernacles (Lev. 23:43). Not just the past is actualized; the future is also present in the present. "The future event of God's salvation may be actualized in the Sabbath, the sabbatical year or even in the institution of the Jubilee (Ps. 92:4; Jer. 25:9–12; Isa. 61:1; Dan. 9:2, 24–7)"; and Creation is re-actualized by the return of the exiles (Isa. 42:5–9). The past event of the return from the exile, in turn, will be re-actualized in the final salvation (Ezek. 37:21–8). Doukhan notes that the thought is made possible by using the "Prophetic Perfect" tense, or "*perfectum propheticum*." "In Jer. 32.37–41, for instance, the Perfect tense is used to express the certainty of the hope of the restoration. This future event is so sure that it is perceived as if it were *already* accomplished." In other words, the future and past event may be perceived "as their own in the present."[20]

It may seem a long way from the *perfectum propheticum* to Proust, but we might think of how Proust talks about the past in *Swann's Way*: it could come straight out of this kind of prophetic tense-merging. What are his moments of recollection after all, when involuntary memory introduces into his present unbidden the colours and smells and happenings of a long-ago afternoon at Combray, but the actualization of the past in the present, in secular form? Proust calls this "the life of the mind." The past is alive, and only waiting for its cue, a door to open, to join the present. In fact, without it, the present is just a shell, a one-dimensional time frame. Reality is where time houses the fullness of experience; reality, Proust writes, "takes shape in the memory alone." The past endures, while the present subsides. Proust finishes the sentence: "the flowers that people show me nowadays for the first time never seem to me to be true flowers."[21] In like manner, the Passover loses its reality, its actuality, if it is nothing but the present, a festival celebrating or pointing to the past; it *is* that very past, and that makes it real.

By contrast, the word "reality" today has a thing-like ontic quality for us that is fixed in space; it is static. We see this in the language: we get the word "reality" from the Latin *res*, meaning "thing." In Biblical Hebrew the word does not exist. The word *davar*, which in later Hebrew came to denote "thing," in biblical Hebrew has various meanings: "speech"; "word"; "message"; "report"; "tidings." Rather than being a sign of linguistic poverty, this suggests a view of the world that does not equate reality with something static, with some "thing." The Old Testament, for example, is not about mapping things in space, or Spinoza's *more geometrico*; it is about time and history. The word "holy" (*qadosh*) in Genesis is not applied to places, but to a time, the seventh day. And prayer has no set places, only set times.[22]

As we know, Bergson apparently did not notice how similar his own concept of *durée* was to this. When he mentions the ancients he is not thinking of his own Judaic ancestors, but writes against the Greek conception of time in Plato, Aristotle, and Plotinus, where temporality is not of the essence (eternity or God) but a quality of the sublunary world. Spinoza does not fare well here with his Cartesian approach to understanding God and the universe. Bergson writes in *Creative Evolution* that with Spinoza the result is a kind of atemporal "universal mechanism" with the universe itself "a system of points" (378). Instead, Bergson cites the temporality of the "artist who creates a picture." Time, he writes,

is no longer an accessory; it is not an interval that may be lengthened or shortened without the content being altered. The duration of his work is part and parcel of his work. To contract or to dilate it would be to modify both the psychical evolution that fills it and the invention which is its goal.

The time taken up by the invention is one with the invention itself. It is the progress of a thought which is changing in the degree and measure that it is taking form. It is a vital process, something like the ripening of an idea. (370)

In Bergson's conception time inheres in the object just the way it does in the Hebrew word for thing, *davar*. This is why scholars like Söderblom wondered at how Bergson could have been so well-versed in Greek philosophy but unaware of the genesis of his own thoughts in his own personal Judaic heritage. His claim that time inheres in and indeed (as Heidegger went on to claim) constitutes the real would be a good way, for example, to help students of the Bible understand the cryptic comments in Ecclesiastes. There we are told that for every thing there is a season, a time to be born, a time to die, a time for every purpose under Heaven, and so on. And we get the same notion elsewhere: a time to gather cattle (Gen. 29:7); a time when kings go out to battle (2 Sam. 11:1); a time for the tree to give its fruit (Ps. 1:3). What is meant is not that everything happens at a particular time appropriate for it, sowing in the spring, harvesting in the fall, and so on, which would be rather pointless to say, but rather that every event possesses actively the time of its happening – that everything has its time the way every body has its blood. Hence a line like "There is nothing new under the sun" hardly means, same old, same old: for the ancient Hebrews it meant that time is immanent in each event and so can never be said to "pass" as long as life exists. Life is not spread across time but is made up of many times. That is how characters in the Old Testament can talk about times in the plural as "my life" – as in "my times are in your hands" (Ps. 31:15; Job 24:1).[23]

Modernists writing under the influence of Bergson, like Proust and Virginia Woolf, are thus bringing us back into contact with prophetic time, rather than just playing with form for form's sake. Woolf cites in *Orlando* the infinitely compressible and expandable nature of time, which is pure Bergson, and she makes it the subject of *Mrs. Dalloway*, *To the Lighthouse*, and *The Waves*. These are at the same time novels, and as such they have to obey to some degree the dictates of Bergson's "cinematographical" presentation of events – a succession of static moments – in order to be comprehended. But the temporality at work here, and in Proust, is more biblical in nature. When Heidegger defines temporality it is also reminiscent of the way times merge – the past and the future in the present – in Hebrew. He is intent on explaining, like Bergson, that we have been misled in our understanding of true "being" by the Greeks, for whom "presence" meant entities. Instead, true being is in "making present," in the coming-into-sight or coming-to-mind of the object. One of the reasons Heidegger's work is such a difficult read for English speakers is perhaps that German, like ancient Hebrew, is a verb-based language, allowing Heidegger much leeway in producing difficult (for us) neologisms: verbs built out of nouns and adjectives, for example, that require in English two or three words with hyphens separating them. On the Greek conception of presence he is more outspoken than Bergson: the Greeks were "without any acquaintance with the fundamental ontological function of time or even any understanding of it" (48; H. 26). Consider his following definition of temporality and "presence" in relation to Hebrew notions of time past and future inhabiting the present: "Coming back to itself futurally, resoluteness brings itself into the Situation by making present. The character of 'having been' arises from the future and in such a way that the future which 'has been' (or better which 'is in the process of having been') releases from itself the Present. This phenomenon has the unity of a future which makes present in the process of having been: we designate it as 'temporality'" (374; H. 326).

Heidegger also chafes against the necessity imposed by his language of using the copulative and making statements like, "Temporality is …" Temporality is not an entity, he warns, despite what grammar requires us to "say." "Temporality temporalizes" (377; H. 328). Rabinowitz and others find the same attitude to essence and entities in the Old Testament, where words for what we would call things (entities) there mean actions. We might also recall the centrality of "care" (Sorge) in Heidegger's definition of Dasein, to which he attaches words like "anxiety," "concern," "and solicitude." "Being-in-the-world is essentially care" (237; H. 193). This condition for the very possibility of Dasein is the presence of the past and future in the present, which is rendered in the awkward English translation as "ahead-of-itself-in-Being-already-in" (236; H. 192). What Heidegger has in mind here with the notion of "care" is the simultaneity of foresight (seeing potentiality) and hindsight (informing the present) in the moment of "making present." This kind of "temporality" would have been familiar to the authors of the Old Testament.

If Bergson and Heidegger redefined temporality in this way, and did so (especially Bergson) in such a convincing way that durée came to be adopted by Proust and his followers as the veritable operating system of their fictions, what does this mean for the way we think of those fictions, and more, of modernism per se, and our tendency to ignore ancient Hebrew culture when we look back to antiquity for the precursors of modernity? Both Bergson and Heidegger point the finger at Greek philosophy for providing us with a misguided, spatial, and static approach not only to existence in general, but to time in particular – what some refer to as "ocularcentrism." Is this fair? I would say that in large it is indeed fair, and that our use of the word "see" to mean "understand" something is no accident of language, but comes from Plato and Eliatic philosophy.

Plato, in his *Timeaus*, talks about both time and space. He thinks of time in terms of his cosmological separation of worlds, in terms of the higher Intelligible world of Ideas, and the lower temporal realm we inhabit. He creates a spatial model. The higher world has no time, it is Eternity, while the lower one is "a moving image of it," a copy, in motion, where the clock is ticking. As he writes, "before the heavens [everything in the copy] came into being there were no days or nights or months or years."[24] Plato may have been the first philosopher in Western culture to think this extra-temporal thought – the thought of Eternity as a timeless place, a background, fixed, infinite, against which or inside of which the universe was created, lives, and dies in time. Timelessness in Plato is not next to godliness, it *is* godliness, while life on earth is 'fallen,' nothing but a "moving image" of the higher realm. The seasons, the crops, the planets, death, and rebirth: it is easy for us to look at the natural world, as the Greeks did, and see how one could believe time was cyclical, not infinite but infinitely repeating, and perhaps (as Bergson says) believe a little too much in the figure of speech, the image. As Plato says in *The Republic*, "destruction comes to everything existing ... when the rounding circles of each come completely round."[25]

We are so fully inside such spatial metaphors that it is difficult to imagine what it would feel like to be outside them. But it would be a mistake to think they belong exclusively to Greek thought, to suggest that the Greeks, for example, had no sense of temporality whatsoever, as Boman sometimes seems to imply; or for that matter that the ancient Hebrews were unable to describe geometrical shapes or think in a very "cinematographical" away about history as a succession of static states, as Bergson might say. One might fairly say, for example, that the Judaeo-Christian view of time is linear, as opposed to cyclical, and the notion of "linear" is no less metaphorical and spatial than the Greek "cyclical" model. Socrates entertains the notion briefly in *Phaedo* only to dismiss it as a possibility: if time is a linear matter, he speculates, a matter of rise and fall, destruction and rebirth, then things would have been getting progressively better. In other words, if time is infinite behind us, as it is in the linear model, as opposed to the cyclical, by now everything should be perfect. Becoming, Socrates says, should therefore have ceased, and we should all be dead.[26] One might even argue that the Old Testament authors had a more spatial (and familiar to us) attitude to history than the Greeks, since establishing a sequence of past events and genealogies ("snapshots of transition," Bergson might say) is what many of the Old Testament books are about. The better approach is probably to allow that all cultures spatialize to one degree or another, and have always done so as a matter of course, in order to "see" and "know" the world.

In sum, I would suggest that the Greek enemy for Bergson and Heidegger is really Plato more than Aristotle. It is to Plato we owe our obsession with entities and essence that Heidegger claims has confounded our thinking about time. In the *Timaeus* Plato tries to explain space itself in its own terms, and the results are dubious at best. Space, he admits, is "difficult and obscure" to talk about. It may be the condition for being, but if it is going to be conceived of it can only be conceived of like everything else, which is to say spatially, visually. Plato therefore refers to it as a "receptacle:" "the receptacle, and, as it were, the nurse of all becoming."[27] But even he seems to find this spatial metaphor inadequate, and does not really seem to think of space as a version of substance or matter.[28] As "difficult" and "obscure" as it might be, space remains the third form of reality, after the realm of the unchanging world of Ideas and the changing visible copy of it. Space itself is the locus of becoming for Plato – something like an incubator or transit lounge where the eternal Ideas pass downward into their worldly shape and form as copies. He has an even more material metaphor for it, calling it "a kind of neutral plastic material on which changing impressions are stamped by the things which enter it."[29] Imagine, he says, someone moulding things out of gold, one after the other, each giving way and transforming itself into the next shape, so if someone pointed to it at any moment and said, "What is it?" you couldn't answer the shape because that would always be in the process of changing. Plato here sounds a bit like Heraclitus, but the change or flux he has in mind is not of the essence. There is something that is of the essence, and that is the gold itself. Think of the receptacle, he tells us, as the gold that may change its characteristics but not its ultimate nature. "We will follow this up another time," he says. For the moment we are directed to think of space as the third reality. It is not the model, or "that which becomes," but "that in which it becomes." It is "invisible and formless, all-embracing, possessed in a most puzzling way of intelligibility, yet very hard to grasp." It is "eternal and indestructible" and "provides a position for everything that comes to be." "We look at [space] indeed in a kind of dream," Plato says. "Everything that exists must be somewhere and occupy some space," he goes on; and "what is nowhere in heaven or earth is nothing at all."[30]

Aristotle could no more think outside the spatial paradigm than Plato, but he did notice what was wrong with his master's idea of space, and that was that it lacked a temporal component. It needed to be wedded to the idea of motion, on which Plato had nothing to say because he saw motion and change as merely attributes. The problem with Plato's space-as-receptacle, Aristotle notices in his *Physics*, is that it cannot play any role in motion. Even though Plato uses the word *chôra*, which does mean "space" and not "matter," and talks about it in terms of *dunamis* or "function," it remains a reified concept. Aristotle prefers the words "*locus* and *topos*, which are used to denote particular spaces here on earth, where things happen. Space for Aristotle must be defined not as something prior to or somehow separate from 'happening' (a third reality between that of the Ideas and that of the World), and certainly not as something nursing or holding the happening; it must be thought of strictly in terms of that happening.[31] And this is surprisingly close to Hebrew thought.

Time itself, Aristotle says in the *Physics*, can only make sense if thought of in terms of motion: "Time cannot exist without change ... nor can it exist without a motion ... Thus time ... must be something belonging to a motion ... and time is continuous because a motion is continuous (for the time elapsed is always thought to be as much as the corresponding motion which took place)."[32] And motion is only understandable as taking place, that is to say, in terms of space. But although time and motion are inseparable for Aristotle, they are not one thing. Time is not identical to movement in Aristotle's language, but pertains to it. Time is "that by which movement can be numerically estimated."[33] Time is a number, the spatial dimension in which motion takes place, so that time and space are a continuum, as Einstein put it. Wicksteed and Cornford write that Aristotle's space-time concept has a clear plus-minus dynamic and could be formulated as R (the dimension of movement) = ST^{-1}. His conception "opens the way to the four-dimensional algebra to which so much attention has recently been directed in connexion with the doctrine of relativity."[34] Einstein's debt to the past, however, is the subject of another book. Suffice it to say in conclusion here that when it comes to Einstein, Bergson, and Heidegger, their ideas on space and time were both new and old.

The Future of Things Past

While at work on *The Hours*, which would become *Mrs Dalloway*, Virginia Woolf wrote in her diary entry for 30 August 1923 about time and how she handled it. She wrote that she preferred to dig down into characters, to hollow out caves beneath them, bringing them into relation with one another so that the caves, once connected, all gave on the light of the present. This was her famous "tunnelling technique," and in *Mrs Dalloway* we see how it produces a series of narrative halts, where the temporal tapeworm, as E.M. Forster called it, is segmented. Instead of forward action in a sequence of events we come to a halt much the way we do when an author introduces a passage of description. The descriptive pause, so called, also puts a hold on the forward action, and Woolf, like any other novelist, uses this often enough – a kind of stopping place from where we look over the scenery. But the interruptions of forward movement she calls "tunnelling" are more like holes in the road that the reader drops into. In fact, they are really just flashbacks, analeptic journeys into the past of individual characters like Septimus Smith or Peter Walsh in *Mrs Dalloway*, filling in their backstory before returning them to the present. The speed of the narrative is reduced since the ratio of narrative to story time is high, so that we feel, almost tangibly, how time is being extended, ballooned, how extensible it is, how fungible, and ultimately, inevitably, how differently it is behaving and being handled from the way it does in what Joyce called "goahead plot." What we are witnessing in modernist (and postmodern) deformations of clock time is of course a treatment of the temporal tapeworm that in fact throws it out and replaces it with Bergsonian *dureé*.

Formalism in its latest instalment, in other words, has brought us into contact, via Bergson, with more than just an artistic practice begun by the Mannerist painters of the early sixteenth century; it reminds us through its temporal dislocations that it has an even older sibling in the ancient Near East. It is a kind of "time" that is always present and that flows around grammatical tense boundaries, alive, like an amniotic bath that nourishes being.

I will end by going back to the epigraph from William Burroughs that I began with. Writing in and of the postmodernist era, Burroughs said: "I feel that the future of writing is in space not time" – a thought echoed by Frederic Jameson. Burroughs was right. The modernists (and their post- followers in the sixties) rejected a certain kind of temporality. Whether this equates to raising space to the status they give it is another question, for another, and different, time.

Notes

Introduction

1 Qtd. in Bockris, 2.
2 James, 241.
3 Abrams, 107.
4 Bennett, 19.
5 Adorno, 21, 23.
6 Heidegger discussed the issue of "enframing" in his essays "The Question Concerning Technology" (1954) and "The Age of the World Picture" (1938).
7 Wundram, 277.
8 Bagrow, 89. See also, Wilford, 56; and Thrower, 59–60.
9 Pettegree, 285–6.
10 See Wilford, 66.
11 Pettegree, 143–4, 287
12 John Kleiner, 1–31, looks at how Renaissance writers attempted to "map" Dante's *Inferno* working from their own aesthetic of proper perspective and just proportion. Kleiner asks how we are to understand the imprecise calculations, disorder, and spatial mismeasurements in the architecture of the lower circles. Are they mistakes; stylistic flourishes designed to create a heightened effect of realism where accuracy is irrelevant, or a parody of the Aristotelian equation of the gravity of the sin and the severity of the punishment (*contrapasso*)? Kleiner suggests it might make more sense to see these incommensurabilities instead as playful and self-ironizing on Dante's part. In any case, the increasing unease created in the reader by these spatial incongruities as Virgil and the Pilgrim get closer to Satan seem appropriately hellish. My thanks to Richard Ratzlaff for bringing this interesting article to my attention.

13 Da Vinci, 2:213.

14 Woodward, 87, claims that the map record in the Renaissance marks the end of the old medieval centre/periphery model.

15 Chastel, 50, suggests that artists felt little interest in projecting their own small ideas in visible form at a time when revising Christian thought mattered far more than aesthetics.

16 Social and economic vectors in the late Renaissance intersect in so many ways it is difficult to isolate a single event as the defining one. Spitz, 28–31, for example, notes that one result of the new opening in global space was the rapid expansion of trade, both between Spain and the New World and, slightly later, to the Indies, which contributed as much to the rapid growth of cities as agrarian reform, especially on the Atlantic side in places like Antwerp. See Gray, 124–6; and Molho, 95–107.

17 Greenblatt, 88.

18 René Wellek, for example, complained in "Auerbach's Special Realism," *Kenyon Review* 16, no. 2 (1954): 299–307, and later in his *History of Modern Criticism*, vol. 7 (1991), that Auerbach tries to write a history of ideas where the ideas are divorced from material and social factors, essentially accusing him of being a "formalist." Spitzer goes the opposite direction and accuses him of a sociological bias (85n36). Cf. Holdheim and DePietro, who come to Auerbach's defence. Perhaps the strongest voice raised against the notion that progress and the advance of realism go hand in hand remains Nietzsche, who famously argued (against Euripides) that the rise of realism signalled the degeneration of art (137).

19 See McKeon, 11–14; and Doody, 2.

20 See, for example, Hervey ("space and time must be viewed through material processes" [204]); and Bulson, who focuses on the actual geography inside novels – for example, "topographical accuracy" in *Ulysses* (66) and "anti-cartographic space" in Kafka and Ishiguro (126).

21 Spengler, 175, 164n4.

22 See Waite; Gluck; and Koss, 149, on abstraction in Worringer's "spiritual aversion to space" [*geistige Raumscheu*].

23 Worringer, 39.

24 Kern, 140–8, writes brilliantly about Cézanne's landscapes as examples not of flatness but of multiple and violated perspectives.

25 See Francastel, 395, for example. Cf. Kubler, 31–53, 83–96, and Belting, 3–23, who warn against a history of ideas approach to art history.

26 Erickson, 21.

27 Bryson, 89.

28 See Kuhn, *Structure*.

29 Donne, *Ignatius*, 17. Editor T.S. Healy reminds us of the comic nature of
    the text, which may explain why Columbus finds himself of the party,
    coming fourth in the satire after Copernicus, Paracelsus, and Machiavelli.
    Copernicus may be there, Healy suggests, "for reasons of mere topicality"
    (xxix).
30 Donne, *Poetical Works*, 213–14.
31 Kuhn, *Structure*, 237. The controversy surrounding Kuhn has always had
    to do with the presumption with which he posited ideas that were philo-
    sophical in import, without being himself a philosopher, or for that matter,
    paying much heed, especially in *The Structure of Scientific Revolutions*, to
    the scholarly context that he was charged with overturning. If logical posi-
    tivism was his target, as was popularly thought, his own approach was
    solidly indebted to the same tradition, hence suspect. From this perspec-
    tive, Kuhn's notions on paradigm shifts seemed totalizing and suspicious-
    ly teleological, suffering from some of the same ills that beset many studies
    in the history of ideas. But Kuhn was a physicist, not a philosopher, and
    the discovery of patterns of the kind he saw are common in the natural
    and social sciences. Where reductivism is a sin in the humanities, it is the
    goal in science, and any disagreement with Kuhn's theory of paradigm
    shifts would have to be based on the same kind of studies in the history of
    science he himself depended on. Kuhn was not interested in defining the
    Zeitgeist for any period, merely studying how the criteria used to judge
    truth claims in science changed over time.
32 Milton tells us in his 1644 *Areopagitica* (where he argues against censor-
    ship) that he visited Galileo, the "Tuscan artist" as he calls him in *Paradise
    Lost* (i. 288), when he was in Florence in 1638.

1. Rabelais and Modernism

 1 Originally self-published (Landshut), the later editions of the
    Cosmographicus liber were published by Gemma Frisius and remain
    untranslated in English. A French translation appeared in 1553. See
    Lestringant, 104ff.
 2 Kuhn, *Structure*, x.
 3 On Aristarchus and Cusa, see Kuhn, *Copernican*, 274–8; 233–5.
 4 Armitage, 14, takes a Kuhnian approach in claiming the new criteria for
    what counts as true in astronomical hypotheses was made necessary by
    Copernicus's discovery.
 5 A paradigm or pattern can emerge unbidden, as an effect without an iden-
    tifiable cause. See Gleick, 151–75.

6 Heidelberger, 272, makes the interesting observation that the result was to make space on an interplanetary scale realistic and empirical for the first time.

7 See Copleston, 3: 283, and Lewis, 2–17.

8 Gingerich, 249. The edition was owned and annotated by many astronomers, Gingerich notes, but also by a wide variety of lay people (x). On Koestler's claim that nobody read *On the Revolutions*, Gingerich writes that "he couldn't have been more mistaken" (255).

9 More, 30.

10 See meanings 1, 4.

11 More, 34.

12 Marin, 110.

13 Ibid. And see Greenblatt, 22–3.

14 See Griffin, 127–8, on the extent to which Renaissance thinkers, including Ariosto, believed that the world was constructed according to mathematical laws, and that numbers controlled time and space. On just proportions at the level of plot in *Orlando furioso*, see Shapiro, 152–91.

15 See *Pantagruel*, chapters 32 and 23. All citations from *Gargantua* and *Pantagruel* are from the Pléiade edition (Gallimard) and will be cited henceforth as *G* or *P* parenthetically in the text. The English translations are from the Modern Library translation by Jacques le Clerq and will also be noted parenthetically in the text.

16 See Screech, 39–40.

17 Screech, 108–9, argues that Rabelais is trying to calm fears generated by the appearance of the comets.

18 Bakhtin notes the presence of Folengo, although he downplays any influence the latter might have had on Rabelais (Bakhtin, 299–300). And on Folengo, see Thuasne, 159–265; and Bowen, 45–53, who calls Folengo and Rabelais "kindred spirits."

19 See Stephens, 6.

20 Barolsky, 115, 117. Cf Shearman, 37–8, who associates literary "mannerism" with "Bembismo" – a movement in early sixteenth-century Rome that reversed the usual understanding of form and content.

2. Swift and *Commensuratio*

1 See Max Dvorak, "El Greco and Mannerism," *Magazine of Art* 46 (1953): 14–23.

2 See de Mourges, *Metaphysical*, 87, 92, 93, 99. See, in the same vein, John Steadman, *Redefining a Period Style: "Renaissance," "Mannerist" and "Baroque" in Literature* (Pittsburgh: Duquesne University Press, 1990).

3 Article 42, *The Present State of the Republic of Letters* (1730), written three years after Newton's death.

4 Newton, *Principles*, Prop.5; Theorem 5:329.

5 Newton, *Treatise*, 223–6.

6 Newton, *Opticks*, book 3, qu. 28.

7 Voltaire, *Works*, 201.

8 Newton, *Principles*, 440, 442. And see Philip Bricker and R.I.G. Hughes, eds, *Philosophical Perspectives on Newtonian Science* (Cambridge, MA: MIT Press, 1990).

9 See Hampson, 34.

10 Kuhn, *Structure*, 92.

11 Fontenelle, 126.

12 Adams, 70.

13 Cohen, 42.

14 Ferguson, 4.

15 Stephen, 8, 69.

16 Swift, 8. All subsequent citations will be from the edition of *Gulliver's Travels* listed in the bibliography and will be included parenthetically in the text.

17 Knowles, 65–6, argues that the fleet and handkerchief items are inconsistencies designed to make us suspect Gulliver's truthfulness.

18 Walpole, 28.

19 Cuffe, vii.

20 Ibid.

21 Voltaire, *Micromégas*, 101.

22 The French foot or *"pied de roi"* Voltaire uses is 1.06 times larger than the English foot, so Sirius is really 127,000 (English) feet tall, or 24 miles.

3. Narcissism: Jonson and the Disfigured Self

Portions of chapter three were previously published as "Getting the "h" Out of Jo(h)nson," *PsyArt* (2006), and are used with permission.

1 Tillyard's spatial metaphor of a "picture" seems to many critics today to be a kind of "formalist" critique whose material nature blinds it to anything outside its "frame." But Tillyard wrote that it was in fact the exceptions that made him aware of the rule. To wit: it was the violence in Shakespeare's plays that led him to conclude that they were only understandable against "a background of order" (vii) – one that he argued was medieval in nature. He also notes the (non) effect of Copernicus on "the ordinary educated Elizabethan [who still] thought the universe was

geocentric" (38). Donne's quite different sensitivity has already been noted (Tillyard, Introduction, 19–21).

2 Greenblatt writes that Spenser and company "all embody ... a profound mobility [that is] social and economic" (7).

3 See *Ben Jonson's Conversations with William Drummond of Hawthornden*, in Jonson, 1:139.

4 Miles, 1–3. Riggs calls dropping the "h" "retrospective self-fashioning" (4–5, 9). And see Chute, 17.

5 He could "loose all father, now," as Jonson wrote the next year after losing his own son in the plague. See Riggs, 114–15.

6 I follow Lawrence Danson, in "Jonsonian Comedy and the Discovery of the Social Self," who understands the "self" in Jonson's plays (after Mead in *Mind, Self and Society*) as socially constructed and unstable. Cf O'Dair 100, who replies to Danson and objects that the contingent self of sociology denies the possibility of an integrated individual self, while the self of the psychologists denies culture and history. Both are "based on and refer to a limited and partial view of the human being." Jonson himself, it might be argued, was never a whole, so that spatializing a part, or parts, of him is all self-fashioning can mean.

7 Kernberg, 228–9.

8 *Diagnostic and Statistical Manual of Mental Disorders (DSM) IV*, 661.

9 Jacobson, 6, writes that the definition comes from H. Hartmann, who introduced the term "self" in "Comments on the Psychoanalytic Theory of the Ego," in *The Psychoanalytic Study of the Child* (New York: International Universities Press, 1950), 5:74–96n2 (my emphasis).

10 "The International Journal of Psycho-Analysis" 53, no. 21 (1972): 22. Reported by Charles Kligerman. For further discussion, see Lynne Layton and Barbara Ann Schapiro, eds, *Narcissism and the Text: Studies in Literature and the Psychology of Self* (New York: New York University Press, 1986).

11 On Jonson's fascination with things and objects, especially in *The Alchemist*, see Eric Wilson, "Abel Drugger's Sign and the Fetishes of Material Culture," *Historicism, Psychoanalysis, and Early Modern Culture*, ed. Carla Mazzion and Douglas Trevor (New York and London: Routledge, 2000), 110–34.

12 Freud, "On Narcissism," 31–2.

13 See Melanie Klein, "A Contribution to the Psychogenesis of Manic Depressive States" (1935), *The Writings of Melanie Klein*, 4 vols (New York: Free Press, 1984), 1:262–89; "Mourning and its Relation to Manic Depressive States" (1940), ibid., 1:344–69; "Notes on Some Schizoid

Mechanisms" (1946), ibid., 3:1–24; et passim. On love, see "Love, Guilt and Reparation" (1937), ibid., 1:311. For objections to Klein on the premise that any discussion of things partial implies a whole, where the whole is always an idealism or fiction, see Gilles Deleuze and Felix Guattari, *Anti-Oedipus: Capitalism and Psychoanalysis*, trans. Helen R. Lane, Robert Hurley, and Mark Seem (New York: Viking, 1977). On making "restitution" as the compensatory motive for literary creation, see Norman N. Holland, *Psychoanalysis and Shakespeare* (New York: Octagon, 1976), p. 46n3.

14 Fineman, 103.
15 D.W. Winnicot speaks of transitional objects that usher the child into the symbolic order; they are the first objects of play, and mark our first cultural acts. See his *The Maturational Processes and the Facilitating Environment* (New York: International Universities Press, 1965).
16 Kernberg, 30.
17 Kohut, Guntrip, and W.R.D. Fairbairn, for example, see it as an important form of self-defence against stress, where the primary impulse is assertiveness, not aggression. See Heinz Kohut, *The Analysis of the Self* and *The Restoration of the Self* (New York: International Universities Press, 1971; 1977).
18 See Klein, "Notes," in *Writings*, 3:13. Otto Kernberg, *Borderline Conditions and Pathological Narcissism* (New York: Aronson, 1975), 227–8, discusses this ambivalence in narcissism: others are solicited for their "tribute and adoration" while at the same time being despised and distrusted. This was something Jonson was famous for.
19 Ibid. For a discussion of the simultaneity of identification and projection, see Meira Likierman, *Melanie Klein: Her Work in Context* (New York: Continuum, 2001), 157–8.
20 Skura, 78–9.
21 Lawrence Danson writes that "the Jonsonian plot ... does not negotiate the passage from nurturing family to adult family to leave us with a sense of self-attainment" (187).
22 After his purchase, Sogliardo says, "I can write my selfe gentleman now" (III.iii.52–3). The plays will be cited in the text by act, scene, and line number.
23 Leggatt writes that "Macilente is not just a role played by Asper; Macilente is Asper" (197).
24 Induction, l. 204.
25 See Hanna Segal, "Some Clinical Implications of Melanie Klein's Work," *The Journal of Psycho-Analysis* 52 (1983), 270–1.
26 See Leah S. Marcus, *The Politics of Mirth: Jonson, Herrick, Milton, Marvell, and the Defense of Old Pastimes* (Chicago: Chicago University Press, 1986), 46–7.

27 See Michel Foucault, *Technologies of the Self: A Seminar with Michel Foucault*, ed. Luther H. Martin, Huck Gutman, and Patrick H. Hutton (Amherst: University of Massachusetts Press, 1988), 41.

28 Greenblatt says the essential action of the play "is the hero's attempt to 'fill himself.'" The narcissist will reveal the emptiness that is there. Volpone empties himself, after which he and the audience realize there is nothing left. See Stephen Greenblatt, "The False Ending in *Volpone*," *Critical Essays on Ben Jonson*, ed. Robert N. Watson (New York: G.K. Hall, 1997), 177; and Thomas M. Greene, "Ben Jonson and the Centered Self," *Studies in English Literature* 10 (1970): 337.

29 Riggs, 146; he qualifies by saying that between 1606 and 1616 Jonson "heeded Sidney's maxim that 'the oblique must be known as well as the right,' and brought these superficially disparate activities into a richly dialectical relationship."

30 Jonson, in the estimation of Riggs, was on one hand a "scoundrel," a view common in "contemporary gossip, satires, court records and private correspondence"; a "notorious reprobate and public nuisance: a drunken, swaggering, murderous sponge" who was a shameless flatterer and back-stabber. On the other hand, "tributes and memorabilia written by his friends, tell a very different story." Jonson was "a discreet and scholarly man" who in his own words "'ever trembled to thinke toward the last prophanenesse'" and sought only to "curb extravagance" (1–2). See Inigo Jones, "To his false friend" (Jonson, 11:385); and *Underwood*, l. 23 (Jonson, 8:174–5).

31 In *Bartholomew Fair*, for example, there is as much emphasis on what goes in as what comes out. Psychoanalytic approaches to Jonson often focus on anality and anal eroticism in the plays. See Edmund Wilson, "Morose Ben Jonson," *The Triple Thinkers: Twelve Essays on Literary Subjects* (New York: Oxford University Press, 1948), 213–32. Bruce Thomas Boehrer, *The Fury of Men's Gullets* (Philadelphia: University of Pennsylvania Press, 1997), surveys the field (8–14), and goes on to discuss the London sewage system in relation to alimentary motifs in Jonson. See especially his excellent chapter "The Ordure of Things" (147–75).

32 The Lacanian phantasm of morcellation and fear of the *corps morcelé* embodies the same set of neuroses in the closeness of bodies and earth. See Jacques Lacan, *The Language of the Self*, trans. Anthony Wilden (Baltimore: Johns Hopkins University Press, 1968), 36.

33 Riggs suggests that the anality of the play is tonic rather than symptomatic, signalling what is overcome in Jonson rather than (as in Eric Wilson, note 11, above) what is not (30–1).

34 Kohut, 324
35 Ibid.
36 For the narcissist, falling in love with another is perceived as a form of emasculation and loss of self. But it is the withdrawal inward, as Christopher Lasch long ago noted , that constitutes true self-obliteration. See Coppelia Kahn, *Man's Estate: Masculine Identity in Shakespeare* (Berkeley: University of California Press, 1981), 43–4.
37 Jonson, 9:533.
38 This aspect of "On my First Sonne" has been noted. See Joshua Scodel, "Genre and Occasion in Jonson's 'On My First Sonne,'" *Studies in Philology* 86 (1989): 235–6n3; G.W. Pigman III, *Grief and the English Renaissance Elegy* (Cambridge: Cambridge University Press, 1985), 88–9; and Katherine Eisamann Maus, *Ben Jonson and the Roman Frame of Mind* (Princeton, NJ: Princeton University Press, 1984), 119–23. I am indebted to David Lee Miller's essay, "Writing the Specular Son," in *Desire in the Renaissance: Psychoanalysis and Literature*, ed. Valeria Finucci and Regina Schwartz (Princeton, NJ: Princeton University Press, 1994), 258n11, for pointing out the three references. On Jonson and dead children, see Riggs, 87–9, and Ann Barton, *Ben Jonson, Dramatist* (Cambridge: Cambridge University Press, 1984), 19. Miller offers a compelling analysis of the famous dream of the son that Jonson recounted to Drummond, suggesting that the boy's premonitory death in the dream can be read as a kind of self-inflicted wound or sacrifice to the author's own identity (234–41).

4. Sade and the Deformed Body

Portions of chapter 4 appeared in "Sade, 'Vanille et Manille': Urology and the Body of the Text," *French Forum* 29, no. 3 (Fall 2004): 13–26, and are used here with the permission of University of Nebraska Press.

 1 *The 120 Days*, 30. De Beauvoir's essay is reprinted in the Grove edition. See "The Marquis de Sade and the Discourses of Pain: Literature and Medicine at the Revolution," in *The Languages of Psyche: Mind and Body in Enlightenment Thought, Clark Library Lectures 1985–86*, ed. G.S. Rousseau (Los Angeles: University of California Press, 1990), 291–330. Cf. Vila, 288, who calls Sade's condition a "jointly medical and philosophical one."
 2 *Juliette*, 582.
 3 Annie Le Brun, 46, claims that in Sade the physical always precedes the moral.
 4 Krafft-Ebbing, 56. All references are to the edition found in the bibliography and will be cited in the text.

5   Gilles de Rais fought alongside Joan of Arc at Orléans and Paris in 1429. Benedetti notes that the court indictment in 1440 put the number of his child victims at 140, but admits that no definitive number exists (180).

6   See Paullini's *Flagellum Salutis* (Stuttgart, 1847).

7   Laborde, *La bibliothèque du marquis de Sade au château de la Coste*.

8   Boileau, 254. All references are to the edition found in the bibliography and will be cited in the text; translations are my own.

9   Tissot, 20–1, 25, 70–107; and see Boisseau's notes.

10 The "Vanilla and Manilla Letter" is in the *Oeuvres Completes*, 11.449–511, Letter 182. The following citations are from Seaver's translation of Sade's *Letters from Prison*, Letter 97, 367–70.

11 Seaver, ibid., 368n. None of Sade's biographers deals with the issue. Gilbert Lely, who first published and decoded the Letter in 1950, notes that the problem dates back to the Rose Keller episode of 1768 but does not discuss it as a medical condition (*Oeuvres*, 2:171–72); Maurice Lever only remarks on it in passing (357); Schaeffer echoes Sade's suspicion that the problem is "congenital" – or perhaps, he writes, a "psychical obstruction" (131); The Laurence L. Bongie biography does not mention it.

12 *Oeuvres*, 12:450–1, Letter 432, my trans.

13 Francine du Plessix Gray, 238. Jean-Jacques Pauvert held a similar view, calling Sade's illness the holdover "of a venereal disease inadequately treated, albeit benign" (my trans., 438).

14 *Oeuvres*, 1:173.

15 See the Wainhouse and Seaver translation of *Juliette*, 55.

16 *The 120 Days*, 239–40.

17 Meacham and Rose (189ff) note that these can be either acquired or congenital, although the symptoms they describe for those who suffer from them today do not match Sade's.

18 Howe, 99, adds that it is appropriate that there is a connection between sexual excess and epilepsy, which he takes to be a disorder of the brain, since the testicle in fact resembles the brain: it too has a three-part structure, with three coverings, a serous, fibrous, and vascular coat.

19 I cite from the Wainhouse and Seaver translation of *The Complete Justine, Philosophy in the Bedroom and other writings*, 672.

20 Lechtenberg and Ohl, 40.

21 Eisendrath and Ralnick, 57.

22 Phillips, 185.

23 Ibid., 188.

24 Eisendrath and Ralnick, 56–7.

25 *Juliette*, 578–9.

26 Carter is right to characterize the sites of sexual release in Sade's underground world as places of "imaginary liberty" (83). In Cell #6 Sade
   laboured mightily and more often than not in vain to gain the kind of
   sexual release his libertines enjoy when they finally emerge into rooms
   like Minsky's. His characters, by contrast, see all the tunnelling as nothing more than protection from the police. In *Juliette*, Delbène says: "If we
   thus burrow far down into the realm of the dead, it is to be at the greatest
   possible remove from the living. When one is a libertine, as depraved, as
   vicious as are we, one likes to be in the bowels of the earth so as the better
   to avoid the interference of men and their ridiculous laws" (55).
27 Ibid., *Juliette*, 582.
28 *Applebee's*, 25 Sept. 1725, in Lee, *Defoe* 3:430.
29 Backscheider, 493.
30 *The 120 Days*, 609.
31 Defoe, *Unparallel'd*, 5–6.
32 Ibid., 3.
33 Krafft-Ebing, 60.
34 Deleuze, 11.
35 Deleuze suggests that just as the fiction or "art" learns from and re-
   embodies the material body, the body can learn from the art (11).

5. Hysteria: Pynchon's Cartoon Space

Portions of this chapter appeared in "Pynchon's Hysterical Sublime," *Critique:
Studies in Contemporary Fiction* 52, no. 4 (2011) and are used here with permission.
 1 All references to works by Pynchon are cited in the text from the editions
   listed in the bibliography and are identified by the following abbrevia-
   tions: *Against the Day=AD, The Crying of Lot 49=CL, Gravity's Rainbow=GR,
   Mason and Dixon=MD, Slow Learner=SL, Vineland=Vl.*
 2 Kermode, 163.
 3 Rosenfeld, 10 11.
 4 See McHale, 91.
 5 O'Donnell, 83. Cf. Mendelson, who argues that "in each book paranoia is
   only a vehicle that bears a larger significance ... none of Pynchon's novels
   is concerned with the self" (15). See also Leo Bersani, "Pynchon, Paranoia,
   and Literature," *Representations* 25 (Winter 1989): 99–118.
 6 Palmieri argues that "Freudian analysis does not explain any of Oedipa's
   problems very well, since she is female, not homosexual, not clearly paranoid, and less narcissistic than the men in the novel" (987); paranoia and
   narcissism can at best provide "only partial truths" (988).

7 Shapiro, *Neurotic*, 56.
8 Freud calls it a "caricature of a philosophic system" (*Totem*, 96).
9 Borossa, 65.
10 Note Septimus Smith in Virginia Woolf's *Mrs. Dalloway* (1925) and the poets-as-patients, Owen and Sassoon, in Pat Barker's *Regeneration* trilogy (1991).
11 Shapiro, *Neurotic*, 108–17, 118.
12 MacKinnon and Michels, 132–3, 118.
13 Horowitz, 5.
14 Bollas, 118.
15 One might recall Robert Coover's "The Phantom of the Movie Palace," for example, in *A Night at the Movies*, where the real space of the movie theatre is run up against, and indeed dissolved into, the fictional space of the film. Coover has commented on why his formalism matters, and how it directly "relates to social forms and structures" (qtd. in Geyh, Leebron and Levy, 226).
16 Jameson, "Postmodernism," 63. Elsewhere Jameson talks about the "postmodernist aesthetic" of "*écriture*, of 'textual productivity' or schizophrenic writing" (*Political Unconscious*, 106).
17 Baudrillard, 133.
18 Jameson, "Postmodernism," 63.
19 Lynn Anne Adam, "Kathy Acker and the Hysterical Sublime: The Movements of Technological Martyrdom, Grotesque Perversity and Post-Freudian Aesthetics," *Dissertation Abstracts International* 62, no. 5 (Nov. 2001): 1831. The article version appears in *Mosaic* (Dec. 2003).
20 See, for example, Mitchell; Showalter; and Clare Hanson, *Hysterical Fictions: The 'Woman's Novel' in the Twentieth Century* (New York: St Martin's Press, 2000).
21 Monk, 58.
22 Burke writes: "Whatever is fitted in any sort to excite the ideas of pain, and danger, that is to say, whatever is in any sort terrible, or is conversant about terrible objects, or operates in a manner analogous to terror, is a source of the sublime" (39).
23 Herz notes that Wordsworth also talks about the mind being "thwarted, baffled" (*Prelude* 2.355) by its encounter with immensity in the natural world (44).
24 Kant 99; Ak. 244–5.
25 See Jameson, "Postmodernism," 77.
26 Kant 99; Ak. 245.
27 Wood, 179.
28 Baudrillard, 133.

29 Sterne, 5, 9. Tristram is a materialist and blames them on a disturbance of the "animal spirits" at his conception, along with the reading of Locke on the association of ideas.

30 Jameson, "Postmodernism," 77.

31 See Roth's essay "Writing American Fiction," *Commentary* 31 (Mar. 1961): 223–33. Lasch discusses the comment (13) and notes the "bafflement and disgust" awaiting anyone "who tries to make sense of contemporary social life."

32 See LeClair, x.

33 LeClair suggests the phrase may also come from 2 Peter 3.7. See his review of *Against the Day* in *Bookforum* Dec./Jan. 2007.

34 Mitchell, 117.

35 On Flaubert, see Showalter, 95; Jan Goldstein, "The Uses of Male Hysteria: Medical and Literary Discourse in Nineteenth-Century France." *Representations* 34 (Spring 1991): 134–65; and Marie Josephine Diamond, "Flaubert's 'Quidquid volueris': the Colonial Father and the Poetics of Hysteria," *SubStance* 27, no. 1 (1998): 71–88. Aragon and Breton call hysteria "la plus grande découverte poétique de la fin du XIXe siècle" (20) and "un moyen suprême d'expression" (22) ["the greatest poetic discovery of the end of the nineteenth century" and "a supreme mode of expression"].

36 Borossa, 77.

37 Barthelme, 82. Physical comedy of the sort we see today in someone like Jim Carrey looks "hysterical" in this sense. In the world of postmodern fiction, Mark Leyner seems to follow Pynchon's idea.

38 Jameson, "Postmodernism," 76.

39 Gordon, 175.

40 Tart, 183, 171.

41 Note the presence in the early story, "Low-lands," of Geronimo Diaz, who thinks he is Paganini and keeps "a priceless Stradivarius in his desk." He reads nonsense syllable lists and mixes cocktails while his patient talks. During one argument Flange "had attempted to brain his psychiatrist with the Stradivarius," but Geronimo jumps on the desk, chaos ensues, and the scene becomes a cartoon. The character comes back as Dr. Hilarius in *Lot 49*. On "skylarking," see *Against the Day*, where the Chums of Chance seek "pretexts for skylarking" (*AD* 4), which they do literally in their balloon; and oppose control freaks like Lindsay, who "just can't abide anybody having too much fun … Anything they can't control is too much like skylarking for those autocratic bastards" (*AD* 427).

42 "Irreverence is always a critique, not only of what has been designated "sacred" and "true" but also of the entrenched power that enforces such designations" (Schaub, 141).

43 Pynchon may have been inspired by Woody Allen's 1971 film *Everything You Always Wanted to Know About Sex But Were Afraid to Ask*, where a giant breast goes on a rampage.
44 Seed claims that "sorting, in various senses, is the book's true subject" (125); and that the letter is a "gesture" – the content is not the issue (141). Mattesich refers to "the torsions of a remorseless identity caught in the compulsion to repeat" (246). "Fragmentation," McLuhan writes, "is the essence of machine technology" (8).
45 Progogine, 133.
46 Schaub, 11.
47 McHale, 97.
48 From *Against the Day*: "Really Traverse you know you must abandon this farcical existence, rededicate yourself to real-world issues …" (802).
49 Mason and Dixon turn into Laurel and Hardy. In the snowstorm in Maryland, Dixon says to Mason, "Another bonny gahn-on tha've got us into" (*MD* 363), echoing the line uttered so many times by Ollie to Stan: "Well, here's another nice mess you've gotten me into," just so we don't miss the point.

6. Modernism and Mannerism

1 Faulkner, 3–4. All subsequent references will appear in the text and are to the edition found in the bibliography.
2 Genette, 115–16
3 Levin, 5, follows Richard Rorty in calling the "enframing" malaise, "ocularcentrism."
4 Raffel notes that "Rabelais is something like a cross between James Joyce and Laurence Sterne" (ix).
5 Kern and Henry unintentionally imply that Einstein might be the muse, or at least have provided the conditions for what followed with Picasso and his followers.
6 Kern claims Einstein "demolished the conventional sense of stability of the entire material universe" (184–5). Henry writes that "Einsteinian relativity had largely reconfigured nineteenth-century conceptions of space and time" (26).
7 See Henderson, 353–8.
8 Henry, 2.
9 The new choice of title for the Modern Library edition, *In Search of Lost Time*, is a more literal translation (by D.J. Enright) of the French original, but has a pedestrian sound, making Proust sound like a detective. The rich

allusiveness of the Moncrieff and Kilmartin original, *Remembrance of Things Past*, which a colleague reminds me is borrowed from the second line of Shakespeare's Sonnet 30, better translates the spirit of Proust's *recherche*.

10 Proust studied under Bergson at the Sorbonne and Bergson's idea of time as *durée* (duration) is much in evidence in *Swann's Way*, which is often called a Bergsonian novel. The two men were related through marriage but were not fond of one another – Proust was sentimental, gay, a Dreyfusard; Bergson was not. Proust did not like being told that *Swann's Way* was "Bergsonian."

11 See Benjamin, 110, 111, 138. Lukács, 121, claims that Proust specializes in "real time – Bergson's *durée*."

12 Heidegger 39; H. 18.

13 Lessing, 349.

14 See Bryson, 35–6.

15 See Frances H. Dowley, "The Moment in Eighteenth-Century Art Criticism," in *Studies in Eighteenth-Century Culture*, ed. Ronald C. Rosbottom (Madison: University of Wisconsin Press, 1976), 5:317–18.

16 See also Riegl's discussion in *Problems of Style* of temporality in painting.

17 In his 1920 essay *Schöpferische Konfession*, Klee writes: "In Lessing's *Laokoön*, the subject of so much mental exercise in our younger years, there is much ado about the difference between time and space in art. Once we examine it more closely, this is really just a bit of erudite hairsplitting, for space, too, implies the concept of time … Only the single dot, which has no life, no energy, lacks the dimension of time." Qtd. in Grohmann, 98.

18 The comment comes in Stein's "Composition as Explanation" (Hogarth Press 1926); qtd. in Lewis, x–xi.

19 Lewis, x-xi.

20 Frank, 9, 57.

21 See Sypher, *Rococo*, 255–330.

22 Joyce influenced painters like Pollock, but also postmodern conceptual artists like Latham and Beuys, who saw his work as an indication of a paradigm shift in thinking (Hayes, 307). See Kronegger, 163–82, on Joyce and de Chirico, who both use otherworldly time and space.

23 For a good modern historical summary of the exercise, see Alistair Fowler, *Renaissance Realism: Narrative Images in Literature and Art* (Oxford: Oxford University Press, 2003), chapter 1.

24 Eliade, 153. Lukács goes even further, arguing that "the entire inner action of a novel is nothing but a struggle against the power of time" (122).

25 See her preface in Walser, viii.

26 Walser, 104–5.

27 Ibid. For a more contemporary example of this, see Thomas Bernhard, the Austrian writer, whose post–SecondWorld War novels also make time stand still. In *Concrete* (1982), writer's block translates into physical immobility; in *The Loser* (1983) the narrator tells practically the whole story as a he hesitates for a moment while crossing the lobby of a train station; in *Woodcutters* (1984) it is a wing chair at a party that imprisons the narrator. In each case temporality is suspended for lengthy passages before suddenly moving ahead briefly at the end.

28 The argument is made more thoroughly in Evans, who writes that Walser "is turning time into circles, into patterns geometrically conceived on the plane"; that in Walser "time relations" are "translated into spatial categories"; and that "Klee and Walser freed themselves provocatively from the representation of space and time as separate categories" (37–8).

29 Copernicus is not mentioned, but the eclipse of Aldebaran that confirmed his heliocentric hypothesis turns up in Callinan's question, "What is the parallax of the subsolar ecliptic of Aldebaran (488)?" Bloom's answer, "K. II." indicates that Joyce was familiar with the classification of stars by temperature. See Gifford, 479.

30 Joyce, 698. Subsequent references are to the edition of *Ulysses* that appears in the bibliography and will be cited in the text. Joyce (Bloom) is not an expert. In 1905 Sirius was thought to be 8.6 light years from earth. His other efforts are similarly off. He is only slightly low with Sirius, but his estimate that the Orion nebula was the size of a hundred solar systems should be compared to information available at the time that said it was another hundred times larger than that (Gifford, 582). S.B. Purdy writes of *Ulysses* that it is "our century's greatest artistic expression of the sense of a changed world science has given us" (216).

31 Wundram, 277. See p. 7 above, and n. 7.

32 Mann, 279. All subsequent references are to the edition that appears in the bibliography and will be cited in the text.

33 Kafka, *Amerika*, 74ff.

34 Kafka, *The Castle*, 360ff.

35 See Kafka, "The Burrow," 325–60; and *The Trial*, 37ff. On other spatial dislocations and disproportion in *Amerika* (including the bridge that leads from Manhattan to Boston), see Anderson, 142–61. Anderson notes "the general shift ... that was taking place in Kafka's society at the turn of the century: a shift away from the representation of people and things securely rooted in a stable, constant environment, and toward a relativized perception of things in motion" (142–3).

36 Qtd. in Janouch, 31.

37 Murray, 150. Murray notes the "haunting preoccupation with space" in the works of Kafka and Céline (1).
38 Céline, 338. All subsequent references are to the edition that appears in the bibliography and will be cited in the text.

7. Space and Time for the Ancients

1 Lewis, 162.
2 Bergson, *Creative Evolution*, 326–33 All references are to this edition and will be noted parenthetically in the text.
3 See note 9 in chapter 6 of the present volume.
4 Marxist writers like Walter Benjamin and Georg Lukàcs cited Bergson and Proust as having the right idea about time. See note 11 in chapter 6 of the present volume. Hans Georg Gadamer does not mention Bergson but invokes his idea of real-time history by using the term *Wirkungsgeschichte* (literally, "working history") to convey the active, dynamic nature of the past. History, he writes, is always a history of effect, of history at work (300–1). T.W. Adorno, writing about Proust, says he "followed Bergson's rule, whether he was acquainted with it or not" (*Notes*, 175).
5 Bergson, *Time and Free Will*, 100–1.
6 Ibid. Cf. Gaston Bachelard, who calls hours and minutes nothing but "the measures and estimates of the surveyor" – a kind of space that has not been touched by the imagination (xxxvi).
7 Heidegger, 38; H. 17. 3
8 Söderblom, 310–11n.
9 Herder, 29–30.
10 Boman, 126, 127, 129; *et passim* claimed in 1954 that "Bergson's thinking is related to Israelite thinking" (22n1).
11 Ibid., 130. For more on the general topic, see R. Laird Harris, ed., *Theological Wordbook of the Old Testament*, 2 vols (Chicago: Moody Press, 1980): 1, 370–1; Francis Brown, S.R. Driver, Charles A. Briggs, *A Hebrew and English Lexicon of the Old Testament* (Oxford: Oxford University Press, 1951): 399a; Gleason L. Archer, *Encyclopedia of Bible Difficulties* (Grand Rapids, MI: Zondervan, 1982), 60; and von Rad, 100–1.
12 Barr warns that is "dangerous to use the existence of an aspect system in Hebrew too confidently as a guide to a peculiar understanding of actions and events and their relation to time" or to see the Hebrew verb system "as a correlate or reflection of certain features of Hebrew thinking as a whole" (81, 84).
13 Ibid., 36, 156.

14 Boman, 31.
15 Heidegger is quite clear that the association of knowledge with "seeing," and vision (ocularcentrism), is a direct legacy of Greek thought. See 215; H. 171. "This thesis has remained the foundation of Western philosophy ever since." See Richard Rorty, *Philosophy and the Mirror of Nature* (Princeton, NJ: Princeton University Press, 1979); and Levin, *Modernity*.
16 Rabinowitz, 3n4.
17 Ibid., 17.
18 Ibid., 60.
19 Eliade, 52–3.
20 Doukhan writes that "Hebrew grammar has the capacity of reversing the two categories of time by the use of the so-called 'consecutive-conversive *vav*.' So, the tense of the Perfect, which is commonly used for action of the past, is suddenly reversed, and points instead to a future event" (92, 206–7).
21 Proust, 258–60.
22 See Heschel, *The Sabbath*. Heschel writes: "Judaism is a *religion of time*" (8). My thanks to Myron and Suri Maron for bringing this book to my attention.
23 See J.G. McConville and J.G. Millar, *Time and Place in Deuteronomy* (Sheffield: Sheffield Academic Press, 1994), 201; and von Rad, 101. John Marsh, *The Fulness of Time* (London: Nisbet and Co., 1952) notes that the Hebrew names for months (those we know) are dynamic rather than static: *'Abib* = ripening ears; *Ziv* = flowers; *'Ethanim* = perennial streams; *Bul* = rain. He points out that in the New Testament, composed in Greek, we find a mix of the Hebrew conception and time, *chronos*, which refers to measurable clock time. In the Old Testament he notes that words starting with *Eth* refer to real-world, happening time (21–2).
24 This and the following are from Plato, *Timaeus*, 49–52.
25 Plato, *The Republic*, in *Great Dialogues*, §546a. The idea of cyclical time also occurs in the *Politicus*.
26 Plato, *Phaedo*, in *Great Dialogues*,§72 bc. The only Greek who believed time was linear was Anaxagoras. Merkley, 49–56, writes that chronology for the Greeks was unimportant and that they had no tradition of historical record-keeping as the Egyptians had, who entrusted it to the priests, or as the Babylonians did with the Chaldeans. Or as the Hebrews did, who had a powerful interest in the continuum that led from Creation to the Present. Agamemnon's importance for the Greeks, by contrast, had nothing to do with his place in any continuum or genealogy. His story, like the whole myth of Troy, could have taken place at any point in the distant past.

27 Plato, *Timaeus*, §49.
28 For an interesting discussion on whether space in Plato's theory is space or matter, see Keimpe Algra, *Concepts of Space in Greek Thought* (Leiden: E.J. Brill, 1995).
29 Plato, *Timaeus*, §50.
30 Ibid., §51–2.
31 Aristotle, *Physics*, trans. Apostle, 234a–237b. Numbers refer to the standard Bekker edition appearing in the margins.
32 Ibid., 218b–219a.
33 See the *Physics*, trans. P.H. Wicksteed and F.M. Cornford, 4.11, 219b.
34 Ibid. See the Commentary for 218b.

Bibliography

Abrams, M.H. *A Glossary of Literary Terms*. 8th ed. Boston: Thomson Wadsworth, 2005.

Adams, John. "Outer Space and the New World in the Imagination of Eighteenth-Century Europeans." *Eighteenth-Century Life* 19 (Feb. 1995): 70–83.

Adorno, T.W. *Aesthetic Theory*. Translated by Robert Hullot-Kentor. Minneapolis: University of Minnesota Press, 1997.

– *Notes to Literature*. Vol. 1. Translated by Shierry Weber Nicholsen. New York: Columbia University Press, 1991.

Anderson, Mark. "Kafka and New York: Notes on a Travelling Narrative." In *Modernity and the Text: Revisions of German Modernism*, edited by Andreas Huyssen and David Bathrick, 142–61. New York, Columbia University Press, 1989.

Aragon, Louis, and André Breton. "Le cinquantenaire de l'hystérie." *La Révolution surréaliste* 11 (1928): 20–2.

Ariosto, Ludovico. *Orlando furioso* [1532]. Translated by W.S. Rose. Indianapolis: Bobbs-Merrill, 1968.

Aristotle. *Aristotle's Physics*. Translated by Hippocrates G. Apostle. Grinnel, IA: Peripatetic Press, 1980.

– *Aristotle's Physics*. Vol. 1. Translated by P.H. Wicksteed and F.M. Cornford. Cambridge, MA: Harvard University Press, 1960–3

Armitage, Angus. *Copernicus and the Reformation of Astronomy*. London: Historical Association, 1950.

Auerbach, Eric. *Mimesis: The Representation of Reality in Western Literature*. Translated by Willard Trask. Princeton, NJ: Princeton University Press, 1953.

Bachelard, Gaston. *The Poetics of Space*. Translated by Maria Jolas. Boston: Beacon Press, 1969.

Backscheider, Paula. *Daniel Defoe: His Life*. Baltimore and London: Johns Hopkins University Press, 1989.

Bagrow, Leo. *History of Cartography*. Revised and Enlarged by R.A. Skelton. Cambridge, MA: Harvard University Press, 1966.

Barolsky, Paul. *Infinite Jest, Wit and Humor in Italian Renaissance Art*. Columbia and London: University of Missouri Press, 1978.

Barr, James. *The Semantics of Biblical Language*. Oxford: Oxford University Press, 1961.

Barthelme, Donald. *Snow White*. New York: Atheneum, 1967.

Baudrillard, Jean. "The Ecstasy of Communication." In *The Anti-Aesthetic: Essays on Postmodern Culture*, translated by John Johnston, edited by Hal Foster, 126–34. Seattle: Bay, 1989.

Belting, Hans. *The End of the History of Art?*. Translated by Christopher S. Wood. Chicago: University of Chicago Press, 1987.

Benedetti, Jean. *Gilles de Rais: The Authentic Bluebeard*. London: Peter Davies, 1971.

Benjamin, Walter. *Charles Baudelaire: A Lyric Poet in the Era of High Capitalism*. Translated by Harry Zohn. New York: Verso, 1983.

Bennett, Tony. *Formalism and Marxism*. Methuen: London, 1979.

Bergson, Henri. *Creative Evolution*. Translated by Arthur Mitchell. New York: Modern Library, 1911.

– *Time and Free Will: An Essay on the Immediate Data of Consciousness*. Translated by F.L. Pogson. New York: Humanities Press, 1971.

Bockris, Victor. *With William Burroughs: A Report from the Bunker*. New York: Seaver Books, 1981.

Boileau, L'Abbé, Docteur de Sorbonne. *Histoire des Flagellans, ou l'on Fait Voir Le bon et le mauvais usage des Flagellations Parmi les Chretiens, traduit du Latin*. Amsterdam: Francois vander Plaats, 1701.

Bollas, Christopher. *Hysteria*. London: Routledge, 2000.

Boman, Thorleif. *Hebrew Thought Compared with Greek*. Translated by J.L. Moreau. London: SCM Press, 1960.

Borossa, Julia. *Hysteria*. Lanham, MD: Icon, 2001.

Bowen, Barbara C. *Enter Rabelais, Laughing*. Nashville, TN: Vanderbilt Press, 1998.

Bryson, Norman. *Word and Image: French Painting of the Ancien Regime*. Cambridge: Cambridge University Press, 1981.

Bulson, Eric. *Novels, Maps, Modernity: The Spatial Imagination, 1850–2000*. New York and London: Routledge, 2007.

Burke, Edmund. *A Philosophical Enquiry into the Origin of Our Ideas of the Sublime and Beautiful*. Edited by James T. Boulton. Notre Dame, IN: University of Notre Dame Press, 1958.

Burkert, Walter. "Impact and Limits of the Idea of Progress in Antiquity," In *The Idea of Progress*, edited by A. Burgen et al., 19–46. Berlin: De Gruyter, 1997.

Carter, Angela. *The Sadeian Woman: An Exercise in Cultural History*. London: Virago, 1979.

Céline, Louis-Ferdinand. *Death on the Installment Plan*. Translated by Ralph Mannheim. New York: New Directions, 1952.

Chastel, André. *The Crisis of the Renaissance 1520–1600*. Translated by Peter Price. Geneva: Skira, 1968.

Chute, Marchette. *Ben Jonson of Westminster*. New York: E.P. Dutton, 1953.

Cohen, Bernard. *The Newtonian Revolution*. Cambridge: Cambridge University Press, 1980.

Copleston, S.J., Frederick. *A History of Philosophy*. Vol. 3. New York: Doubleday, 1953.

Cuffe, Theo. "Foreword." In Voltaire, *Micromégas* [1752]. Translated by Theo Cuffe. Harmondsworth, UK: Penguin, 1994.

Danson, Lawrence. "Jonsonian Comedy and the Discovery of the Social Self." *PMLA* 99.2 (March 1984): 179–93.

Da Vinci, Leonardo. *The Notebooks of Leonardo da Vinci*. 2 vols. Edited by Edward MacCurdy. London: Reprint Society, 1938.

Defoe, Daniel. *Unparallel'd Cruelty: Or, the Tryal of Captain Jeane of Bristol*. London: T. Warner, 1726.

Deleuze, Gilles. *Presentation de Sacher-Masoch*. Paris: Les Editions de Minuit, 1967.

de Mourges, Odette. *Metaphysical Baroque and Précieux Poetry*. Oxford: Clarendon Press, 1953.

DePietro, Thomas. "Literary Criticism as History: The Example of Auerbach's *Mimesis*." *Clio* 8 (1979): 377–87.

Diagnostic and Statistical Manual of Mental Disorders IV. Washington, DC: American Psychiatric Association, 1994.

Donne, John. *Ignatius His Conclave*. Edited by T.S. Healy. Oxford: Clarendon Press, 1969.

– *Poetical Works*. Edited by H.J.C. Grierson. Oxford: Oxford University Press.

Donoghue, William. "Pynchon's Hysterical Sublime," *Critique: Studies in Contemporary Fiction* 52, no. 4 (2011): 444–59.

Doody, Margaret Anne. *The True Story of the Novel*. New Brunswick, NJ: Rutgers University Press, 1996.

Doukhan, Jacques B. *Hebrew for Theologians: A Textbook for the Study of Biblical Hebrew in Relation to Hebrew Thinking*. New York: University Press of America, 1993.

du Plessix Gray, Francine. *At Home with the Marquis de Sade*. New York: Simon and Schuster, 1998.

Eisendrath, Daniel N. and Harry C. Ralnick. Urology. Philadelphia: Lippincott, 1938.

Eliade, Mircea. *The Myth of the Eternal Return*. New York: Bollingen, 1954.

Erickson, Erik H. *Life History and the Historical Moment*. New York: Norton, 1975.

Evans, Tamara S. "'A Paul Klee in Prose:' Design, Space, and Time in the Work of Robert Walser." *German Quarterly* 57, no. 1 (Winter 1984): 27–91.

Faulkner, William. *As I Lay Dying*. New York: Vintage, 1985.

Ferguson, James. *Astronomy Explained* [1778].

Fineman, Joel. "Fratricide and Cuckoldry: Shakespeare's Doubles." In *Representing Shakespeare: New Psychoanalytic Essays*, edited by Murray M. Schwartz and Coppélia Kahn: 70–109. . Baltimore: Johns Hopkins University Press, 1980.

Fontenelle, Bernard le Bouvier de. *A Plurality of Worlds* [1688]. London: Nonesuch, 1929.

Francastel, Pierre. "The Destruction of a Plastic Space." In *Art History: An Anthology of Modern Criticism*, edited by Wylie Sypher, 379–98. New York: Vintage, 1963.

Frank, Joseph. *The Widening Gyre: Crisis and Mastery in Modern Literature*. New Brunswick, NJ: Rutgers University Press, 1963.

Freud, Sigmund. "On Narcissism: An Introduction." In *Collected Papers*, vol. 4, 30–59. New York: Basic Books, 1959.

– *Totem and Taboo*. New York: Vintage, 1946.

Gadamer, Hans Georg. *Truth and Method*. 2nd rev. ed. Translated by Joel Weinsheimer and Donald G. Marshall. New York: Continuum, 1993.

Genette, Gérard. *Narrative Discourse*. Translated by Jane E. Lewin. Ithaca, NY: Cornell University Press, 1980.

Geyh, Paula, Fred G. Leebron, and Andrew Levy, eds. *Postmodern American Fiction: A Norton Anthology*. New York and London: W.W. Norton, 1998.

Gifford, Don, with Robert J. Seidman. *Ulysses Annotated*. 2nd ed. Berkeley: University of California Press, 1988.

Gingerich, Owen. *The Book Nobody Read: Chasing the Revolutions of Nicolaus Copernicus*. New York: Walker, 2004.

Gleick, James. *Chaos: Making a New Science*. New York: Penguin, 1987.

Gordon, Andrew. "Smoking Dope with Thomas Pynchon: A Sixties Memoir." In *The Vineland Papers: Critical Takes on Pynchon's Novel*, edited by Geoffrey Green, Donald J. Greiner, and Larry McCaffery, 167–78. Normal, Ll.: Dalkey Archive Press, 1994.

Gluck, Mary. "Interpreting Primitivism, Mass Culture and Modernism: The Making of Wilhelm Worringer's *Abstraction and Empathy*." *New German Critique* 80 (Spring–Summer 2000): 149–69.

Gray, Madeleine. *The Protestant Reformation: Belief, Practice and Tradition*. Portland, OR: Sussex Academic Press, 2003.

Greenblatt, Stephen. *Renaissance Self-Fashioning from More to Shakespeare.* Chicago: University of Chicago Press, 1980.

Griffin, Robert. *Ludovico Ariosto.* New York: Twayne, 1974.

Grohmann, Will. *Paul Klee.* New York: Harry N. Abrams, 1954.

Hampson, Norman. *The Enlightenment.* Harmondsworth, UK: Penguin, 1968.

Hayes, Christa-Maria Lerm. *Joyce in Art: Visual Art Inspired by James Joyce.* Dublin: Lilliput Press, 2004.

Hayles, N. Katherine. "'A Metaphor of God Knew How Many Parts': The Engine that Drives *The Crying of Lot 49.*" In *New Essays on The Crying of Lot 49*, edited by Patrick O'Donnell, 97–125. Cambridge: Cambridge University Press, 1991.

Heidegger, Martin. *Being and Time.* Translated by John Macquarrie and Edward Robinson. New York: Harper and Row, 1962.

Heidelberger, Michael. "Some Intertheoretic Relations between Ptolemean and Copernican Astronomy." In *Paradigms and Revolutions*, edited by Gary Cutting, 271–83. Notre Dame, IN: University of Notre Dame Press, 1980.

Henderson, Linda Dalrymple. *The Fourth Dimension and Non-Euclidean Geometry in Modern Art.* Princeton, NJ: Princeton University Press, 1983.

Henry, Holly. *Virginia Woolf and the Discourse of Science: The Aesthetics of Astronomy.* Cambridge: Cambridge University Press, 2003.

Herder, J.G. *The Spirit of Hebrew Poetry.* 2 vols. Translated by J. Marsh. Burlington, VT: E. Smith, 1833.

Hervey, David. *The Condition of Postmodernity: An Enquiry into the Origins of Cultural Change.* Oxford: Blackwell, 1989.

Herz, Neil. *The End of the Line: Essays on Psychoanalysis and the Sublime.* New York: Columbia University Press, 1985.

Heschel, Abraham Joshua. *The Sabbath.* New York: Farrar, Straus and Giroux, 1951.

Holdheim, W. Wolfgang. "Auerbach's *Mimesis*: Aesthetics as Historical Understanding" *Clio* 10, no. 2 (1981): 143–54.

Horowitz, Mardi J. *Hysterical Personality Style and the Histrionic Personality Disorder.* Northdale, NJ: Jason Aronson, 1991.

Howe, Joseph. *Excessive Venery.* New York: E.B. Treat, 1887.

Jacobson, Edith. *The Self and the Object World.* New York: International Universities Press, 1964.

James, Henry. *The Novels and Tales of Henry James.* New York: Scribner's, 1909.

Jameson, Fredric. *The Political Unconscious: Narrative as a Socially Symbolic Act.* Ithaca, NY: Cornell University Press, 1981.

– "Postmodernism, or the Cultural Logic of Late Capitalism." *New Left Review* 146 (July–August, 1984): 53–89.

Janouch, Gustav. *Conversations with Kafka*. Translated by Goronwy Rees. New York: New Directions, 1971.

Jonson, Ben. *Ben Jonson*. 11 vols. Edited by C.H. Herford, Percy Simpson and Evelyn Simpson. Oxford, 1925–52. 1:139.

Joyce, James. *Ulysses* [1922]. Edited by H.W. Gabler. Harmondsworth, UK: Penguin, 1986.

Kafka, Franz. *Amerika*. Translated by Edwin Muir. New York: New Directions, 1946.

– "The Burrow." In *The Complete Stores*. Edited by Nahum N. Glatzer. New York: Schocken, 1971.

– *The Castle*. Translated by Willa and Edwin Muir. New York: Schocken, 1992.

– *The Trial*. Translated by Willa and Edwin Muir. New York: Schocken, 1992.

Kant, Immanuel. *Critique of Judgment* [1790]. Translated by Werner S. Pluhar. Indianapolis: Hackett Publishing, 1987.

Kermode, Frank. "Decoding the Trystero." In *Pynchon: A Collection of Critical Essays*, edited by Edward Mendelson, 162–6. Englewood Cliffs, NJ: Prentice Hall, 1978.

Kern, Stephen. *The Culture of Time and Space 1880–1918*. Cambridge, MA: Harvard University Press, 1983.

Kernberg, Otto. *Internal World and External Reality: Object Relations Theory Applied*. New York: Aronson, 1980.

Kleiner, John. "Mismapping the Underworld." *Dante Studies* 107 (1989): 1–31.

Knowles, Ronald. *Gulliver's Travels: The Politics of Satire*. New York: Twayne, 1996.

Kohut, Heinz. *The Analysis of the Self*. New York: International Universities Press, 1971.

Koss, Juliet. "On the Limits of Empathy." *Art Bulletin* 88, no. 1 (March 2006): 139–57.

Krafft-Ebing, R. von. *Psychopathia Sexualis*. Translated by C.G. Chaddock. 7th rev. German ed. Philadelphia and London: F.A. Davis, 1893.

Kronegger, Maria Elisabeth. *James Joyce and Associated Image Makers*. New Haven, CT: College and University Press, 1968.

Kubler, George. *The Shape of Time: Remarks on the History of Things*. New Haven, CT: Yale University Press, 1962.

Kuhn, T.S. *The Copernican Revolution: Planetary Astronomy in the Development of Western Thought*. Cambridge, MA: Harvard University Press, 1957.

– *The Structure of Scientific Revolutions*. Chicago: University of Chicago Press, 1962.

Laborde, Alice. *La bibliothèque du marquis de Sade au château de la Coste (en 1776)*. Geneva: Slatkine, 1991.

Lasch, Christopher. *The Minimal Self: Psychic Survival in Troubled Times*. New York: W.W. Norton, 1984.

Le Brun, Annie. *Soudain un bloc d'abîme, Sade*. Paris: Jean-Jacques Pauvert chez Pauvert, 1986.

LeClair, Tom. *In the Loop: Don DeLillo and the Systems Novel*. Urbana, Ill. 1987.

Lechtenberg, Richard, and Dana A. Ohl. *Sexual Dysfunction: Neurologic, Urologic and Gynecologic Aspects*. Philadelphia: Lea and Febiger, 1994.

Lee, William. *Daniel Defoe: His Life and Hitherto Unknown Writing*. 3 vols. London: Hotten, 1869.

Leggatt, Alexander. *Ben Jonson: His Vision and His Art*. London: Methuen, 1981.

Lessing, Gotthold Ephraim. *Laocoön*. Translated by Sir Robert Phillimore. In *Critical Theory Since Plato*, edited by Hazard Adams, 348–52. New York: Harcourt, Brace, Jovanovich, 1971.

Lestringant, Frank. *Mapping the Renaissance World: The Geographical Imagination in the Age of Discovery*. Translated by David Fausett. Berkeley: University of California Press, 1994.

Lever, Maurice. *Donatien Alphonse François, marquis de Sade*. Paris: Fayard, 1991.

Levin, David Michael, ed. *Modernity and the Hegemony of Vision*. Berkeley: University of California Press, 1993.

Lewis, C.S. *English Literature in the Sixteenth Century*. Oxford: Oxford University Press, 1954.

Lewis, Wyndham. *Time and Western Man* [1927]. Boston: Beacon Press, 1957.

Lukács, Georg. *Theory of the Novel*. Translated by Anna Bostock. Cambridge, MA: MIT Press, 1971.

MacKinnon, R.A., and R. Michels. *The Psychiatric Interview*. Philadelphia: W.B. Saunders, 1971.

Mann, Thomas. *The Magic Mountain* [1924]. Translated by John E. Woods. New York: Vintage, 1996.

Marin, Louis. *Utopiques: jeux d'éspaces*. Paris: Minuit, 1973.

Marvell, Andrew. "To His Coy Mistress." In *The Complete Poems*, edited by Elizabeth Story Donno, 50–1. Harmondsworth, UK: Penguin, 1972.

Mattessich, Stefan. *Discursive Time and Countercultural Desire in the Work of Thomas Pynchon*. Durham, NC: Duke University Press, 2002.

McHale, Brian. "Modernist Reading, Post-Modern Text: The Case of Gravity's Rainbow." *Poetics Today* 1, nos. 1/2 (Autumn 1979): 85–110.

McHoul, Alec, and David Wills. *Writing Pynchon: Strategies in Fictional Analysis*. Chicago: University of Illinois Press, 1990.

McKeon, Michael. *The Origins of the English Novel 1600–1740*. Baltimore: Johns Hopkins University Press, 1987.

McLuhan, Marshall. *Understanding Media: The Extensions of Man*. London: Routledge and K. Paul, 1964.

Meacham, Randall B., and Julia A. Drose. "Evaluation and Treatment of Ejaculatory Duct Obstruction in the Infertile Male." In *Male Infertility and Sexual Dysfunction*, edited by Wayne J. G. Hellstrom, 189–200. New York: Springer, 1997.

Mead, George Herbert. *Mind, Self and Society from the Standpoint of a Social Behaviorist*. Chicago: University of Chicago Press, 1934.

Mendelson, Edward. "Pynchon's Gravity." In *Thomas Pynchon: Modern Critical Views*, edited by Harold Bloom, 15–21. New York: Chelsea House, 1986.

Merkley, Paul. *The Greek and Hebrew Origins of Our Idea of History*. Lewiston, NY: Mellen Press, 1987.

Miles, Rosalind. *Ben Jonson: His Life and Work*. London: Routledge, 1986.

Mitchell, Juliet. *Mad Men and Medusas: Reclaiming Hysteria*. New York: Basic, 2000.

Molho, Anthony. *Social and Economic Foundations of the Italian Renaissance*. New York: Wiley, 1969.

Monk, Samuel. *The Sublime: A Study of Critical Theories in Eighteenth-Century England*. Ann Arbor: University of Michigan Press, 1960.

More, Sir Thomas. *Utopia* [1517]. Translated and edited by Robert M. Adams. New York: Norton, 1992.

Murray, Jack. *The Landscapes of Alienation: Ideological Subversion in Kafka, Céline and Onetti*. Stanford, CA: Stanford University Press, 1991.

Newton, Sir Isaac. *The Mathematical Principles of Natural Philosophy* [1687]. Translated by Andrew Motte. Amherst, NY: Prometheus, 1995.

– *Opticks: or A treatise of the Reflections, Refractions, Inflections and Colours of Light*, 4th ed. London: William Innys, 1730.

– *A Treatise of the System of the World* [1731]. 2nd ed. London: Dawsons, 1969.

Nietzsche, Friedrich. *Birth of Tragedy*, in *Basic Writings of Nietzsche*. Translated by Walter Kaufmann. New York: Modern Library, 1968.

O'Dair, Sharon K. "The Social Self and Science." *PMLA* 100, no. 1 (Winter 1985): 99–100.

O'Donnell, Patrick. *Latent Destinies: Cultural Paranoia and Contemporary U.S. Narrative*. Durham, NC: Duke University Press, 2000.

Olsen, Lance. "Pynchon's New Nature: The Uncertainty Principle in *The Crying of Lot 49*." *Canadian Review of American Studies* 14 (1983): 153–63.

Palmieri, Frank. "Neither Literally Nor as Metaphor: Pynchon's *The Crying of Lot 49* and the Structure of Scientific Revolutions." *ELH* 54 (1987): 979–99.

Pauvert, Jean-Jacques. *Sade Vivant*. Paris: Laffont, 1989.

Pettegree, Andrew. *The Book in the Renaissance*. New Haven, CT: Yale University Press, 2010.

Phillips, G.M. *Handbook of Genito-Urinary Surgery and Venereal Diseases*. N.p., 1898.

Plato. *Great Dialogues of Plato*. Translated by W.H.D. Rouse. New York: New American Library, 1956.

– *Timaeus and Critias*. Translated by Desmond Lee. Harmondsworth, UK: Penguin, 1977.

Prigogine, Ilya, and Isabelle Stengers. *Order out of Chaos: Man's New Dialogue with Nature*. Boulder, CO: New Science Library, 1984.

Proust, Marcel. *Swann's Way*. Vol. 1 of *In Search of Lost Time*. Translated by C.K. Scott Moncrieff and Terence Kilmartin. Revised by D.J. Enright. New York: Modern Library.

Purdy, S.B. "Let's Hear What Science Has to Say: Finnegans Wake and the Gnosis of Science." In *The Seventh of Joyce*, edited by Bernard Benstock, 207–18. Bloomington: Indiana University Press, 1982.

Pynchon, Thomas. *Against the Day*. New York: Penguin, 2006.

– *The Crying of Lot 49*. New York: Harper Perennial, 1999.

– *Gravity's Rainbow*. New York: Viking, 1973.

– *Mason and Dixon*. New York: Picador, 1997.

– *Slow Learner: Eight Stories*. Boston: Little Brown, 1984.

– *V*. Philadelphia: Lippincott, 1961.

– *Vineland*. New York: Penguin, 1990.

Rabelais, François. *The Five Books of Gargantua and Pantagruel*. Translated by Jacques Le Clerq. New York: Modern Library, 1944.

– *Oeuvres complètes*. Edition established, presented, and annotated by Mireille Huchon, with the collaboration of François Moreau. Paris: Gallimard, 1994.

Rabinowitz, Isaac. *A Witness Forever: Ancient Israel's Perception of Literature and the Resultant Hebrew Bible*. Edited by Ross Brann and David I. Owen. Bethesda, MD: CDL Press, 1993.

Raffel, Burton. "Translator's Preface," *Gargantua and Pantagruel*. New York: W.W. Norton, 1990.

Riegl, Alois. *Problems of Style: Foundations for a History of Ornament*. Translated by Evelyn Kain. Princeton, NJ: Princeton University Press, 1992.

Riggs, David. *Ben Jonson: A Life*. Cambridge, MA: Harvard University Press, 1989.

Rosenfeld, Aaron. "The 'Scanty Plot': Orwell, Pynchon, and the Poetics of Paranoia." *Twentieth Century Literature* 50, no. 4 (Winter 2004): 337–67.

Sade, D.A.F. *The Complete Justine, Philosophy in the Bedroom and Other Writings*. Translated by Austryn Wainhouse and Richard Seaver. New York: Grove, 1966.

– *Juliette*. Translated by Austryn Wainhouse and Richard Seaver. New York: Grove, 1966.

– *Marquis de Sade: Letters from Prison*. Translated by Richard Seaver. New York: Arcade, 1999.

– *Oeuvres Completes du Marquis de Sade*. Paris: Au Cercle du Livre Précieux, 1966.

– *The 120 Days of Sodom and Other Writings*. Translated by Austryn Wainhouse and Richard Seaver. New York: Grove, 1966.

Schaefer, Neil. *The Marquis de Sade: A Life*. New York: Knopf, 1999.

Schaub, Thomas. *Pynchon, the Voice of Ambiguity*. Urbana: University of Illinois Press, 1981.

Screech, M.A. *Rabelais*. Ithaca, NY: Cornell University Press, 1979.

Seed, David. *The Fictional Labyrinths of Thomas Pynchon*. Iowa City: University of Iowa Press, 1988.

Shapiro, David. *Neurotic Styles*. New York: Basic Books, 1965.

Shapiro, Marianne. *The Poetics of Ariosto*. Detroit: Wayne State University Press, 1988.

Shearman, John. *Mannerism*. Harmondsworth, UK: Penguin, 1967.

Showalter, Elaine. *Hystories: Hysterical Epidemics and Modern Culture*. New York: Columbia University Press, 1997.

Siegel, Mark R. "Creative Paranoia: Understanding the System of *Gravity's Rainbow*." *Critique* 18 (1976): 39–54.

Skura, Meredith Anne. *The Literary Use of the Psychoanalytic Process*. New Haven, CT: Yale University Press, 1981.

Söderblom, Nathan. *The Living God: Basal Forms of Personal Religion*. Oxford: Oxford University Press, 1933.

Spengler, Oswald. *The Decline of the West*. Translated by C.F. Atkinson. New York: Knopf, 1962.

Spitz, Lewis W. *The Protestant Reformation 1517–1559*. New York: Harper, 1985.

Spitzer, Leo. *Linguistics and Literary History: Essays in Stylistics*. Princeton, NJ: Princeton University Press, 1948.

Stephen, Leslie. *History of English Thought in the Eighteenth Century* [1876]. Vol. 2. New York: Harcourt, Brace and World, 1962.

Stephens, Walter. *Giants, in Those Days: Folklore, Ancient History and Nationalism*. Lincoln: University of Nebraska Press, 1989.

Sterne, Laurence. *Tristram Shandy*. Edited by Howard Anderson. New York: Norton, 1980.

Swift, Jonathan. *Gulliver's Travels* [1735]. New York: Norton, 1970.

Sypher, Wylie. *Rococo to Cubism in Art and Literature*. New York: Random House, 1960.

Tart, Charles T. *On Being Stoned: A Psychological Study of Marijuana Intoxication*. Palo Alto, CA: Science and Behavior Books, 1971.

Thrower, Norman J. W. *Maps and Civilization: Cartography in Culture and Society*. Chicago: University of Chicago Press, 1972.

Thuasne, Louis. *Etudes sur Rabelais*. Paris: Bouillon, 1904.

Tillyard, E.M.W. *The Elizabethan World Picture*. New York: Vintage, n.d.

Tissot, A.D. *De la sante des gens de letters* [1766]. Paris: Bailliere, 1826, with notes by F.G. Boisseau, doctor of medicine and member of the Royal Academy of Medicine.

Vila, Anne C. *Enlightenment and Pathology*. Baltimore and London: Johns Hopkins University Press, 1998.

Voltaire. *The Complete Works of Voltaire*. Vol. 15. Oxford: Voltaire Foundation, 1992.

– *Micromégas* [1752]. Translated by Roger Pearson. Oxford: World's Classics, 1990.

von Rad, Gerhard. *Old Testament Theology*. 2 vols. Translated by D.M.G. Stalker. New York: Harper and Row, 1965.

Waite, Geoffrey C.W. "Worringer's *Abstraction and Empathy*: Remarks on its Reception and the Rhetoric of Criticism." In *Invisible Cathedrals: The Expressionist Art History of Wilhelm Worringer*, edited by Neil H. Donahue, 13–40. University Park: Pennsylvania State University Press, 1995.

Walpole, Horace. *The Castle of Otranto* [1764]. New York: Macmillian Publishing, 1963.

Walser, Robert. *Selected Stories*. Translated by Christopher Middleton et al. New York: New York Review of Books, 1982.

Weber, Samuel. *The Legend of Freud*. Minneapolis: University of Minnesota Press, 1982.

Wilford, John Noble. *The Mapmakers*. New York: Vintage Books, 1981.

Wood, James. *The Irresponsible Self: On Laughter and the Novel*. New York: Farrar, Straus and Giroux, 2004.

Woodward, David. "Maps and the Rationalization of Geographic Space." In *Circa 1492: Art in the Age of Exploration*, edited by Jay Levenson, 83–7. New Haven, CT: Yale University Press, 1991.

Worringer, Wilhelm. *Abstraction and Empathy*. Translated by Michael Bullock. Cleveland and New York: World Publishing Co., 1948. Originally published as *Abstraktion und Einfühlung*. Munich: Piper, 1908.

Wundram, Manfred. *The Dictionary of Art*. Vol. 20. Edited by Jane Turner. London: Macmillan, 1966. 277–81.

Index